S0-BXD-933

PLEASE STAMP DATE DUE, BOTH BELOW AND ON CARD

| DATE DUE | DATE DUE | DATE DUE | DATE DUE |
|---|---|---|---|
| NOV 5 1980 | | | |
| MAR 1 7 1981 | | | |

# SOCIOECONOMIC SUCCESS
## A STUDY OF THE EFFECTS OF GENETIC ENDOWMENTS, FAMILY ENVIRONMENT, AND SCHOOLING

# CONTRIBUTIONS TO ECONOMIC ANALYSIS

## 128

*Honorary Editor*

J. TINBERGEN


*Editors*

D. W. JORGENSON

J. WAELBROECK

NORTH-HOLLAND PUBLISHING COMPANY
AMSTERDAM · NEW YORK · OXFORD

# SOCIOECONOMIC SUCCESS

## A study of the effects of genetic endowments, family environment, and schooling

JERE R. BEHRMAN
*University of Pennsylvania*

ZDENEK HRUBEC
*National Research Council*

PAUL TAUBMAN
*University of Pennsylvania*

TERENCE J. WALES
*University of British Columbia*

1980

NORTH-HOLLAND PUBLISHING COMPANY
AMSTERDAM · NEW YORK · OXFORD

ISBN 0-444-85410-X


Publishers:

NORTH-HOLLAND PUBLISHING COMPANY
AMSTERDAM · NEW YORK · OXFORD


Sole distributors for the U.S.A. and Canada:

ELSEVIER NORTH-HOLLAND, INC.
52 VANDERBILT AVENUE
NEW YORK, N.Y. 10017

Library of Congress Cataloging in Publication Data
  Main entry under title:

  Socioeconomic success.

    (Contributions to economic analysis ; 128)
    Bibliography:  p.
    1.  Nature and nurture.  2.  Nature and nurture--
  Economic aspects.  3.  Twins.  4.  Social mobility.
  5.  Success.  I.  Behrman, Jere R.  II.  Series.
  HQ751.S63        305.5        80-13402
  ISBN 0-444-85410-X

PRINTED IN THE NETHERLANDS

# INTRODUCTION TO THE SERIES

This series consists of a number of hitherto unpublished studies, which are introduced by the editors in the belief that they represent fresh contributions to economic science.

The term *economic analysis* as used in the title of the series has been adopted because it covers both the activities of the theoretical economist and the research worker.

Although the analytical methods used by the various contributors are not the same, they are nevertheless conditioned by the common origin of their studies, namely theoretical problems encountered in practical research. Since for this reason, business cycle research and national accounting, research work on behalf of economic policy, and problems of planning are the main sources of the subjects dealt with, they necessarily determine the manner of approach adopted by the authors. Their methods tend to be "practical" in the sense of not being too far remote from application to actual economic conditions. In addition they are quantitative rather than qualitative.

It is the hope of the editors that the publication of these studies will help to stimulate the exchange of scientific information and to reinforce international cooperation in the field of economics.

The Editors

# PREFACE

The research reported in this book springs from several different sources. During the 1960s many economists studied the relationship between education and earnings. These studies were partly motivated by the desire to understand why the distribution of income is skewed and the extent to which inequality in schooling led to inequality in earnings. The answer to the last question requires, in part, an unbiased estimate of the coefficient of schooling in an earnings equation. Yet it has long been recognized that the coefficients obtained from regressing earnings on schooling will be biased if the more able also obtain more education and if the labor market rewards ability.

To try to overcome this ability problem, several economists and other social scientists had developed samples which included IQ tests or other measures of cognitive ability. Two of the authors of this book, Taubman and Wales, had helped to develop and to analyze the NBER-TH sample which contains several measures of ability. Shortly after that book was written, Taubman had the pleasure of teaching a senior seminar in the general area of income distribution. A paper was required for the course. Two students, Mr. J. Rotwitt and Mr. H. Rosenthal, wished to undertake a study similar to that but using a sample of twins.

Believing that no such sample existed, Taubman told them they could look around for a week or two and then he would help them find a more feasible topic. Within a week they returned with a reprint indicating the nature and availability of the National Academy of Science–National Research Council (NAS-NRC) twin sample. Too much planning was needed for them to be able to use the NAS-NRC twin sample and so they had to be satisfied with basing their paper on a survey conducted with twins identified in Philadelphia high school books. However, because of their curiosity and initiative the research project reported in this volume began. We owe a large debt to them which is hardly paid by the heartiest thanks that we offer.

The research would also have been impossible without the availability of the NAS-NRC twin sample. The construction and characteristics of this sample are described in detail in subsequent chapters. As an example of the need to conduct long-term research, and the unexpected fruits of such research, we wish to point out here that the sample was originally designed to study various illnesses. While the project was conceived in 1955 by Dr. William B. Wartman, Professor of Pathology at Northwestern University, the first article based on the sample was published in 1967. Since then many projects have benefited from this sample. Moreover, when convinced that the NAS-NRC twin sample could make an important and unique contribution to a problem in economics, the NAS-NRC generously allowed us to undertake the extensive survey work that forms the basis of this study.

Many of the empirical results are obtained from ordinary least squares regressions. Some, however, require the use of a special latent variable model. Only within the last decade have such models been examined within the field of economics. This study would have been much different without the extensive research of Goldberger on this class of models.

Chapter 5 was written primarily by Z. Hrubec. Behrman, Taubman and Wales have the primary responsibility for the other chapters. A portion of the work described in Chapter 5 was supported with funds from the National Science Foundation, grant no. SOC73-05543-A02 (formerly GS-40430X). The National Science Foundation also supported the activities of the Medical Follow-up Agency, National Research Council. The Medical Follow-up Agency program was developed by the Committee on Veterans' Medical Problems and is carried out with the cooperation of the Veterans Administration and the Department of Defense. These organizations and the individual military services kindly provided access to the required material which was obtained with the cooperation of the National Archives and Records Service of the General Services Administration. The use of these materials in the preparation of this report is acknowledged, but it is not to be construed as implying official approval by these agencies of the conclusions presented. Dr. Robert Hauser, Department of Sociology, University of Wisconsin, kindly provided data on U.S. males and on veterans for comparison with those of this study.

The NRC Twin Registry is an activity of the Medical Follow-up Agency established with funding support from the Veterans Administration and the National Institutes of Health. In the period during which this study was conducted the Registry was receiving operating fund support from the National Heart and Lung Institute. The preparation of Chapter 5 was supported from contract no. N01-HV-53010 with the National Institutes of Health.

The acquisition of the education, occupation, and earnings questionnaire of this study was carried out by the Medical Follow-up Agency, and was the responsibility of Dr. James E. Norman, Jr. The operations staff was directed by Mr. A. Hiram Simon, the questionnaire mailing operation was managed by Miss Hatsumi Hamamura and Ms. Deborah Maloff. Ms. Dorothy Mahon supervised the abstracting of Navy personnel records. Mr. Thomas Preston coordinated data processing and other project activities. Their contribution to this work is deeply appreciated.

Our research has benefited greatly from the comments of many colleagues. Those who contributed the most to our understanding of the issues raised in this book are Professors Chamberlain, Goldberger, Griliches, Hauser, Jencks, and Olneck. We wish to thank each while noting that none of them may agree with all that is written.

Excellent research assistance in the analysis of the data by Barbara Atrostic, Shah Fardost, and Fred Slade. The research was generously supported by NSF through grant SOC73-05543-A02 formerly GS40430X.

# CONTENTS

# LIST OF TABLES

# LIST OF FIGURES

# CHAPTER 1

# INTRODUCTION

In this book we examine the inter- and intragenerational determinants of inequality in schooling, initial and mature occupational status, and mature earnings for a group of white male veterans born in the United States. In the chapters below we provide the details of our theoretical model, statistical methodology, data, empirical estimates, and their implications.

Before turning to those details, however, a more general perspective is useful to place this study in context. We address ourselves to that task in this chapter. In section 1.1 we discuss why we are interested in the subject under examination. In section 1.2 we summarize some previous related research and the problems therein. In section 1.3 we indicate the main purposes and major findings of this study.

## 1.1. Why be concerned with the inter- and intragenerational sources of inequality?

To many people the answer to this question is obvious. The degree of intragenerational inequality among these various socio-economic indicators constitute fundamental normative characteristics of a society. In the value judgements of many individuals the basic goodness or justness of a society is intimately tied to the degree of equality of such indicators. Knowledge of the determinants of the distribution of these indicators is important both in

2          *Socioeconomic success*

judging the fairness of societies and in considering policy alternatives.

However, the degree of intragenerational inequality is not the sole concern in many such evaluations. Also significant is the pattern over time. The degree of inter- and intragenerational mobility for schooling, occupational status, and earnings are basic indices of the openness of society.[1] An important, if far from perfectly realized, traditional ideal in the United States (and in a number of other countries) is that the opportunity to achieve schooling, occupational status, and earnings should be equal, given the distribution of natural ability, and that merit (i.e. ability and effort) should be rewarded by achievement. In addition, at least from the time of de Tocqueville, observers have maintained that the stability of democracy in the United States is related to the widespread perception of considerable possibilities for upward mobility. The same perception reputedly has been an important supply factor both in the earlier waves of immigration and in continuing migration. Moreover, greater mobility probably implies better leadership in that the composition of the elite is based more on merit than on ascription. Finally, some people have hypothesized that mobility could decrease with the maturation of industrial society, perhaps reversing some of the positive results suggested above. Knowledge of the determinants of inter- and intragenerational mobility is therefore critical in understanding a range of important phenomena.[2]

A crucial question in the evaluation of the degree of inequality and the determinants of inter- and intragenerational mobility, and in the evaluation of policies designed to affect inequality and

[1]Inequality within a generation and intergenerational social mobility are separable concerns. As Conlisk (1974) has shown, some policies to reduce intragenerational inequality may lessen intergenerational mobility and vice versa. The distinction between such policies depends upon the extent to which they affect systematic family environment versus random environments.
[2]These issues are discussed much more extensively in Blau and Duncan (1967), Jencks et al. (1972), Bendix and Lypsett (1966), and Reiss et al. (1961).

mobility is: to what extent would increases in the equality of opportunity lead to increases in the equality of outcomes as measured, for example, by the reduction in the variance of income? There always has been a strong constituency in the United States which has emphasized the importance of assuring equality of opportunity and letting individual characteristics determine the degree of equality of outcomes rather than attempt to affect outcomes directly. This has been the rationale of programs such as Head Start and free school lunches which have been instituted to offset poor family environment. Family environment is a broad concept which often is defined to include parental role models. It may be very difficult to design policies to equalize all aspects of family environment. In any event, the more important are genetic factors in determining the distributions of various socioeconomic indicators, the less probable it is that elimination of inequality of opportunity will lead to significant increases in the equality of outcomes.

Equality of outcomes can be affected by programs other than equality of opportunity. It is possible to institute training programs or school lunches for the poor to compensate for poor genetic endowments or poor family environment. It is also possible to alter equality of outcomes through income (and other) transfer programs. Both compensatory and transfer programs have been adopted by society to aid certain groups such as the blind or physically handicapped. Some people, however, advocate negative income taxes, food stamps, and other programs to achieve greater equality of outcomes for society as a whole.

Many specific examples of the "opportunity" versus "outcome" question are found in the institutions and policies in the United States and many other countries. Perhaps the dominant focus of debate has been the area of education. Can the school system be used to ensure an adequate degree of equality of opportunity? Or, are educational benefits best utilized by those who come from advantaged family backgrounds so that equality of educational opportunity will not lead to the desired degree of equality of outcomes?[3] In the past decade or so there have been considerable defections from a previous wide consensus about the extent to which schooling could provide sufficient equality of opportunities. Key to this change is a shift in the perception of the level of the rate of return (in terms of income) of investment in schooling. Fägerland (1975, p. 11) provides contrasting quotations from Samuelson (1964, p. 118) and Jencks et al. (1972, p. 224) which illustrate this substantial change:

> "How do education and training affect lifetimes income? Are they worth their cost? The evidence answers, 'decidedly yes'" (Samuelson, 1964).

> "Rate of return estimates do tell us that efforts to keep everyone in school longer make little economic sense. The average rate of return for postsecondary education is quite low" (Jencks et al., 1972).

These quotations point not only to increasing doubts about the earlier belief that formal education is the most important factor in promoting significant equality of opportunity, but also increasing scepticism about whether the benefits of additional schooling warrant the costs. Moreover, as cited above, some people have come to the view that equality of opportunity will still leave such inequality of outcomes that further steps are required.

Thus far we have focused on concerns of equity at a point of time or over time. The question about the rate of return on schooling, however, raises broader questions about efficiency which are also of considerable interest. Given the goals of society and the scarcity of resources, is it efficient to use programs such

---

[3]Conceivably, in such circumstances, programs instituted in the name of equality of opportunity could increase the inequality of outcomes. For example, consider the introduction at low cost to the individual of an advanced program which is supposedly designed to increase advanced training for the disadvantaged. Those capable of exploiting the program, however, may be primarily from advantaged backgrounds especially if there are educational prerequisites which have been previously obtained largely in this group. If the advanced program results in increased income and status for the participants, the net result may be greater inequality of outcomes.

as schooling to attempt to achieve those goals? Are there preferable programs? Do labor markets permit sufficient mobility among
occupations to allow adjustments towards the more efficient allocation of labor in a dynamic context? Would improvements in
capital markets lead both to greater efficiency and to greater equity,
as Mincer (1970) and others have suggested might be the case? On
the other hand, are there conflicts between equity and efficiency?
Traditionally, economists have tended to focus more on these
positive questions than on normative ones related to equity.
Greater knowledge of the determinants of inter- and intragenerational mobility and of the returns from programs such as
schooling would enhance considerably our understanding of important efficiency issues such as those which are raised in the
above questions.

## 1.2. Previous related research

Economists, sociologists, and other social scientists have
produced substantial related research on these questions in the
past decade or so. Most of this research is concerned with one or
more of the equations in a largely recursive model which determines: (1) early cognitive ability; (2) educational attainment; (3)
occupational status; and (4) earnings.[4] In the last part of this
section we review some of the important previous research on the
relations determining each of these four indicators. While we
attempt to present a concise review of a number of important
recent works, we are sure that our coverage is not exhaustive
given the rapid expansion of studies in this area. Before reviewing
the recent studies of these four indicators, however, it is important to indicate important limitations of the estimated relations
under discussion.

First, the lack of data has precluded the exploration of the
impact of many important family effects – whether the effects are

---

[4]We assess the appropriateness of the recursive structure in Chapter 2.

direct or through intervening factors such as schooling. Since such family effects are critical in the exploration of the determinants of inter- and intragenerational inequality, many questions posed in the previous section have been difficult to explore.

Secondly, in most estimates of the determination of educational attainment, occupational status, and earnings, *a priori* possibly important variables such as motivation and many (if not all) aspects of ability and family environment are excluded because of unavailable data. As is well known, if such excluded independent variables are correlated with the included independent variables, the estimated coefficients of such included variables are biased.[5] The resulting biases may make it very difficult to identify the true impact of the included variables, and obscure their role in determining inequality and mobility.

Thirdly, the data which are used generally are cross-sectional instead of time series even though many of the questions posed in the previous section relate to phenomena over time. Under special conditions, such as in a stationary state, cross-section estimates may capture well longitudinal relations. The necessary assumptions, however, seem quite strong and probably often are not fulfilled.

Fourthly, the results obtained at best describe marginal changes, but not large ones. This is so for three reasons. (1) Large changes would result in significant variations in the returns to determinants and thus, in parameters which are assumed to be constant in most estimates. If advanced schooling were increased substantially, for example, the returns to this type of schooling probably would fall owing to the relatively great increase in the supply of individuals so trained as compared to the demand for their services. (2) Many of the data sets which have been utilized are limited to a particular population (as identified, for example, by geography, institutional affiliation, age). The extension of the results beyond groups included in the sample may be quite risky.

---

[5]The size of the bias is dependent upon the slope coefficient between the included and excluded variables and the true structural coefficient of the excluded variables. See Chapter 4 for details.

(3) The simple functional forms generally utilized (with few nonlinearities and interactions terms) may be appropriate as Taylor series approximations to more complicated functions over the range of the sample, but may be quite misleading if used outside of the sample.

Fifthly, for each of the four indicators, in principle, the determining relationship can be thought to be the reduced form resulting from the interaction of structural demand and supply curves. To illustrate, consider Becker's (1967) analysis of the human capital investment-earnings relationship as a reduced form of (1) demand functions, $D_i$, which relate individual investments to their marginal rates of return and (2) supply functions, $S_i$, which relate the obtainable funds for such investments to their marginal interest-equivalent costs (fig. 1.1).[6] The demand functions are downward sloping because of diminishing returns to investment in one's self. Differences in marginal productivities or abilities cause there to be different levels of demand curves for different in-

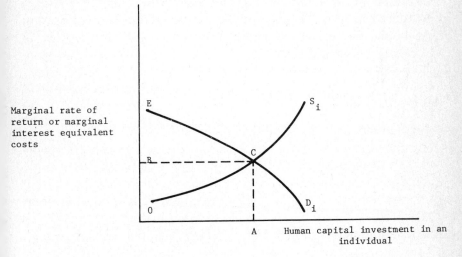

Figure 1.1. Supply and demand curves for human capital investment.

[6]This model will be discussed in more detail in Chapter 2.

dividuals. The supply function is upward sloping because of
increasing difficulties of financing larger investments in an individual. Differences in access to capital markets and in family
wealth cause there to be different levels of supply curves for
different individuals. For any individual the intersection of his or
her demand and supply curves determines his or her optimal
investment in human capital, *OA*, earnings, *OACE*, and average
and marginal, *AC*, rates of return. A number of important insights
can be obtained from this analysis.[7] An important one is that in
general the estimated relation between earnings and the marginal
rate of interest (or between any of the other three indicators
mentioned above and their respective "prices") is a reduced form
based on the *n* different intersections of the *n* sets of demand and
supply curves for the *n* individuals in the sample. Only under
special conditions can the underlying structural supply and/or
demand curves be identified statistically.

Despite these five general limitations, the previous research
gives some insight into the determinants of the four indicators
mentioned at the start of this section. Now each of these is
considered in turn. Because of the nature of the data set used in
this book, we focus on results pertaining to white males in
developed countries.

### 1.2.1. Early cognitive ability

Although most recursive models posit early cognitive ability to be
determined prior to schooling, much of the empirical work reported here uses measures of cognitive ability obtained after some
schooling. Since there exists evidence, moreover, that the amount
of formal education affects measured cognitive ability, in some of
these studies it may be preferable to reverse the recursivity or to
use a simultaneous model. For organizational purposes, however,

[7]For example, dispersions in the demand curves can be considered broadly to
represent inequalities of opportunity (at least in regard to access to the capital
market), but not all of the factors affecting the two curves are independent (e.g.
discrimination may lower the demand curve and raise the supply curve). For
more details see Chapter 2 below or the original Becker (1967) study.

here we follow the ordering of most recursive systems and first discuss the determinants of cognitive ability and next turn to educational attainment.

Debate has been considerable – and often almost ideological in ferver – about the determination of early cognitive ability or "intelligence". Usually, this debate has focused on the distinction between genetic and environment sources, or "nature versus nurture". At one extreme is the position of those such as Hunt (1961) and Halsey (1961) that cognitive ability is determined primarily by environment; changes over time; and is potentially about equal for all individuals. The opposite end of the spectrum has been most prominantly represented recently by Jensen (1969, 1972, 1974, 1975) and Hernstein (1971) who argue that intelligence is almost entirely inherited; almost constant over time; and therefore is inherently unequal across individuals (unless mating were regulated appropriately). Others have taken intermediate positions on this spectrum.

One point of focus of this debate has been on the calculation of heritability measures for cognitive ability (i.e. the proportion of the total variation in cognitive ability which is due to heredity, as opposed to environment).[8] We explore the meaning and limitation of this concept in Chapter 3. At this point we merely summarize the literature. To investigate heritability, one must attempt to separate the effects of genes from the effect of environment by investigating data concerning differences and similarities among various blood relatives.[9] But relatives tend to have environments with many common characteristics, so the main data sets which have been used to try to estimate heritability have contrasted identical (monozygotic, MZ) twins and fraternal (dyzygotic, DZ) twins, twins separated at birth and twins raised together, and adopted children and own children.[10] On the basis of an extension

---

[8]Of course, heritability measures may be defined for any trait, not only for cognitive ability.

[9]Alternatively, one can study unrelated, adopted individuals raised in the same environment.

[10]See, however, Eaves (1975) and Jinks and Eaves (1974) who use many kin groups. See also Goldberger's (1975) analysis of the data and model in the latter piece.

of the classical twins method to include the covariance between genetics and environment, Jensen estimates that 65% of the variance in measured cognitive abilities originate in genetic factors, 28% in environmental factors, and 7% in the covariance term. He claims that these estimates are tightly bounded. Jencks et al. (1972) summarize the available estimates, respectively, to be 45, 35, and 20%.[11] They are much less sure what policy implications these estimates have, since they argue correctly that in many examples compensatory environments can offset the distribution of a trait even if heritability is quite high. (We return to this point in Chapter 3.)

In addition to this last point, a number of other criticisms have been made of heritability estimates.[12] (1) Heritability is a concept that cannot be attributed to a trait itself, but only to a trait in a particular population in a particular environment. (2) Jensen's interpretations of the primary studies on which he bases his estimates are quite questionable. (3) The Jensen approach of searching over variances and covariances to find a narrowly bounded set of estimates does not in fact lead to a narrowly bounded set of estimates. (4) In order to identify the parameters in a heritability model, very strong *a priori* assumptions need to be made (e.g. the correlation between environments is the same for MZ and DZ twins).

This very concise summary hopefully gives a taste of the nature of the issues concerning heritability estimates. Although measures of and debates over heritability have focused on the variance in cognitive ability, it should be obvious that both such measures and criticisms thereof can be transferred to other characteristics, including the other three indicators considered below. We come back to several of these issues below in our

[11]Loehlin et al. (1975) discovered an error in these estimates that would raise the estimate of the covariance by about 0.1 and lower the estimate of environment by the same amount.

[12]See Jencks et al. (1972), Light and Smith (1969), Kamin (1974), Bowles and Gintis (1973), Lewontin (1970), Goldberger and Lewontin (1976), Goldberger (1975, 1976a, 1976b, and 1978), and Scarr-Salapetek (1975).

discussion of identification of our model in Chapter 4 and in the discussion of the implications of our results in Chapters 6–9.

Aside from the debate over heritability, there have been a number of recent attempts to estimate family effects on cognitive ability. Usually, these studies do not attempt to distinguish between genetics and home environments, but occasionally attribution is made to one or the other of these two sources without convincing arguments concerning the identification problem to which reference is made above. Even more rarely, a plausible argument is made concerning the identification question, such as Leibowitz's (1974) conjecture that the relatively greater significance of maternal than of paternal education on the child's IQ reflects in part the quality of home environment since the mother is much more important in shaping that environment, but both parents are equally important in the genetic determination of intelligence.[13]

Examples of these studies include Husen (1950, 1974, 1975), Anastasi (1958), Bloom (1964), Williams (1973, 1974), Bulcock, Fägerlind and Emanuelsson (1974), Wolf (1964), Mosychuk (1969), Majoribanks (1970), Leibowitz (1974), Lindert (1976), Sewell and Hauser (1975), Fägerlind (1975) and Kadane et al. (1976). Typically, many of these studies are based on a sample limited to a fairly narrowly prescribed population (e.g. the 1554 children in the third grade in 1938 in Malmo, Sweden for Husen, for Bulcock, Fägerlind and Emanuelsson, and for Fägerlind; the Terman sample of 821 males and females in Californian schools around 1921, in grades three through eight and with IQ test scores in the top 2% of the national average for Leibowitz; the 1087 siblings of 312 senior male employees of a New Jersey utility company in 1963 for Lindert).

The specific independent variables which generally are fairly important in these studies are: the positive effects of parental (or father's) socioeconomic status; positive effects of parental education; the positive effects of parental time spent with chil-

---

[13]The greater importance of maternal education is not found universally. See, for example, Sewell and Hauser (1975).

dren; the positive effects of birth order (perhaps with some positive effect also of being the last child as compared to middle children); and the negative effects of number of siblings (although Leibowitz in a very special sample finds that the coefficient of this variable is insignificant once birth order is included). These variables, however, are generally only able to explain a modest proportion of the variance in cognitive ability (e.g. $\bar{R}^2$'s of 0.19 for Leibowitz and 0.11 for Fägerlind). The coefficients, moreover, may have been subject to substantial biases because of excluded variables (e.g. the general result of the significant negative effect of the number of siblings, as contrasted with an insignificant coefficient estimate obtained by Leibowitz once birth order is included).

## 1.2.2. *Educational attainment*

As was suggested in section 1.1, during the early 1960s an almost euphoric belief in education widely prevailed. Education was thought not only to be a very important source of economic growth, but also a great social equalizer. In many Western societies equal availability of educational opportunities was thought to permit equality of opportunity in the eighteenth-century enlightenment sense of permitting any person to rise to that position in society which corresponded to his or her inborn capacity. It was also felt that inequality of outcomes was largely the result of inequality of opportunity in schooling. For such reasons, expenditures on education increased rapidly. In the developed market countries such expenditures increased at approximately twice the rate of increase of GNP in the 1960s. The rates of growth of educational expenditures were even higher in many developing countries, in some cases reaching 20–30% of the national budget. In this subsection we review some evidence on the determinants of individual educational attainment.[14] We turn

---

[14]Most of these studies are for the U.S. where it is appropriate to assume no capacity constraints limited individuals from obtaining schooling.

to the question of the impact of such attainment on occupational status and earnings in the next two subsections.

Estimates of the determination of educational attainment are subject to all the general limitations mentioned above. In addition, there is a question about data regarding the dependent variable.[15] If educational attainment is defined broadly to include all types of formal and informal education and training (e.g. on-the-job training), then no study adequately measures the dependent variable. If educational attainment is defined more narrowly to mean formal schooling, then problems remain with the measure generally used: years of schooling. The way this measure normally is used is that the assumption is made that each additional year of schooling represents the same additional increment in educational attainment. No adjustment generally is made for the differential quality of various schools.[16] Nor is an adjustment made for possible diminishing returns to schooling, or for other similar phenomena. The consequence is a problem of error in the dependent variable. If the error is randomly distributed it causes no problem in the estimates of the function for the determination of schooling attainment, but may result in biases when schooling is used as a right-hand-side variable. If the error is systematic, it may cause problems in the estimation of this function as well as biases in the estimation of other relations in which schooling attainment is a right-hand-side variable.[17]

[15]Realistically, of course, this same question arises to various degrees for all four of the indicators under discussion in this section.

[16]Some attempts have been made to represent the quality of schooling by such variables as expenditures per student, particular resources per student, or average achievment of students in a school (e.g. Coleman et al. 1966; Plowden, 1969; Morgenstern, 1973; Taubman and Wales, 1974). Smith and Welch (1975) and Freeman and Gordon (1974) have argued that black–white earning differences are partially due to differences in quality – expenditure per pupil or days attended per year. Recent work on education production functions indicate that there is substitution among inputs, that inputs are not allocated efficiently, and that coefficient estimates differ significantly across levels of schooling and across socioeconomic categories (e.g. racial composition, mean family income). These studies, of course, raise questions about most of the proxies for quality which are used. For example see Summers and Wolfe (1974).

[17]Griliches and Maston (1972) explore the biases introduced when years of schooling is independent of the quality of schooling, but the latter is correlated with ability.

Among the recent studies of the determinants of years of schooling are Blau and Duncan (1967), Duncan (1968), Jencks et al. (1972), Bulcock, Fägerlind and Emanuelsson (1974), Fägerlind (1975), Conlisk (1971), Sewell and Hauser (1975), Bowles and Nelson (1974), Morgenstern (1973), Hauser and Featherman (1976), Leibowitz (1974), Lindert (1976), Jencks and Brown (1977), Olneck (1977), Hill and Stafford (1977), and Gordon (1977). Because of the use of many specialized samples, once again it is difficult to be very specific in summarizing the results. Some general characteristics, however, are clear.

(1) There is considerable evidence of a significant effect of early cognitive ability on years of schooling. In some cases, such as those discussed by Fägerlind, early cognitive ability seems to interact with various observed socioeconomic variables.

(2) Whether or not some measure of ability is included, generally significant coefficients are obtained for socioeconomic background variables related to the parents such as their income, occupational status, and education. The few exceptions (e.g. the lack of significance of parents' schooling which Conlisk reports and the lack of significance of family income which Leibowitz reports) may only reflect multicollinearity between parents' schooling and income or very small samples with attendant large variances. While these variables may represent the abilities of the child other than measured cognitive skills, they probably also serve as proxies for family wealth and access to capital markets. Therefore, it seems likely that the ideal alluded to in first paragraph of this subsection of having educational attainment reflect *only* inborn capacities and not family status has not been met in reality.

(3) Although the estimated impact of measured ability usually tends to be no smaller than that of the socioeconomic background variables, the evidence is not conclusive. Bowles and Nelson demonstrate, for examble, that Duncan's conclusion in this respect is reversed with plausible assumptions about the relative magnitudes of measurement errors.

(4) Relatively little exploration has been undertaken for specific family effects (i.e. aside from the general characteristics men-

tioned above). However, Fägerlind, Leibowitz, Mattes, Hauser and Featherman, and Gordon present evidence of a significant negative impact of the number of siblings, broken families, and the birth order. Lindert and Hill and Stafford find significant effects of estimated parental time inputs in early childhood.

(5) The $R^2$, the variance explained by these variables, ranges from about a tenth to about a half. The differences reflect differences in the sample populations, statistical methodology, and included variables. Even in the cases in which the coefficients of determination are highest, however, the unexplained variance is at least as large as the explained variance. Important variables may be excluded. Examples might be family wealth, noncognitive abilities, and other measures of specific home inputs. The exclusion of such variables may cause substantial biases in the estimated coefficients for the included variables. For example, Jencks and Brown find that controlling for all of genetic endowments and family environments reduces the coefficient on IQ by about half.[18] Olneck reports that controlling for all aspects of family environment reduces the same coefficient by about 40%.

## 1.2.3. Occupational status

One major indicator of overall socioeconomic success is occupational status.[19] For some time sociologists and, more recently, economists have used socioeconomic indices of economic status such as the Duncan (1961) index as a primary indicator of intra- and intergenerational social mobility. This index was derived by regressing 1947 United States prestige rankings (scaled from 0 to 96) from a large sample for 45 occupational titles on two summary

[18]Jencks and Brown (1977) use a statistical technique that does not require genetic endowments and family environment to be observed. Similarly, Olneck (1977) does not require family environment to be observed.

[19]Most models posit that occupational status is determined recursively prior to earnings. We are following this ordering in our presentation. Nevertheless, it might be preferable to consider earnings to be determined simultaneously with occupational status, depending on the definitions of the particular variables utilized.

age-standardized measures from the 1950 census: the percentage
of male workers in that occupation with at least four years of high
school and the percentage with incomes of at least $3500.[20] The
regression estimates were then used as weights to construct an
index for 446 detailed occupational categories using the same two
measures from the 1950 census. The resulting scale closely
resembles the scale of the United States Bureau of the Census
and other similar scales. These scales show a considerable (and
perhaps surprising) degree of invariance over time and place
(Hodge, Siegel and Rossi, 1964; Hodge, Treiman and Rossi, 1966).

Representative recent multivariable studies of the determinants
of occupational status include Blau and Duncan (1967), Duncan
(1968), Hauser (1973), Sewell and Hauser (1975), Bulcock, Fägerlind and Emanuelsson (1974), Hauser, Sewell and Lutterman (1973),
Griliches and Mason (1972), Bowles and Nelson (1974), Lindert
(1976), Jencks et al. (1972), Featherman (1971b), Kelly (1973),
Coleman (1973), Fägerlind (1975), and Olneck (1977). The major
characteristics of these studies are as follows:

(1) In the early studies in which few variables are included, the
direct effect[21] of father's occupation status is systematic and
significant. However, the magnitude of this direct impact declines
substantially and often becomes insignificant when other variables, especially years of schooling, are included.[22] The magnitude
and significance of any remaining direct effect also seems to
decline over the life cycle. Other aspects of family backgrounds
seem even less robust, although in the work of Sewell and Hauser
there is some support for a direct impact of parents' income, at
least in early occupational status.[23]

[20]The multiple correlation of this regression is 0.91.
[21]Throughout this book a direct effect is defined as the partial regression
coefficient. The size of this coefficient depends upon what intervening variables
are also included in the regression. By indirect effect we mean that which is
transmitted through intervening variables.
[22]Haller and Portes and Sewell (1971) also would include personal motivation.
[23]Jencks, however, in a personal communication questions if the stronger
effect of education on first occupation than on later occupations occurs when
one controls for work experience and age.

(2) Both early and late cognitive ability measures have been used in occupational status studies. Univariate correlations between the cognitive ability measures and occupational scales generally range from about 0.3 to 0.5. However, the magnitude of any direct effect generally is reduced considerably (and often to an insignificant level) once father's socioeconomic status and (even more so) education are included. Nevertheless, Bowles and Nelson, Sewell and Hauser, and Olneck still find some significant impact, albeit small.

(3) In the previous subsection, we described the hypothesized importance of education in economic progress and social equality – as well as growing recent doubts. A number of studies support the conclusion that years of schooling is the most important observed determinant of occupational status (e.g. Blau and Duncan, Featherman, Kelly, Sewell and Hauser, Coleman, Bowles and Nelson, Fägerlind, and Olneck). Featherman, Kelly, Fägerlind and Olneck, however, find that this factor declines somewhat over time on the basis of longitudinal data for a given birth cohort.

Of course, such a result does not necessarily imply that schooling leads to social mobility. As is indicated in the previous subsection, parents' socioeconomic background, which seems to have a systematic, fairly substantial impact on years of schooling, can be considered a primary casual element. Moreover, the education coefficient is probably biased upwards because some aspects of genetics and family environment have not been controlled for. For example, Olneck finds an upward bias of about 20% in an equation for mature occupational status when total family environment is not controlled. For this and other reasons there has been considerable questioning of the belief that education is an important channel for social mobility.

(4) Much less systematic evidence is available for other possible variables, partly because of the paucity of data. There are a few suggestions, however. For example, Lindert presents evidence of the significance of a number of variables related to the family environment (i.e. positive for estimated time inputs of the parents and negative for broken home, birth order, and number of

siblings) and Sewell and Hauser give evidence of the significance of intervening motivational variables.

(5) Different studies tend to be more consistent with the variance of occupational status than of the other three indicators discussed in this section. Coefficients of determination generally range from 0.3 to 0.6. Nevertheless, the unexplained variance still is considerable.

## 1.2.4. Earnings

Another major indicator of overall socioeconomic success is earnings.[24] Economists have focused primarily on this variable, and sociologists have given it substantial emphasis. Much of the recent work, at least by economists, has been conditioned by the human capital model developed by Schultz (1961), Becker (1964, 1967) and Mincer (1957, 1958, 1960, 1962a, 1962b, 1969, 1970, 1974).[25] Because of this influence, many of the earnings functions estimated by economists use a semilog form with the natural logarithm of earnings as the dependent variable. Of course, the general observations which we present above also apply to the estimated earnings functions.

Representative recent studies of earnings[26] (or ln earnings) functions include Conlisk (1971), Sewell and Hauser (1975), Bowles and Nelson (1974), Morgenstern (1973), Leibowitz (1974), de Wolff and Van Slijpe (1973), Blau and Duncan (1967), Duncan (1968), Bulcock, Fägerlind and Emanuelsson (1974a), Griliches and Mason (1972), Hauser, Sewell and Lutterman (1973), Jencks

[24]Of course, earnings might be divided into wage rates and number of hours worked. Some studies have taken this approach. However, the success in estimating the latter function has been relatively limited. To limit the length of this review, here we focus on the estimates of earnings rather than on the wage rate and hours worked component.

[25]For a description of this human capital model see the discussion of identification at the start of this section and Chapter 2 below. For other recent surveys by economists of the literature on income distribution including non-human capital models, see Taubman (1975), Tinbergen (1975) and Blaug (1976).

[26]Or, in a few cases, wage rates or income.

et al. (1972), Spaeth (1974), Mincer (1969, 1974), Klevmarken (1972), Klevmarken et al. (1974), Eriksson (1970), Gustavsson (1974), Taubman and Wales (1974, 1976), Taubman (1975), Featherman (1971b), Blum (1972), Rainwater (1974), Ducan, Featherman and Duncan (1972), Húsen (1959), Eriksson (1971), Johansson (1971), Fägerlind (1975), Chamberlain and Griliches (1975, 1976), Hauser and Daymont (1977), and Olneck (1977). The major characteristics of these studies are as follows:

(1) Generally, the direct effects of indicators of parents' socioeconomic success (e.g. schooling, occupational status, earnings) on earnings are small or insignificant. Apparently, such influences are largely transmitted through years of schooling or, perhaps, occupational status (see Hauser, Sewell and Lutterman for an example of the latter). However, there are some cases in which significant positive direct influences are reported for father's occupation (Bowles and Nelson, Duncan, Featherman and Duncan, Jencks et al., Sewell and Hauser, Griliches and Mason), father's or parents' income (Sewell and Hauser, Bowles and Nelson, Leibowitz, Hauser, Sewell and Lutterman, Conlisk), and father's schooling (Bowles and Nelson, Morgenstern).[27] The interpretation given to these estimates is speculative, but generally relates to the effect of some noncognitive abilities and/or motivations which are shaped by one's parents or parents' financial capabilities. In any case, the Sewell and Hauser estimates suggest that the impact changes over the life cycle, with only parents' income continuing to have a significant coefficient around age 30. Taubman presents some evidence that, although the most commonly used indicators of parents' background do not have significant direct effects, some other measures of family environment (e.g. religion) may have an increasing direct impact over the life cycle. Of course, in some cases, the lack of significance reported may reflect the small sample sizes used.

[27]In most studies in which father's schooling is included it does not have a significantly zero coefficient if father's income and/or father's occupational status are included. In the Morgenstern study data are not available for these last two variables. Thus, his significant coefficient on father's schooling is suspect.

(2) The evidence on the direct impact of cognitive ability on earnings is mixed. Duncan, Hauser and Sewell, Hauser, Bowles and Nelson, de Wolff and Van Slijpe, Taubman and Wales, and Taubman all report a fairly significant effect (although Bowles and Nelson emphasize that this effect is much smaller than that of socioeconomic background measures). Conlisk, Leibowitz, and Griliches and Mason report insignificant or small coefficients. In part this difference may reflect whether early or mature cognitive ability measure is used, but the discriminatory power of this distinction is not perfect (e.g. Bowles and Nelson use childhood IQ, Griliches and Mason use mature ability). In addition, the samples that find large effects tend to be those in which the individuals have at least ten years of labor market experience while the small effect group generally have five or fewer years of labor market experience.

(3) The prevalent result is that years of schooling has a significant and quite substantial effect on earnings (Mincer, Klevmarken, Sewell and Hauser, Conlisk, Bowles and Nelson, Morgenstern, Leibowitz, de Wolff and Van Slijpe, Klevmarken et al., Erikson, Bustavsson, Taubman and Wales, Fägerlind, Griliches and Mason, Featherman, Blum, Kelly). There also is evidence that this effect increases initially, perhaps to peak in the 40–44 age range.

The estimated rates of returns to education calculated exclusively from income from these studies generally are in the 6–10% range. The question often has been raised about the extent to which such estimates are biased upward due to the failure to hold ability constant. Griliches and Mason report estimates that the exclusion of an index of mental ability causes a relatively small bias of 7–15% in the coefficient of years of schooling. As shown in Welch's (1975) survey, many other people have found the bias to be small. Taubman and Wales report different results for two samples. The Wolfle-Smith data indicate that a very limited bias if cognitive ability is excluded. But in the larger NBER-TH sample, which was conducted first when the men were about 33 and later when they were 47, the bias is around 25%. Olneck reports a similar result. Hauser and Daymont indicate that for men in a given cohort the absolute bias increases with work experience.

In contrast to the predominant result about the importance of years of schooling in determining earnings, some studies have concluded that this impact is much less once socioeconomic background is properly controlled for (Husen et al., Erikson, and Olneck; for an opposite view see Chamberlain and Griliches). Jencks et al. at times present estimates in which the positive effects of education are not significantly different from zero once current occupation is controlled. Of course, analogous to the above discussion of occupational status, even if education has an important role in determining earnings, intergenerational mobility may be quite limited because of the role of socioeconomic background variables in determining years of schooling.

(4) Several studies report estimates that support a strong direct relationship between occupational status and earnings (Duncan, Jencks et al., Rainwater, Duncan, Featherman and Duncan, Sewell and Hauser, Olneck).[28] To some extent this correlation reflects the way the occupational status measures are constructed, as is described above.

(5) Nearly every study has found that earnings increase with age or work experience till about age 50. The few samples in which it has been possible to obtain separate estimates of age and years of work of experience have found both to be statistically significant. There is also some indication that skills gained from work experience in one occupation are not fully transferable to another occupation, i.e. some training is occupation specific.

(6) The extent to which these models are consistent with the variance in earnings range from 5 to almost 50%. If there is any consistent pattern across the indicators for a given sample it is that the relations used are less consistent with the variance in earnings than in occupational status (and possibly than in years of schooling). Once again, of course, the unexplained variance is

[28]As was noted in the previous subsection, we might posit a simultaneous relation between occupational status and earnings instead of a recursive system. If the true relation is simultaneous, the recursive estimates may suffer from simultaneity bias.

substantial – perhaps with the implication that important variables are excluded, which may imply significant biases in the estimates of the included variables.

## 1.3. Major purposes and findings of the present study

In section 1.1 we discussed why we think that concern with the sources of inter- and intragenerational equality is a very important one. In section 1.2 we reviewed most of the important recent applied studies on the topic. We identified certain empirical regularities in this review, but on a number of questions there remains considerable ambiguity in respect to the significance and/or the magnitude of possibly important determinants. Moreover, we noted a number of general problems with most of these studies: (1) the exclusion of many possibly important variables, such as a whole range of family effects and noncognitive abilities and motivations; (2) the possible introduction of biases in the coefficients of included variables which are correlated with significant excluded ones; (3) the use of cross-section data to investigate longitudinal phenomena, without much evidence to suggest that such an interpretation is justified; (4) the obtaining of results which are applicable to marginal but not large changes; and (5) the problem of identifying the underlying structural supply and demand relations.

Our purpose in this study is to develop methodologies and to apply them to a major new longitudinal data source never before exploited by social scientists, in order to obtain better estimates for the population of the sources of inequality and mobility for years of schooling, early and mature occupational status, and mature earnings.[29] In developing these methodologies we have benefited immensely from the comments and concurrent work of Goldberger, Chamberlain, Griliches, and Jencks. The sample

---

[29]In this book we extend significantly preliminary results reported in Taubman (1976), Behrman and Taubman (1975a, 1976), Behrman, Taubman and Wales (1977), and Taubman, Behrman and Wales (1978).

which we analyze is the NAS-NRC twin sample, which includes 2478 pairs of white male twins who were born in the decade after 1917, served in the military, and were alive and answered the most recent of a series of questionnaires in 1974.[30] The methodology which we develop combines latent variable and variance components techniques. It enables us to estimate the contribution of unobservable variables, such as family effects broadly defined, and to estimate the extent of the bias introduced in the estimates of coefficients of observable variables if the impact of the unobservable variables is not included. Given the special genetic relations between twin brothers, this methodology also enables us to separate the total family effects into two components: one which is perfectly correlated between MZ (monozygotic or identical) twins but less than perfectly correlated between DZ (dizygotic or fraternal) twins and one which is less than perfectly correlated across both MZ and DZ twins. We identify these components under assumptions which are somewhat controversial, but which we feel are justifiable.[31] For brevity of exposition, we generally refer to these two components as "genetics" and "environment", respectively. We further divide the latter into that part which is common to the two brothers and that which differs between them. We interpret the common environmental component to represent primarily family environmental effects.

The estimates that we present do not overcome all of the five general problems encountered in most related research which were discussed in the previous section and were reiterated concisely at the start of this one. No contribution is made to the resolution of the identification question in the fifth problem area. The fourth problem of representing at most marginal changes also

[30]The sample is discussed extensively below in Chapter 5. The existence of individuals who responded to other questionnaires but not to the 1974 questionnaire enables us to make some estimates of the biases introduced by self-selection of the respondents.

[31]This identification question obviously is related directly to the discussion of heritability estimates in subsection 1.2.1 above. Also, see the discussion of identification Chapter 4 below.

largely remains. Substantial extrapolation outside of the sample might be misleading because of changes in underlying prices which are assumed constant, the question of the representativeness of the sample,[32] and the simple functional forms. By virtue of adding another large and interesting data set to those already utilized for exploration of sources of inequality, however, some contribution is made to the resolution of this fourth problem merely through the extension of the coverage of data utilized in such studies.

In respect to the first three problems our estimates represent major improvements over most related studies. They reflect the use of longitudinal kinship data to obtain estimates of the contribution of unobservable family effects (whether or not subdivided into genetics and environment) on inter- and intragenerational equality and to eliminate biases in the estimated coefficients of important observed variables, such as years of schooling. Thus, significant advances are made over most studies in these important dimensions.

To provide some perspective for the reader, in the rest of this section we summarize quite briefly the methodology which we use and the results which we obtain. The rest of the book, of course, provides much more detail on both of these topics.

## 1.3.1. Methodology

Below we present estimates from two basic methodologies: (1) ordinary least squares regressions on individuals and on differences within pairs of MZ and DZ brothers; and (2) maximum likelihood estimates of a variance component, latent variable model. In both cases we assume a recursive model for our four indicators, with the possibility of genetic and environmental indices having direct effects beyond those transferred indirectly by the observed variables.

---

[32]See Chapter 5 for comparisons of our sample with the white male United States population of the same age cohort.

The basic ordinary least squares methodology itself needs no discussion. It is useful to note, however, that for the DZ within-pair estimates we are holding constant environment common to the brothers and for the MZ within-pair estimates we are holding constant genetics and the common environment. Under certain assumptions, therefore, we can estimate the biases if genetics and common environment are excluded. For within-pair DZ twin data, for example, the estimate of the coefficient of schooling in a linear earnings function in the limit approaches the true parameter if schooling is measured without error and (i) if there is no correlation between the differences in years of schooling and the weighted average of the difference in genetics, the noncommon environment, and the difference in the disturbance (where the weights are given by the true relation) or (ii) if genetics and noncommon environment have no direct effect on earnings and there is no correlation between the difference in years of schooling and the difference in the disturbance term.[33] For within-pair MZ data these two conditions simplify since the difference in genetics is zero. If either of these conditions hold, the MZ within-pair estimates give unbiased estimates. A test of the null hypothesis that the MZ and DZ within-pair estimates are the same is a partial test of the hypothesis that there are no genetic effects.[34] If the MZ estimates are biased, no general statement can be made about the magnitude of this bias as compared to the magnitude of possible biases in the DZ within-pair or individual estimates.

The maximum likelihood, variance components, latent variable

---

[33]If there is more than one genetic or environmental index then these conditions should be rewritten to refer only to the indices which enter into the schooling relation.

[34]This test may be important since it does not depend upon the assumption that MZ and DZ brothers have the same environmental correlation, which is a controversial assumption utilized for some of our variance components, latent variable estimates. The test is only partial because (i) it is possible for genes to affect earnings but not bias the coefficient of the years of schooling, in which case the MZ and DZ within equations would not differ, and (ii) it depends upon there being no correlation between the difference in years of schooling and the true coefficient of the environmental index times the difference in the index.

methodology brings together several analytical procedures. The rapidity of recent developments in this area has been quite remarkable.[35] In this book we proceed as follows. In each of the relations[36] within our recursive model we hypothesize some impact of unobservable genetic and environmental indices.[37] We solve these relations to eliminate the right-hand side observable variables, and take the variances of the resulting "reduced form" system.[38] The most general model which we would like to estimate is underidentified, so we cannot test all of the interesting hypotheses. However, we can identify a number of important parameters under sets of assumptions which we think are interesting. We estimate sets of parameters by maximizing the likelihood of observing the actual covariance matrices among the MZ and DZ twins and individuals under the assumption that the "reduced form" residuals are independently normally distributed.

Thereby, we obtain estimates of the parameters of both the observable and the unobservable variables in the original relations for the four indicators and of the variances in the unobservable genetic and environmental indices, all conditional upon our identifying assumptions and our assumptions about the distributions of the disturbances. We can explore how robust are the estimates of the key parameters when changes occur in the identifiying restrictions.

[35]Important recent developments and applications in this area are presented in Zellner (1970), Goldberger (1973), Griliches and Maston (1972), Chamberlain (1974, 1977a, 1977b), Chamberlain and Griliches (1975, 1976), Taubman (1974, 1975), Behrman and Taubman (1975, 1976), Behrman, Taubman and Wales (1976), Taubman, Behrman and Wales (1977), Olneck (1977), and Jencks and Brown (1977).

[36]In our case we have four relations. There is a tradeoff in regard to the number of identified parameters (which increase with the number of observable correlations and, thus, with the number of relations) and the difficulties of estimating large systems by maximum likelihood methods.

[37]Other studies generally do not attempt to divide the family effects into the genetic and environmental components.

[38]Here reduced form refers to the system resulting from substituting for all observable variables. In the other supply and demand sense discussed in section 1.2 all of our original relations are reduced forms.

## *1.3.2. Results*

First we summarize the ordinary least squares results. In the reduced form equations, in which years of schooling and occupational status are not included among the right-hand-side variables, many of the standard socioeconomic background variables have significant coefficients with the standard sign when they are included in the equations based on individuals for all four of the indicators. For example, we find positive effects for Jewish religion and parental education and occupation and negative effects for number of siblings, Catholic religion, and rural background. When education and/or occupational status are included as right-hand-side recursive variables, the estimated coefficients of the background variables generally decline and sometimes become insignificant. Thus, many of the effects of these background variables are mediated by years of schooling and occupational status.

Of more interest is the comparison of particular parameters estimated from observations on individuals, and within DZ and within MZ pairs.[39] For initial occupational status, mature occupational status, and the logarithm of mature earnings, the highest estimates of the coefficients of years of schooling are from the individual equations, the next highest from the DZ within-pair equations in which common environment is controlled for, and the lowest is from the MZ within-pair equations in which common environment and genetics are controlled for.[40]

To be more explicit, consider the estimated coefficient of schooling in the logarithm of mature earnings equation. For individuals the estimate is 0.08, about the same as is reported in many of the studies reviewed in subsection 1.2.4 above. If family background variables are added, this coefficient falls to about 0.07. When common environment is controlled for in the DZ within-pair equation, the estimate drops to 0.06. When both

---

[39]For years of schooling we have no within equations since the background variables are the same for the two variables.

[40]In the mature occupational status relation, however, the equations for DZ within-pair and MZ within-pair are not significantly different.

common environment and genetics are controlled for in the MZ within-pair equation, the estimate drops to less than 0.03!

The implied bias of over two-thirds in the individual estimate of this coefficient probably is an upper bound since the variance of the measurement error to variance in true schooling is almost surely greater in the within than in the individual equations. Nevertheless, it is unlikely that measurement error accounts for most of this difference. Apparently, the failure to hold family effects constant, especially those genetic in origin, may result in substantial overestimates of the return to education. And many of the usual proxies for family background (which in our study does not include family income) do not capture much of this family effect.

For the overall sample we do not have measures of cognitive ability the omission of which is often assumed to cause a bias in the education coefficient in an earnings equation. However, we do have a measure of cognitive ability for a subset of our sample. When we include this variable in the earnings equation for individuals the coefficient is reduced by about 35%. This is a substantial bias although it is in agreement with the few samples which have had cognitive skill data for men with substantial amounts of labor force experience.[41] However, 35% is only about one-half of the apparent bias suggested by the MZ within-pair equations.

We begin the exploration of the maximum likelihood, variance components, latent variable model with a set of assumptions which embodies those made in estimating the MZ within-pair equations, although four separate genetic indices are included. The results for the coefficients of the observable variables indirectly are very similar to the MZ within-pair ordinary least squares estimates, with implications similar to those discussed above.

These estimates also are quite robust under various assumptions about assortive mating, the correlation between environmental and genetic indices, the correlation(s) between the

[41] See Fägerlind (1975), Taubman and Wales (1972), and Olneck (1977).

environment(s) of the twins, and the number of genetic and environmental indices. The above conclusions about probable biases in those estimates due to the inadequate representations of family effects are therefore reinforced. These results contrast with the smaller biases estimated within a latent variable framework with sibling data by Griliches and Chamberlain (1975, 1977), but are quite similar to those presented by Olneck (1977) with sibling data. In part, this difference may occur because Griliches and Chamberlain use younger samples with less work experience (especially in the 1977 study) than do we or Olneck. Another possibility is that Griliches and Chamberlain structure their model to depend more heavily on cognitive abilities, which might miss some important noncognitive factors.

Aside from the question of the robustness of the estimated coefficients of the observed variables, the results of the exploration of alternative assumptions are interesting in themselves.

(1) The possibility that the environment affecting the four indicators (or some subset greater than thereof) includes some of each sibling's specific environment is rejected. This is an important consideration because within MZ estimates do not eliminate specific environments whose presence, were they important, might cause a bias.

(2) The relaxation of the assumption of random mating or of additive genetic effects results in a significant improvement in the fit of the model. The estimate of 0.34 for the relevant coefficient is explicable in terms of negative assortive mating and/or nonadditive genetic effects. This model reduces the importance of genetics versus environment in the overall variance of the various indicators.

(3) When we drop the restriction that the covariances between genetic and environmental indices are zero, we seem to encounter a very flat section of the likelihood function on which we have considerable difficulty in finding a maximum. If we impose *a priori* values on this covariance, the only change is a tradeoff between its coefficient and the variance of the environmental index.

(4) If we add another environmental index to the model, the

other estimates and the overall goodness of fit are not changed substantially. If we compare the results of a model with four environmental indices and no genetic indices to one in which one genetic index is added, the latter is considerably more consistent with the observed data. In pure environmental cases the model can be identified only if the unknown correlation between all the environmental indices is the same for a given type of twin, although they may differ across types of twins. The estimated value of these correlations are about 0.95 for MZ pairs and 0.6 for DZ pairs, respectively.

We thus briefly have summarized the nature of the estimated coefficients and some of the variations which we have explored. Throughout these results the total family effects which are the sum of genetic and family environment are identified and are quite important. The family effects account for from about 50% of the variance in mature occupational status to over 75% of the variance in years of schooling. Their greater importance in the latter than in the former case is plausible since schooling decisions are more directly influenced by parents.

We now turn to a more controversial area: the decomposition of the variance of the family effects into genetic and environmental components. A number, but not all, of the necessary assumptions for this decomposition are tested within the model, which is a considerable advancement over the traditional heritability studies summarized in subsection 1.2.1 above. The critical remaining untested assumption is that the covariance between common environments is the same for MZ and DZ twins. In Chapter 3 we discuss some weak evidence in support of this assumption.

Under the assumptions that the sibling environmental correlations are equal to one for both MZ and DZ twins and that there is a zero correlation between genetics and environment, with a genotypic correlation for fraternal twins estimated at 0.35 genetics accounts for about 35% of the variance in occupational status and 45% of the variance in mature earnings.[42] Common

---

[42]Most of the genetic effects are attributable to specific genetic indices, but the general genetic index has noticeable effects on all four indicators.

environment accounts for 42% of the variance in schooling, 22% in initial occupation, and 10% of mature occupational status and mature earnings. The remainder are attributable to specific environment and account for 25–60% of the total.

Other variants of the model have somewhat different, but predictable, changes in decomposition. Assuming that there is random mating and that all genetic effects are additive increases the genetic contributions by about one-quarter for the general genetics index. Dropping one genetic index or adding one environment index (with a correlation of one across twins) has little effect. If a nonzero correlation between genetics and environment is allowed, most of the results are not affected very much. The arbitrary allocation of the covariance term would, if anything, increase the genetic contribution. In a pure environmental model, of course, all the family effects are attributed to environmental variances.

The above discussion focuses on the sources of earnings differences within a generation. Our results also let us examine certain aspects of intergenerational mobility. We can estimate directly the parent–child correlation for education and occupational status as 0.3 and 0.2, respectively. We can also obtain indirectly an upper bound estimate for this correlation for the logarithm of earnings of 0.25. At least for schooling and occupational status, a majority of this intergenerational correlation arises because the relevant environments of parents and children are correlated.

These results, are obtained from a particular sample of white male United States twin veterans born between 1917 and 1927. The differences between this sample and the population as a whole may mean that all of our results, but especially the partition of variance, do not have broader generality.

Assuming that our results are approximately correct for the whole United States, they have the following implications. First, schooling, *per se*, does not have a large effect on earnings and is not a major source of inequality in earnings or occupational status. Thus, policies to equalize schooling will have little effect on inequality in earnings or status. Secondly, the family plays a major role in generating inequality of education, occupational status, and earnings. It appears, however, that most of the family effects arise out of genetic endowments; thus, policies designed to equalize opportunity defined solely in terms of family environment will leave substantial inequality of outcomes within a generation. Such inequalities can be overcome by transfer schemes and perhaps by large compensatory training programs. However, policies that eliminate family environmental differences will reduce the intergenerational correlation in earnings to about 0.1 which, to all intents and purposes, would mean parents' position in the income distribution would not influence their child's position. The difference in results and implications for inter- and intragenerational inequality is explained in Chapter 8.

CHAPTER 2

# THE MODEL

## 2.1. Introduction

We posit a four-indicator model of socioeconomic development within a generation. This model determines years of schooling, initial civilian occupation, mature occupation, and mature earnings. We choose these four variables because (1) they are important indicators of socioeconomic success in economies such as that of the United States, (2) they permit the exploration of family and key policy (e.g. schooling) effects over the life cycle, (3) we are able to obtain satisfactory measures for them, and (4) the interconnections among these variables facilitate the statistical estimation procedure presented in Chapter 4. The model allows us to follow the time path by which individuals acquire skills and earnings capacity.

We can conceive of other indicators which might be of about the same importance in determining overall human welfare. Examples include health, marital status, and the quantity and quality of children. While there is available a substantial amount of information on these other characteristics for this sample, we reserve explanations of these important dimensions of human welfare for a separate study because of the huge additional complexities that would be involved to incorporate them into the present work.

We also have information on cognitive ability for a subset of the sample. We do not consider cognitive ability to be a socioeconomic indicator of the same ilk as the four on which we focus. However, to try to distinguish cognitive from noncognitive processes and to provide a firmer basis for comparing our analysis with others, we integrate it into the model for that subset of data.

Until recently most theoretical developments have been for earnings. Therefore, in this chapter we first discuss the theoretical underpinnings of the earnings function. We then turn briefly to the other three indicators, building considerably upon our discussion of the determinants of earnings.

## 2.2. The determination of earnings

The basic model used by economists to explain why wage rates or earnings vary is one in which the concepts of marginal productivity, skills, attitudes, genetic endowment, and training play major roles.[1] The model essentially assumes that a person's real gross rate of compensation – the sum of wage and of the value of nonpecuniary rewards, divided by prices – equals his marginal product which is defined as the output he produces, given all other factors of production.[2]

The simplest version of the model assumes that there is perfect competition and no labor market discrimination. It is also assumed that there are nonpecuniary rewards and that there are no deductions from gross wages to pay for investment in on-the-job training. For the moment let us make these simple assumptions with prices normalized to 1. Then we can write,

$$w_i = MP_i, \tag{2.1}$$

where $w$ is the wage rate, $MP$ is marginal product, and the subscript $i$ is for an individual.

The focus in many models is on why individuals have different marginal products. A trivial or tautological answer to this question

[1]This framework is used, for example, by Meade (1973), Becker (1964), Mincer (1974), Rosen (1976) and Welch (1975), among others.
[2]The implications of these assumptions are discussed below. For elegant and more complete descriptions of both issues see Rosen (1976) and Mincer (1974).

is that individuals have different skills and attitudes. However, once we invoke the term "skills", we can begin to ask questions such as what skills matter in the labor market and what determines the level and the composition of a person's skills.

Many different skills and attitudes can help determine earnings. A partial list would include such diverse items as judgement, leadership, physical strength, emotional stability, eye and hand coordination, memory, and reasoning. Many of these skills and attitudes are of more use in some occupations (defined as the performance of particular tasks) than others, and one can probably think of occupations which require skills and attitudes entirely separate from those listed above. The demand function for each skill and attitude by each occupation can be derived from marginal productivity conditions. The supply of various skills and attitudes to the different occupations can be written as a function of relative wages and following, e.g. Tinbergen (1956), a general equilibrium solution of wages for each type of skill and attitude can be found. In general, the set of equilibrium wages changes as supply or demand shifts for the various occupations. But as others do, we generally assume the economy is on a steady state growth path with a constant set of relative prices. Furthermore, we assume in what follows that individuals select those occupations or career paths which are expected to yield the largest present discounted value (PDV) of earnings (or compensation). This condition is consistent with the supply curves assumed above.

Any skill or attitude can be thought of as being produced by an individual combining his innate or genetic endowments with various other inputs which we will label "environment".[3] The relevant aspects of the environment can include, but are not limited to, such elements as prenatal diet, parental love and affection, peer group pressure, schools, military service, and on-the-job training.

A wide variety of economists including, for example, Meade (1973) and Conlisk (1974), have used this framework to study

[3]The genetic concept is discussed in more detail in Chapter 3.

several different problems including the sources of inequality within generations and intergenerational mobility. The human capital model to which Schultz (1961), Becker (1964), Ben-Porath (1967), and Mincer (1974) have made notable contributions also fits into this framework, although within that model the emphasis is on the determination of the optimal amount of schooling and other aspects of environment in which a person should invest.

## 2.3. The human capital model

At this point we consider in some detail a particular version of the human capital model. In this model a person wishes to maximize the present discounted value, $V$, of lifetime earnings, as given in eq. (2.2):

$$V(S, A) = \int_X^N Y(S, A)\, e^{-rt}\, \mathrm{d}t, \tag{2.2}$$

where $r$ is the fixed discount rate, $A$ is "ability" which, in our language, is a combination of genetic endowments and some parts of environment, $t$ is time, $S$ is years of schooling, $X$ is date of completion of schooling $= S +$ preschool years, $N$ is the fixed retirement date, and $Y(S, A)$ is the level of income which is fixed over the life cycle for a given combination of schooling and ability. Embedded in the material that follows are several key assumptions including: perfect competition; perfect knowledge (or risk neutrality); forgone earnings as the only cost of schooling (this ignores G.I. bill benefits which were available to members of our sample); all returns to schooling accruing in the form of increased wage rates; hours worked being exogenous; the interest rate being constant; and productivity being independent of age and experience. But perhaps the most important assumptions in this version of the human capital model are that there are constant returns to investment in schooling, and that the dollar amount of returns from investment is equal to the constant interest rate times the amount of investment.

## 2.3.1. Education and equalizing differences in earnings

Each individual should invest in schooling until the expected present discounted value of further investments in schooling are zero. With our assumptions for any level of schooling the value of (2.2) is given by

$$V(S, A) = \frac{1}{r}[e^{-Sr} - e^{-Nr}] Y(S, A). \tag{2.3}$$

If $N$ is large, the last term in the brackets goes to zero and for any two levels of schooling, $S_0$ and $S_1$,

$$\frac{V(S_0, A)}{V(S_1, A)} = \frac{Y(S_0, A) e^{-S_0 r}}{Y(S_1, A) e^{-S_1 r}} = \frac{Y(S_0, A) \exp [(S_1 - S_0)r]}{Y(S_1, A)}. \tag{2.4}$$

In this version of the human capital model, $r$ and the retirement date $N$, are generally considered fixed and the same for all individuals. Eq. (2.4) therefore is an equilibrium condition for the economy. Suppose that the economy is not in equilibrium. Then the left-hand side of (2.4) is not equal to one, and it would pay for some individuals to alter their schooling levels. The adjustment of the supplies of variously schooled individuals causes wage rates $Y(S, A)$ and $V(S, A)$ to alter. The adjustment in supply and wages continues until the left-hand side of (2.4) is equal to 1.0 for all individuals.[4] Then in equilibrium we can write

$$\ln Y(S_1, A) = \ln Y(S_0, A) + r(S_1 - S_0). \tag{2.5}$$

With no loss in generality, $S_0$ can be set equal to zero and the subscript of $S_1$ can be dropped.[5] In this version of the model, $r$ is a constant at all levels of education because it is assumed that all individuals can borrow at the market rate of interest; earnings, however, are a function of "ability" and the more able will

[4] We discuss an important exception below in section 2.3.2.
[5] The semilog form of eq. (2) with the coefficient on $S$ being $r$ need not hold if we drop assumptions such as that all returns to schooling accrue in wages or any of the other assumptions in section 2.3 are violated. The first assumption will not hold if there are consumption benefits to schooling or if nonpecuniary rewards are correlated with education.

receive more education and more earnings. Indeed, part of the difference of earnings by education level is due to ability.

Schooling is, of course, only one type of environment in which the individual can invest to acquire skills. The individual or his parents could invest optimally in any other type of environment.[6] For example, Grossman (1975) has examined models in which health affects earnings and in which parents or the individual invest optimally in expenditures on health care. In addition, Leibowitz (1974), Lindert (1976), and Hill and Stafford (1977) among others have examined models in which parents invest their own time to augment their offspring's IQ or other marketable skills. More recently Becker and Tomes (1976) among others have examined models of the optimal provisions of family environment as a whole. We return to these works shortly but for the moment we continue to concentrate on investment in schooling.

The model sketched above, of course, makes a number of simplifying assumptions such as perfect knowledge of the shape of the skill production function and of the prices of various inputs. A more realistic model, which has been examined by Weiss (1972) among others, would allow for risk and uncertainty. Since empirical implementation of the model with risk substantially complicates matters, we assume risk neutrality in this book. In the future we plan to return to this issue. In the meantime the reader is referred to Fardoust (1978) who uses the sample we employ to examine the responses to and effects of risk.

### 2.3.2. Equalizing differences and marginal supply and demand curves for individuals

There is, however, a more fundamental problem which has been highlighted by Rosen (1976). Following up on Becker's (1967) Woytinsky Lecture, Rosen asks why people invest in different amounts of education and what are the implications of such differences for the human capital model. He considers his answer

---

[6]Parents and children may not agree on what is optimal; see Ishikawa (1975).

under two different formats. The first is one in which schooling creates a variety of skills and in which annual earnings adjust so as to equalize the present discounted value (PDV) of lifetime earnings. The second model is one based on efficiency units in which schooling augments all existing skills proportionately. Since Rosen comes to similar conclusions in either case, we consider only the equalizing difference approach.

In fig. 2.1 we have drawn an individual's demand curve, *DD*, and the marginal curve to the supply curve (hereafter referred to as the marginal supply curve), *SS*, for investment in education. Contrary to the assumptions in the previous section, the demand curve is drawn so that for a person each additional dollar of investment yields successively smaller rates of returns, i.e. there are diminishing returns to investment. The supply curve indicates how the interest rate, which is the cost of borrowing financial capital, increases as investment in human capital increases. Contrary to the previous assumption that everyone can borrow whatever he wants at the same market rate of interest, we now assume that $r$ increases with the quantity of funds borrowed for investment and that the marginal supply curve is higher the lower

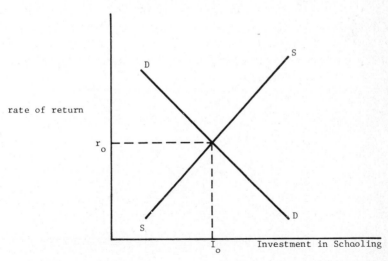

Figure 2.1. Hypothetical marginal supply and demand curves.

is family income. In equilibrium a person would invest $I_0$ and receive $r_0$ on his or her marginal investment. His or her income (before deductions for interest expenses) would be the area under the demand curve up to $I_0$. Fig. 2.1 applies to an individual. If all persons had the same supply and demand curve, fig. 2.1 would apply to the economy.

Assume, however, that some individuals have different marginal supply or demand curves. For example, suppose in fig. 2.2 that everyone had the same supply curve, *SS*, but that some people had *DD* and others, $D_1D_1$. Then equilibrium would be found at either *B* or *E*. Leaving aside for a moment why some people have *DD* and others $D_1D_1$, note that the observed points in the market place trace out the marginal supply curve. That is to say, the points do not give us information on the slope of the demand curve but only allow us to identify the slope of the marginal supply curve. Note also that even in equilibrium people with various amounts of education receive different earnings and eq. (2.5) would not hold exactly since *r* is not fixed but varies with the level of schooling.

Now let us ask why the demand curves differ. The argument in

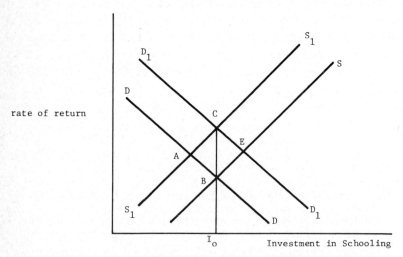

Figure 2.2. Hypothetical marginal supply and demand curves.

Becker and in Rosen is that people with more ability (prior to the investment) obtain higher yields from investment in schooling. That is, either the skill production function, an example of which is eq. (2.9), is not separable so that there is an ability–schooling interaction term or the investment costs are lower for the more able.[7] If this view is correct, then in some sense those who have greater education receive larger earnings partly because of their greater "ability".

Now suppose everyone has the same demand curve but some people have $SS$ and others $S_1S_1$ in fig. 2.2. Then some people will be at equilibrium at $A$ and others at $B$. The observed points *identify* the slope of the demand curve. In this case the equalizing difference approach will allow us to estimate the demand for education and $r$ for each level of $S$, although eq. (2.5) still would not hold since $r$ would not be a constant.

Next consider what happens if both marginal supply and demand curves differ over individuals. In this case we observe points $A, B, C$, and $E$ in fig. 2.2. Following the usual approaches to identification, it seems that we may be able to estimate the slopes of $DD$ and $SS$ if we can find variables that shift marginal demand but not marginal supply curves and vice versa.[8] But the fact that the rate of return to investment varies in schooling for people with the same investment in schooling, e.g. $I_0$ in fig. 2.2, causes a major complication. Recall that in the equalizing difference approach, wage rates alter until in equilibrium the rate of return on investment equals the cost of financial capital. The market does not adjust wage rates for an individual but only for occupations and education levels. However, if both marginal

[7] It is possible to construct models in which the more able receive more earnings at all education levels but there is no interaction so that the demand for education is the same. The available evidence on interaction effects is ambiguous. See Becker (1964), and compare Taubman and Wales (1974) and Hauser (1973). In Chapter 7 we present some new information on the subject. The costs may differ because the more able receive more scholarships or forgo less leisure while mastering the academic curriculum. On the other hand the more able have higher forgone earnings.

[8] For example, we may be able to measure ability and family wealth, the first of which might affect only demand and the second only supply.

supply and demand curves differ across individuals, there is not *a* rate of return at each education level but an average rate of return with dispersion.

It is not clear that information on these average rates of returns allows us to estimate the slope of *DD* since the average return at each education level depends upon the distribution of marginal demand and supply curves at that quantity. Hence, the estimated relationship of ln earnings to education is a market clearing relationship which need no longer be consistent with the originally examined human capital model. That is to say, if individuals in our sample choose their investment in schooling or other aspects of the environment so that their expected rate of return equals their interest rate, we will be estimating changes in average rates of return as schooling or environment varies. While we agree that for many purposes it would be more desirable to estimate the marginal return to education, we think that information on how the average return varies with years of schooling is of value.

Figure 2.2 also illustrates another important problem which we study in our empirical analysis. At $I_0$, the two individuals invest in the same amount of schooling but receive different earnings. In the figure we have paired $S_1 S_1$ with $D_1 D_1$ and $SS$ with $DD$. Let us call the person with $D_1 D_1$, person 1, and with $DD$, person 2. As drawn in the figure, 1 pays more to finance schooling. If, however, 1 faced the $SS$ supply curve and 2 faced the $S_1 S_1$ curve, then 1 would have more schooling and more income than 2 because 1 was both more able and had readier access to financing.

Most people suspect that there is a positive correlation between "ability" and access to financing because the more able – those with better genes and/or family environment – tend to come from families with more income. Thus, earnings differences by education level incorporate the differences in ability and in financing as well as the returns to education, *per se*. In the model which we estimate we allow for differences in genetic endowments and family environment which are some of the factors that shift the education supply and demand curves. Thus, we can control for the joint determinants of schooling and earnings and can, in principle, eliminate the bias in the estimate of the average return to education arising from these sources.[9] Put another way, our model controls for variables that normally induce the residuals for schooling and earnings to be correlated. We cannot, however, estimate the marginal relationship between $r$ and schooling along $DD$ or $SS$ without additional assumptions.

Figures 2.1 and 2.2 purportedly indicate how a rational individual with given expectations should behave when making his investment decision. If, as we have assumed, the economy were in a steady state, expected and actual outcomes would agree. However, over time the actual return on these investments are affected by shifts in the supply and demand curves which undoubtedly are not all anticipated. We find it difficult to believe that the expectations of the 1920s and 1930s, etc., even on the average, have been borne out in the 1950s, 1960s and 1970s.[10] Thus, we think any simultaneity problem is small. We can, however, use the existing data to estimate what have been the influences of parental effects and schooling on the actual distribution of earnings. Of course, if the economy is not or has not been in a steady state, the applicability of our results to future periods depends on the nature of future unexpected developments.

Becker has built upon the approach used in his Woytinsky Lecture in his subsequent work on child quality. In Becker and Tomes (1976), for example, parents maximize a utility function whose arguments include the quality of each child ($Q_i$). Using our notation they define quality as the stock of human capital which is the sum of its genetic and environmental components, i.e.

$$Q_i = G_i + \hat{N}_i, \tag{2.6}$$

where $\hat{N}_i$ is the dollar value of all investments in the child's

---

[9]The method we use allows us to estimate the factors that shift schooling and earnings jointly, even if these factors have a positive influence on one and a negative on the other.

[10]Consider, for example, the marked, and to a large extent, unexpected shifts in birth rates and life expectancy which have affected supplies. Demand for various skills must have changed because of technological progress.

human capital.[11] Using this analysis one can derive demand functions for each child's $N$ which depend upon prices, $P$, parental income, $Y_F$, interest rates, $i$, tastes, $T$, and genetic endowments, $G$. A linear version of such a demand function is

$$\hat{N}_i = bP + ci + dY_F + eT + fG = N_i + fG. \qquad (2.7)$$

Since we are assuming that tastes shift the marginal supply curve as does income and since tastes is an unobservable variable whose normalization is arbitrary, we can set $d = e$.

Economists such as Becker (1967) Okun, (1975), and Tawney (1961) define inequality of opportunity as those variations in investment or income that arise because of differences across family in $P$, $i$, $Y_F$ and (in some cases) $T$. In Chapters 3 and 4 we demonstrate how we can use data on twins to estimate the contribution of inequality of opportunity to inequality of earnings.

It is instructive at this point to consider the various factors which affect the allocation of resources within a twin pair. Suppose that hours of work are fixed and that the parents utility function is

$$U = U(X, Q_1 \ldots Q_N), \qquad (2.8)$$

where $X$ is parental consumption of goods and $Q_i$ is the quality or income of the $i$th child.

It is well known from the public finance literature that the effects of a tax (or subsidy) are the same regardless of whether the tax is legally levied on the supplier or demander. Therefore to simplify the presentation assume that the utility function is such that there is no diminishing marginal utility to $Q_i$, although there are diminishing returns to investments. Parents still can express preferences for one sibling over another by "charging" one sibling a higher price for his or her investment funds. This point can best be illustrated by redrawing fig. 2.2 under the assumption that

---

[11]Becker and Tomes would include in $G_i$ any inputs into human capital not subject to parental or the child's decisions. However, they acknowledge that their primary example of an exogenous input, school quality, is only exogenous with neighborhood schools if locational choices are ignored.

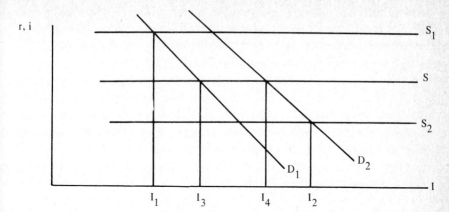

Figure 2.3. Hypothetical supply and demand curves for siblings.

the marginal supply of funds curve is horizontal.[12] In fig. 2.3, $S$ represents the supply of funds curve that would be available if parents wished to provide the twins with the same opportunities and had no preferences for one child over the other. If $S$ were to prevail, the optimal investment for the two siblings would be $I_3$ and $I_4$.

If parents prefer child 2 to child 1, they can offer $S_1$ and $S_2$. Then optimal investments would be $I_1$ and $I_2$ and child 1 would have less investment than if his parents were neutral in their preferences. We would define parents as having compensatory (reinforcing) preferences if they preferred the less well (better) endowed child. We warn the reader that Becker and Tomes define the terms "compensatory" and "reinforcing" in terms of outcomes rather than parental preferences. In their vocabulary, parents reinforce if the better endowed child ends up with greater investments than the less well endowed child.

$Q_i$ depends upon many different investments. However, if the parents prefer one child to the other, we assume that they impose

---

[12]While the analysis is more complicated if the supply curve is upward sloping, the same conclusions are reached.

a tax or shift $S$ in the same direction for each investment.

In general the optimal investment function for each type of investment depends on prices, interest rates, family income, tastes, and genetic endowments as in eq. (2.7). For twins reared together it seems reasonable to assume that prices, interest rates, and parental income are the same. As just argued, tastes may or may not vary within a family. As discussed in Chapter 3, in general siblings have different genetic endowments although identical twin pairs have identical genetic endowments. That prices, family income, etc. are the same for twins causes twins to share a common environment.

### 2.3.3. Investments in on-the-job training

As indicated in Chapter 1, most economic research on earnings functions has included variables for years of schooling and of work experience with more focus on the former and only secondary attention on cognitive ability and family background including parental time and resources. Years of work experience is generally considered to be a proxy for investment in on-the-job training (OJT).

Economists have examined in great detail models of investment in OJT. A simplified version of this theory, as developed by Mincer (1958, 1974), Ben-Porath (1967) and others, is the following. Suppose at date of entry into the labor market an individual could receive the same wage in many occupations. Furthermore, assume that a particular occupation in a given firm provides general training in the initial period to the worker at a marginal cost $C_0$. Such general training can, by definition, be used in all occupations in all firms. Once training is completed the person has an increased marginal product in all firms. To prevent him from switching to another firm, the training firm must pay the worker a wage equal to his new higher marginal product. Since the individual captures all the benefits of his training, the training firm is not willing to pay any and the individual must pay for all of the training costs.[13] The firm could sell the training directly for a stated fee, but generally the individual in effect pays for the training by receiving a wage less than his or her marginal product while being trained. That is, his or her initial wage is reduced by $C_0$. Subsequently his or her wage will be increased because of the investment in new skills. In equilibrium, the increases in the value of his marginal product is $rC_0$.

Once again the model can be thought of in the equalizing difference framework with all its strengths and weaknesses. Thus, if an individual is initially equally skilled in two occupations, A and B, but only A provides training and higher future incomes, initial wages adjust so that the PDV of lifetime wages in the two occupations are equal. If training is provided in only year 0, at costs $C_0$, initial year wages then will be $\bar{W} - C_0$, where $\bar{W}$ is earnings without training. If the market rate of interest which is available to all is $r$, then in equilibrium for training which will generate benefits for many years

$$W_t - \bar{W} = \left(\frac{r}{1+r}\right)C_0, \qquad t > 0.$$

This of course implies that after the initial year earnings will be constant. Mincer, however, argues that investment occurs not only in the initial year of work but for many years. The rate of investment, however, decreases annually, i.e. $dI_t/dt < 0$. Thus, $W_t - \bar{W} = rK_t - C_t$ where $K_t = \Sigma C_t = $ capital stock of on-the-job training.[14]

While Mincer uses years of work experience as a proxy for $K_t$ to explain the age profile in the variance of earnings he argues

---

[13]If there is specific training a firm might pay all the costs, but in general it is felt that individuals and firms share the costs in order to give both an incentive to remain in an employee–employer relationship which allows the returns to accrue.

[14]This version does not allow for depreciation which is incorporated in later works.

that there is individual variation in such investment.[15] He also
explains the steeper experience earnings profiles of the more
educated by the greater (average) investment in OJT by the more
educated. In other words, the use of years of work experience as
a proxy for $K_t$ results in an omitted variable correlated with $S$
and the covariance of this omitted variable and $S$ varies over the
life cycle.

## 2.4. The model

In this section we present the basic model which we wish to
estimate.[16] We build upon the human capital model, but incorporate explicitly information on genetic endowments and
family environment. For simplicity we suppose that no measures
of skills are available. The model is easily modified to allow for
any skills that are measured.

### 2.4.1. The earnings function

Assume that there are $M$ different skills which are produced by
combining $r$ different genes and $t$ different environments. (Some
of the genes and environments may have zero coefficients in a
particular function.) The skill production function can be written
as

$$\text{skill}_m = f(G_1, \ldots, G_r, N_1, \ldots, N_t), \qquad m = 1, \ldots, M. \qquad (2.9)$$

Since a person may not use all of his $M$ skills in a particular
occupation, his or her marginal product and wage need not be a
linear combination of the $M$ skills. We assume that a person

[15]Ross, Taubman and Wachter (1977) show that they can explain everything
the OJT theory does by assuming a sequential sorting model based on on-the-job
performance.
[16]In Chapter 6 we incorporate IQ into this model. We do not include IQ in the
basic model because information is only available on a nonrandom subset of our
sample.

selects the occupation which yields the highest PDV of the sum of lifetime earnings plus the value of nonpecuniary rewards. In the chosen occupation his or her wage depends on his or her $M$ skills. With prices normalized to one, we can write,

$$w_i = MP_i = h(\text{skill}_1, \ldots, \text{skill}_M), \tag{2.10}$$

$$w_i = h[f_1(G_1, \ldots, G_r, N_1, \ldots, N_t), \ldots, f_M$$
$$\times (G_i, \ldots, G_r, N_1, \ldots, N_t)]. \tag{2.11}$$

For simplicity we assume that each production function, $f_m$, is of a generalized Cobb–Douglas form and that the $h$ function is also of this form. Then, supressing the subscript for an individual, we can write

$$w = (G_1^{\alpha_1} G_2^{\alpha_2}, \ldots, G_r^{\alpha_r})(N_1^{\beta_1} N_2^{\beta_2}, \ldots, N_t^{\beta_t}). \tag{2.12}$$

Note that these assumptions lead to a wage function which is separable in the genetic and environmental indices. For the statistical methodology presented in Chapter 4 this separability, which precludes interaction terms between genetic and environmental indices after taking logarithms, is *not* an innocuous assumption. It saves degrees of freedom in a model which is underidentified even with this assumption.

For some purposes we can further simplify (2.12) by defining,

$$G = \prod_{j=1}^{r} G_j^{d_j} \tag{2.13}$$

and

$$N = \prod_{k=1}^{t} N_k^{B_k}. \tag{2.14}$$

Then we have,

$$\ln w = \ln G + \ln N. \tag{2.15}$$

Note that we can rewrite (2.15) in the semilog form of (2.15a) since the unobservable genetics and environmental indices can be replaced by any monotonic transform.

$$\ln w = G + N. \tag{2.15a}$$

In eq. (2.13) $G$ is an overall genetic index which is a

geometrically weighted average of the separate genetic components of each of the $M$ skills. Similarly, $N$ is an overall environmental index. (We can modify this by letting $N$ be the unobserved environment while letting schooling or other observed aspects of the environment enter directly into (2.15).)

Our model has been developed in terms of wage rates. The data in our, and in most other, samples are for annual earnings, although we and others often have available information on hours worked.[17] We can of course develop a labor supply model which can be expressed as a function of wage rates of family members, nonwage income, genetics, and environment. Multiplication of the wage and hours function yields annual earnings, which would have the same arguments as $\ln w$ – except for nonwage income and other family members' wage rates which we ignore. The resulting equation is the fourth one in table 2.1. The numerous $G_i$ and $N_i$ variables in that table are explained in the next section.

### 2.4.2. The determinants of initial civilian and mature occupation and of years of schooling

The first equation in the model is for schooling which we have made dependent on genetics and family environment. The actual schooling of an individual is determined by his or her own preferences and opportunities and by societal actions.[18] The material included in fig. 2.1 can be used to generate a derived demand function which is related to a person's ability, relative wage, schooling costs, and cost of borrowing funds which depend upon family income and perhaps other elements of background. As argued earlier, in the human capital model ability and back-

---

[17]Obviously, we can divide the earnings series by hours worked to obtain an estimated wage rate. We choose not to do so because we are suspicious of the hours series, e.g. we would be hard pressed to give an accurate appraisal for ourselves. Moreover, in the sample, Atrostic has found wage rates and most economic type variables are not correlated with hours. See also Griliches (1975).

[18]The societal constraints would be important if society refuses to make available all the education slots demanded at the given set of prices, etc.

Table 2.1
Structural and reduced forms for four-indicator model of socioeconomic success.[a]

---

*Structural equations*

$$Y_1 = \alpha_1 N_1 + \beta_1 G_1 \qquad\qquad\qquad\qquad\qquad + u_1$$

$$Y_2 = \gamma_1 Y_1 + \alpha_2 N_1 + \beta_2 G_1 + \delta_1 G_2 + \mu_1 N_2 \qquad\qquad + u_2$$

$$Y_3 = \gamma_2 Y_2 + \gamma_3 Y_1 + \alpha_3 N_1 + \beta_3 G_1 + \delta_2 G_2 + \mu_2 N_2 + \theta_1 G_3 + \psi_1 N_3 \qquad + u_3$$

$$Y_4 = \gamma_4 Y_3 \qquad + \gamma_6 Y_1 + \alpha_4 N_1 + \beta_4 G_1 + \delta_3 G_2 + \mu_3 N_2 + \theta_2 G_3 + \psi_2 N_3$$
$$+ \eta G_4 + \epsilon N_4 + u_4$$

*Reduced forms*

$$Y_1 = k_{11} N_1 + d_{11} G_1 \qquad\qquad\qquad\qquad + v_1$$

$$Y_2 = k_{12} N_1 + d_{12} G_1 + d_{22} G_2 + k_{22} N_2 \qquad\qquad + v_2$$

$$Y_3 = k_{13} N_1 + d_{13} G_1 + d_{23} G_2 + k_{23} N_2 + d_{33} G_3 + k_{33} N_3 \qquad + v_3$$

$$Y_4 = k_{14} N_1 + d_{14} G_1 + d_{24} G_2 + k_{24} N_2 + d_{34} G_3 + k_{34} N_3 + d_{44} G_4 + k_{44} N_4 + v_4$$

---

[a] *Notes*:

$Y_1 = S$ is years of schooling.

$Y_2 = OC_i$ is status score on initial full-time civilian occupation, as measured by the Duncan scale.

$Y_3 = OC_{67}$ is status score on 1967 occupation, as measured by the Duncan scale.

$Y_4 + \ln Y_{73}$ is the natural logarithm of earnings in 1973.

$N_1, N_2, N_3, N_4$ are unobserved environmental indices.

$G_1, G_2, G_3, G_4$ are unobserved genetic indices.

$u_1, u_2, u_3, u_4$ are unobserved random structural errors.

$v_1, v_2, v_3, v_4$ are unobserved reduced form errors which are functions of the $u_1$ and $\gamma_i$ as is indicated in (4.25).

The Greek letters are parameters in the structural relations.

The $k_{ij}$ and $d_{ij}$ $(i = 1, \ldots, 4; j = 1, \ldots, 4)$ are parameters in the reduced form relations which are functions of the structural parameters (only nonzero values are included in this table).

ground in the schooling equation may also appear in the earnings function. On the other hand, schooling may not depend in exactly the same way as earnings on the individual components of genetic factors and family environment. For example, earnings at age 50 may be affected by diseases that only occur after completion of schooling but are related to genetics or family environment. The demand for schooling also may be dependent upon consumption aspects which are related to family environment. To clarify this point suppose that we examine only the genetic elements that influence earnings. Let the two indices defined as in (2.13) by $G_y$ and $G_s$. Then we might have

$$G_y = \prod_{j=1}^{r} G_j^{\epsilon_j} \tag{2.16}$$

and

$$G_s = \prod_{j=1}^{r} G_j^{\sigma_j}. \tag{2.17}$$

We can then write

$$G_y = G_s \prod_{j=1}^{r} G_j^{(\epsilon_j - \sigma_j)}. \tag{2.18}$$

$G_y$ will differ from $G_s$ if any of the $(\epsilon_j - \sigma_j)$ terms are nonzero.

It is possible to express the four structural equations in table 2.1 in terms of at most four aggregate genetic and four aggregate environmental indices. Note that it is immaterial whether these indices enter into the structural relations in the triangular fashion which we posit in table 2.1 or with separate environmental and genetic indices for each relation. One structure can be transformed into the other.

By similar reasoning we need define at most four environmental variables to include in our four-equation model. However, it may be possible to reduce the dimensionality of the environmental indices. The optimal investment for each of the $t$ types of investment can be expressed as in eq. (2.7). All the variables in that equation may vary across families, but to a first approximation the major across-family variations would occur in $Y_F$, $T$, and $G$. The effects of $G$ on $N$ can be incorporated into our estimate of genetic effects. Since the effect of $T$ is to raise or lower a child's supply of funds curve for all $N$, and since the position of the supply curve depends on $Y_F$, the across-family variations in the endogenous (nongenetic related) portions of each $N$ depend primarily on $Y_F$ adjusted for the "tax" implicit in preferences. We could, of course, relabel the $N$ variable as family income but we choose not to do so in order to keep the notation similar to that generally used in the nature–nurture literature. In subsequent work we test whether there are different $N$ values for our four equations. These additional variables would be required if price variations are important or, for reasons explained in Chapter 3, if post childhood investments depend upon resources made available to a person by his inlaws.

Our model also contains measures of occupation at two points in the life cycle: initial civilian occupation and mature occupation. These status measures use the Duncan scale, which is a weighted average of the percentage of males in the occupation in 1950 who had graduated from high school[19] and the percentage who had annual earnings above $3000. Both the initial and the mature indices may be thought of as indicators of normal income in an occupation, with some adjustments for nonpecuniary returns. As such, the same general model as for earnings seems appropriate.

The model in table 2.1 would be fully recursive if initial occupation, $Y_2$, were allowed to have direct effects on earnings in 1973, $Y_4$. It seems plausible that a person's initial occupation can have implications for his or her earnings throughout his or her career. For example, a person can choose an occupation with a little or large amount of general or specific training. He or she also may choose an occupation which subsequently undergoes an unexpected shift in demand and change in equilibrium wages. Also, a person's initial occupation may indicate particular skill levels that are not directly measured but which persist over time. It is for these reasons that we allow initial occupation to have a direct effect on the mature occupation. However, since we include the mature occupation in our earnings equation and since we include the $G_i$ and the $N_i$ indices throughout our model, there seems to be no need to permit initial occupation to have direct effects on 1973 earnings.[20] As we demonstrate in Chapter 4, imposing this zero coefficient restriction allows us to estimate another important parameter.

---

[19]For a discussion of this index see the references given in section 1.2.3.
[20]Others often impose restrictions of this type. See, for example, Griliches and Maston (1974).

In these equations we include a number of genetic and
environmental indices. To the extent possible we use measured
variables, such as mother's education, to represent these indices.
But we are certain that many aspects of $G_i$ and $N_i$ are not
measured in our sample. We develop and use a technique to
control for and measure these variables in Chapters 4 and 7.

Table 2.1 presents both "structural" and "reduced form"
parameters.[21] The reduced form parameters are obtained by substituting the appropriate structural equations for any of the four
dependent variables that appear as right-hand variables in the
structural equations. The *total* effect of any variable is obtained
from the reduced form equations while the *direct* effect is given
by the structural equations. The difference between the total and
direct effects are the *indirect* effects.

The distinction between total and direct effects is important
when considering variables such as family environment since
much of its effect on earnings flows through schooling. Thus, an
earnings equation with both schooling and background variables
understates the total effects of family background. On the other
hand, there is a bias on the education coefficient in the earnings
structural equation only if the $G$ and $N$ variables have direct
effects on earnings.

The reduced form idea is also important in another way. A key
question in the estimating technique we use is whether the cross-
sibling correlation in family environment can be expected to be
the same for twin pairs with more or less correlated genetic
endowments, i.e. for identical and fraternal twins. (See Chapter 3
for formal definitions.) The major reason for expecting the correlation to be smaller for fraternal twins is that either parents,
peer group, and other people react to the genetic differences in
providing the environment such as schooling or that choices of
the twins depend on their genetic endowments. That is, environ-

---

[21]The term "structural" may be a misnomer since we have already argued that
for earnings we are observing market clearing relations that reflect both supply
and demand considerations. Similar comments apply to the other equations.
Nevertheless, we continue to make the structural versus reduced form distinction because we have not been able to think of a more satisfactory shorthand
nomenclature.

ment partly depends on genetic endowments. In our models genes are exogenous and we generally adopt the assumption that a reduced form expression properly attributes any potential difference in the cross-sibling covariance of expenditures on the child by twin type to genetic endowments. Put another way, the parents select the appropriate expenditures on the child (and thus the cross-sibling covariance in such expenditures) out of a distribution which is the same for both types of twins. Thus, our estimate of the contribution of genetics includes any indirect effects via choices of family environment as well as direct effects. This definition is appropriate for answering the question of how much of the inequality of earnings is attributable to inequality of opportunity or across-family differences in prices, interest rates, family income, and tastes.

## 2.4.3. *Cognitive skills*

For a subset of the sample, a measure of cognitive skill is available which is discussed in Chapter 5. This is a vocabulary test which was administered as part of the general classification test (GCT). A similar test is the major component of most IQ tests. Denote this variable by *GCT*. To aid in examining the contribution of cognitive skills to labor market success and to provide comparability with other studies, we also re-estimate our model including *GCT* for the subset. The model is then specified so that there is a fifth equation for *GCT* which depends on an additional genetic and an additional environmental variable ($G_5$ and $N_5$) and another random variable, $u_5$. Both $G_5$ and $N_5$ and *GCT* enter all the other structural equations.

Posing the model in this form implies that *GCT* is not affected by schooling. Such a formulation would be correct if either the cognitive skills test had been administered prior to schooling or if the particular test was independent of material taught in schools. Since our measure is a vocabulary test administered in the military when people had different amounts of education, there are reasons to doubt that the scores are independent of schooling. However, in Chapter 6 we use a method originally proposed by Griliches and Mason to solve this issue.

# CHAPTER 3

# GENETIC ENDOWMENTS AND TWINS

## 3.1. Introduction

Many economists have proposed models like that in Chapter 2 in which earnings depend in part on genetic endowments; however, until now there have been no attempts to control for or to estimate the effects of all possible genetic endowments.[1] The major obstacle, of course, has been the lack of data. We do not have direct data on genetic endowments but we have a special sample which allows us to substitute statistical methodology for direct observations. To understand this methodology it is necessary to discuss briefly some principles and concepts of biology.

---

[1]Jencks and Brown (1977), sociologists, and their colleagues have estimated models similar to ours for IQ and education but have not yet extended their analysis to earnings or occupational status. A number of studies of earnings have included IQ which is an ability that presumably is rewarded in the market place. Since we can think of IQ as being produced by combining genetics and environment, controlling for IQ will control for this genetic variation. Very few other abilities have been included in earnings equations. For the most extensive effort on noncognitive abilities see Mueser (1979). Moreover, even if IQ is the only ability which is rewarded in the market and which is partly produced by genetic endowments, the coefficient or $R^2$ of IQ in an earnings equation will not provide an estimate of the contribution of genetics to the mean or variance of earnings.

## 3.2. Biological concepts and twins

Males and females normally have twenty-three pairs of chromosomes, which pairs do not differ in shape and size by sex except for the sex chromosomes, X and Y. There are thousands and maybe millions of genes located along the chromosomes. Each gene also occurs in pairs, one member of each pair having come from each parent. The available members in the population of each gene pair may be of the same form (homozygotic) such as AA, BB, or different (heterozygotic) such as AB, AC. We assume that each skill or trait considered in this work is influenced by many genes, some of which are heterozygotic or have more than one variety in the population. These assumptions mean that there is genetic diversity among individuals and that the distribution of genetic endowments can be considered to be normally distributed.

Normally when cells divide each of the new cells contains all the genes of the original cells. However, only a randomly determined member of each pair of genes (and of each chromosome) is transmitted to the next generation via the egg or the sperm, each of which is a gamete of one parent. But once the egg is fertilized, i.e. the two gametes combine, the developing individual has received one member of each gene from each gamete.

There are two types of twins – monozygotic (MZ) and dizygotic (DZ).[2] The MZs, often known as "identical", are the result of the splitting of an already fertilized egg. The DZs, or fraternal twins, are the result of two different eggs fertilized by two different sperm. The DZs, from a genetic viewpoint, are siblings born at the same time. DZ twins do not have the same genetic composition, although they are more alike than randomly drawn individuals.[3] The MZ pairs, however, have the same genetic make-up because

---

[2]The literature, at times, refers to a third type which is hypothesized to occur when part of the single egg released by the woman splits (before fertilization) and both parts become fertilized by separate sperm. Such pairs would be more alike than DZ and less alike than MZ pairs. Most empirical studies have rejected the presence of such third types.
[3]Below we give the formula that indicates how much alike DZ twins are.

each piece of the split fertilized egg contains all and only the information of the original fertilized egg (barring mutations).[4]

The frequency of twin births – at least before the introduction of fertility drugs – is 1–1.5% of all human births depending upon the population being studied. For the U.S. white population the twinning rate is about 1.25% with about 25–30% of the twin births being MZ pairs. The rate varies by population because the DZ twinning rate varies by race, ethnic origin, and age of mother; but the twinning rate for MZs does not so vary. As an example of the variation in DZ and constancy in MZ twinning rates, consider fig. 3.1 which is taken from Cavalli-Sforza and Bodmer (1971). The MZ twin rate is increased only slightly as the age of the mother grows. On the other hand the rate for DZ twins goes from less than 4 per 1000 maternities for mothers who are 18 years old to nearly 16 for mothers age 40. The rate then drops dramatically,

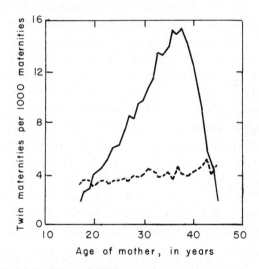

Figure 3.1. Twin maternities per 1000 maternities for given age of mother. Solid line: births of DZ twins; dashed line: births of MZ twins. Italian data, 1949–54. *Source*: Cavalli-Sforza and Bodmer (1971, p. 568).

[4]For a more complete discription of the biological aspects, see Cavalli-Sforza and Bodmer (1971).

perhaps because of sample size. While the graph is based on
Italian data, the situation is similar for the U.S. white population.
An issue which we explore in Chapter 5 is whether the marked
difference in the mean and distribution of age of mother by twin
type results in differences in the mean and distribution of income
or of other variables.

Besides mother's age there is another major distinction between
MZ and DZ pairs. MZ pairs are always of the same sex while DZ
pairs can be either same sex or mixed sex.[5] Since about 50% of
the DZ pairs born are mixed sex pairs, MZs account for 40–45%
of like-sex pairs.


*Identification of twin type*

The methodology we construct below requires us to separate
twins into MZ and DZ groups. In principle, there are several
mechanisms available which can discriminate perfectly, but the
available information is no longer available or is too costly to
obtain.[6] Most empirical separations are based on one of two
methods. The first is biochemical evidence. There are some
human features – such as blood type – which are determined
solely by genes and which can be classified into various groups by
a variety of tests. Identical twins have the same genes, and have
the same test results – ignoring measurement error. Fraternal
twins do not have the same test results in all cases even if there is
no measurement error. With enough tests one can reduce the
probability of misassignment to as low a level as is desired. This
method is costly for large samples since individuals must be
examined personally but it has been used in some studies.

[5]It is possible for a MZ pair to be a mixed-sex pair only if when the fertilized
egg splits there is mutation solely on the X or Y chromosomes, which determine
sex. Such a mutation would occur very infrequently though biologists in oral
conversation have mentioned one case being known.
[6]One technique uses evidence from the placenta. The other involves whether
or not the body of one twin can accept permanently a skin graft from his sibling.
This technique relies on the proposition that many different genes determine
immunity to foreign bodies.

Another method uses certain information obtained from the twins themselves by mail or telephone surveys. Cederlöf et al. (1961) have compared the answers on such surveys with those obtained from biochemical analysis for Swedish twins. They find that a question which reads, "As children were you and your twin alike 'as two peas in a pod' or only of ordinary family resemblance?" provides correct answers about 92% of the time.[7] Jablon (1967) used a mail questionaire on a subset of 232 twin pairs from the NAS–NRC sample which we are using. Jablon et al. defined the terms "identical" and "fraternal" in terms of the peas in a pod question and asked the twins which kind they were. A comparison with earlier blood samples revealed a correct classification of 96.1% of the cases (after eliminating 14 pairs for which the two brothers gave different answers and 7 pairs thought to be erroneously classified as MZ by the laboratory procedure). Also for the NAS–NRC sample, Hrubec (1976) reports that the "peas-in-a-pod" question gives the same classification as blood tests 94.0% of the time. There appears to be some tendency for one member of a MZ pair not to so identify himself if the other member has a severe disability or mental disorder. For further details, see Chapter 5.

## 3.3. Genotypic and phenotypic correlations for kin[8]

In this book to estimate the model we use information about variances, covariances, and correlations calculated for individuals and across twins. We also use the model to examine intergenerational mobility. In estimating and using the model, we make use of certain formulae which give the expected value of correlations for twins or other kin. In this section we present and examine the formulae.

[7]The authors must confess that they do not know how alike are two peas in a pod. Fortunately, these men who come from an earlier generation have such knowledge. Other studies with different samples and information report greater misclassification. See Jencks and Brown (1977) and Scarr-Salapatek (1975).

[8]The presentation in this section has benefited enormously from comments by A. Goldberger.

Some definitions are required. Suppose that we are interested in a trait or characteristic such as income, $Y$, which is produced by a combination of genetic factors, $G$, and environment, $N$. $G$ and $N$ may be normalized so that their coefficients are each 1:[9]

$$Y_j = G_j + N_j. \tag{3.1}$$

The observed value of $Y$ is known as the *phenotype* while the level that would occur if $N$ were at its average value is the *genotype*. Throughout the formal analysis and in our empirical work we assume that both the genotype and environment are not observed though we assign numbers for some examples. We remind the reader that among the determinants of $\hat{N}$ in eq. (2.7) is $G$. Eq. (3.1) can be considered a reduced form in which the effects of $G$ include both the direct effects of genetic endowments and the indirect effects through the choice of environment, i.e. the $fG$ term in eq. (2.7) is incorporated into the genetic effect in (3.1). As indicated in the discussion of (2.7), the $N_j$ term consists of the effects of prices, interest rates, family income, and tastes. Random errors also are included in $N$.

Equation (3.1) holds for all individuals in the population. If we calculate the variance in the phenotype over all individuals, we obtain

$$\sigma_Y^2 = \sigma_G^2 + \sigma_N^2 + 2\sigma_{NG}. \tag{3.2}$$

We can, if we wish, divide through by $\sigma_Y^2$ to obtain

$$1 = \frac{\sigma_G^2}{\sigma_Y^2} + \frac{\sigma_N^2}{\sigma_Y^2} + \frac{2\sigma_{GN}}{\sigma_Y^2}. \tag{3.3}$$

The three terms in order in eq. (3.3) indicate the proportion of the total variance attributable to the additive effect of variations in genotype, to the additive effect of variations in environment, and to their covariance. The first term is also known as the "broad heritability". We discuss below the reasons for this term and more importantly the implication of heritability for various issues.

[9]Eq. (3.1) is the reduced form for the various indicators in table 2.1, except that for simplicity we have combined all the $N$'s and the $u$'s in table 2.1 into one variable denoted $N$.

Think of $Y_j$ as the $j$th element in a vector of observations of sample size $J$. Suppose we take another sample of size $J$ with data on $Y$. Denote the vector of observations in this sample by $\hat{Y}$. Now suppose we pair up persons in each vector and calculate the cross-pair covariance $\sigma_{Y\hat{Y}}$ defined as

$$\frac{1}{J} \sum (Y_j - \bar{Y}_J)(\hat{Y}_j - \hat{\bar{Y}}_J) = \sigma_{Y\hat{Y}}. \tag{3.3a}$$

$\sigma_{Y\hat{Y}}$ is known as the *phenotypic covariance*. We can express the phenotypic covariance in terms of $G$ and $N$ as

$$\sigma_{Y\hat{Y}} = \sigma_{G\hat{G}} + \sigma_{N\hat{N}} + 2\sigma_{G\hat{N}}. \tag{3.4}$$

Assuming that the expected value of covariances are the same for the people in the two vectors, we can transform this into correlation coefficients as

$$\frac{\sigma_{Y\hat{Y}}}{\sigma_Y^2} = \frac{\sigma_{G\hat{G}}}{\sigma_G^2}\frac{\sigma_G^2}{\sigma_Y^2} + \frac{\sigma_{N\hat{N}}}{\sigma_N^2}\frac{\sigma_N^2}{\sigma_Y^2} + \frac{2\sigma_{G\hat{N}}}{\sigma_G\sigma_N}\frac{\sigma_G\sigma_N}{\sigma_Y^2}, \tag{3.5}$$

or more compactly as

$$c = gh^2 + ne^2 + 2rhe, \tag{3.6}$$

where

$c = \sigma_{Y\hat{Y}}/\sigma_Y^2 =$ phenotypic correlation,
$g = \sigma_{G\hat{G}}/\sigma_G^2 =$ genotypic correlation,
$h^2 = \sigma_G^2/\sigma_Y^2 =$ broad heritability,
$n = \sigma_{N\hat{N}}/\sigma_N^2 =$ environmental correlation,
$e^2 = \sigma_N^2/\sigma_Y^2 =$ environmentability, and
$r = \sigma_{G\hat{N}}/\sigma_G\sigma_N =$ correlation of $G$ and $N$.

Thus the phenotypic correlation is a weighted average of $g$ and $n$.

If individuals are paired randomly, the expected values of $c$, $g$, and $n$ are zero. When individuals are paired with kin, however, the expected value of each of $c$, $g$, and $n$ is nonzero.

The genotypic correlation of kin arises because of the process, described earlier, by which genes are transmitted from one generation to another. Consider, for example, brothers or DZ twins who have the same parents. At a particular location on a chromosome each brother has a gene pair with one member contributed by each parent. Each parent contributes a randomly selected member of his or her two genes at the same location. Thus, if the father had an A and a B gene pair while the mother had a C and a D gene pair, each brother could have AC, AC, BC, or BD with equal probability. One-quarter of the time the brothers have the same gene pair at this location and half the time one of the genes is the same.

*Assume that the value of Y produced directly or indirectly by each gene is independent of the other gene.* Let the numerical contribution to the phenotype associated with each of 8 hypothetical genes be those in table 3.1. Assume that each gene appears with probability 1/8 in the population. This mean genotype will be 0 and the variance will be 168. For the pair of brothers under consideration, the possible gentypic values, each with a probability of $\frac{1}{2}$, are given in table 3.2. Under the conditions which we have specified, the expected value of each brother's genotype is $\Sigma P_k G_k$, where $P_i$ is the probability that the gene will take on the $k$th value. In our example the expected genotype for the two brothers is 8, although the actual values can be 6, 8, or 10. Note that the actual values for the father and mother are 4 and 12, the average of which is 8.

Since we are assuming that all genetic effects are additive, we can express the genotypic value for each offspring as the average value for each parent plus a random error $v$. That is

$$Y_j = \tfrac{1}{2}\bar{G}_{F_j} + \tfrac{1}{2}\bar{G}_{M_j} + v = \tfrac{1}{4}(G_{1F_j} + G_{1M_j} + G_{2F_j} + G_{2M_j}) + v_j, \qquad (3.7)$$

where $\bar{G}_{F_j}$ and $\bar{G}_{F_j}$ are the average value of the two genes of the $j$th person's father and mother, respectively. For siblings for whom $v$ is uncorrelated, the genotypic covariance of $Y$ can be expressed as

$$\sigma^g_{\hat{Y}\hat{Y}} = \tfrac{1}{4}\sigma^2_{\bar{G}_F} + \tfrac{1}{4}\sigma^2_{\bar{G}_M} + \tfrac{1}{2}\sigma_{\bar{G}_F\bar{G}_M}. \qquad (3.8)$$

Suppose that the expected value of $\sigma_{\bar{G}_F\bar{G}_M}$ is zero, which means there is no linear correlation between the genotypic level of the

Table 3.1
Hypothetical example of gene types and phenotypes.

| Gene type | Contribution to phenotype[a] |
|---|---|
| A | 1 |
| B | 3 |
| C | 5 |
| D | 7 |
| E | −1 |
| F | −3 |
| G | −5 |
| H | −7 |

[a]Includes any indirect effects that occur if environmental choices depend on genotype.

Table 3.2
Hypothetical example of gene combinations and phenotypes.

| Gene combination | Phenotypic value if $N = 0$ |
|---|---|
| AC | 6 |
| AD | 8 |
| BC | 8 |
| BD | 10 |

parents.[10] Then assuming that $\sigma_{\bar{G}_F} = \sigma_{\bar{G}_M} = \sigma_G^2$, we find for siblings and DZ twins that

$$\sigma_{Y\hat{Y}} = \tfrac{1}{2}\sigma_G^2. \tag{3.9}$$

The particular result obtained in eq. (3.9) depends crucially on the assumption that the effect of each gene on the phenotype is additive, e.g. is the same for all $k$ states both of the other member of the gene pair at the same location on the chromosome and of all other genes at other locations. If the genotypic effect of one gene depends upon which of the $k$ states is taken on by the other

[10]While $\sigma_{\bar{G}_M\bar{G}_F}$ sometimes is referred as "assortive mating", that term is more often used to refer to the covariance of the average phenotype of the parents.

member of the gene pair, the gene is dominant or recessive. For example, eye color is determined by genes. As is well known, two "blue" genes produce blue eyes, two "brown" genes produce brown eyes, but one "blue" and one "brown" gene produce brown eyes. If the genotypic value varies with genes located elsewhere there is epistacy. Dominant and recessive genes and epistacy imply that the average genotypic value of a gene pair is not the average of the individual components. In the above example the one blue and one brown gene do not produce bluish/brown eyes.

Commencing with the pioneering work of R.A. Fisher (1918), geneticists have examined the effects of a variety of factors which affect kin genotypic correlations. If it is assumed that there is an equilibrium distribution of genotypes,[11] that there is no difference in reproduction rates by genotype, and that mating is based on phenotypic (rather than genotypic) levels, it can be shown for DZ twins that[12]

$$c_{DZ}^{g} = \tfrac{1}{2}d(1 + bdh^2) + \tfrac{1}{4}(1 - d),\qquad(3.10)$$

where

$h^2$ = ratio of total genetic variance to total phenotypic variance, i.e. the previously defined broad heritability,
$d$ = ratio of additive genetic variance to total genetic variance, and
$b$ = the phenotypic correlation of parents, i.e. $c_{PP}$, where P refers to parents.

With the same assumptions the parent–child genotypic correlation, $c_{PC}^{g}$, is

$$c_{PC}^{g} = \tfrac{1}{2}d(1 + b).\qquad(3.11)$$

The dominance or nonadditive portion of genetic variation does not enter into the parent–child correlation. Thus, for studies of

---

[11]If, for example, a new gene is introduced by mutation or by immigration of a few people into a population, and this gene has a higher reproduction rate, correlations will change as the gene becomes more common.
[12]See for example, Burt and Howard (1957, pp. 113–116).

intergenerational mobility it is necessary to examine narrow heritability rather than $h^2$.

Equation (3.6) defines the phenotypic correlation of kin in terms of cross-kin genotypic and environmental correlations. There are several reasons for expecting the environment of certain kin to be correlated. First, there are what Cavalli-Sforza and Feldman (1973), who are biologists and geneticists, call cultural reasons – offspring in part *learn* values, attitudes, and technologies from listening to, observing, and imitating their parents.[13] Secondly, part of the environment such as diet, books, and the quality of life may depend on parents' income which is partly genetically determined. Thirdly, prices for various goods are the same for both sibs even if there is variation across families. Siblings are also generally raised in the same family but may share a less common environment since for example family income and social norms can change during the interval between births. Cousins and other kin may also share some common environment especially if they are raised in the same region of the country. There are no formulae available to predict cross-kin environmental correlations. However, we estimate this correlation for twins in our empirical work in Chapter 7 and we use this estimate to calculate the contribution of inequality of opportunity to the variance of earnings. Thus, we define inequality of opportunity as arising because of cross-family differences in prices, family income, and tastes.

## 3.4. Twins and the total population

The methodology presented in Chapter 4 allows us, in some cases, to apportion the variance of any variable into components of genetic, common environment, and other environment. Of course, from any sample we only obtain estimates of these components for the population from which the sample is drawn.

---

[13]It is not important at this stage of the argument if parents teach their offspring consciously or subconsciously. Easterlin (1975) and other economists have used similar ideas to explain taste formation.

The hope in any study is to draw inferences about an important element of a society. Our sample consists of white males which is a group often studied. The results from our sample, however, need not generalize to the population of white males if the people who responded to our survey are atypical of twins or if twins are atypical of the population. We discuss in Chapter 5 the extent to which our sample is a random drawing from the population of twins. Whether or not a particular sample suffers from response and success bias is an issue common to all surveys. But a more general issue in twin research is whether the population of twins constitute a random subset of the total population and whether twins can be used to make inferences about the population. Some of these questions are also examined in Chapter 5.

Basically there are two different reasons why twins may not be an appropriate group from which to draw inferences about the population. Consider first the incidence of twinning. A variety of studies have shown that the rates of MZ twins are independent of factors such as mother's age, ethnic and socioeconomic backgrounds. The rate for DZ twins, on the other hand, varies with mother's age and by ethnic backgrounds.[14] An example of the age–twinning rate relationship is given in fig. 3.1. Age of mother can be correlated with her religious and socioeconomic background and with family environment. Moreover, older mothers tend to have had more children. Thus, DZ twins have more siblings and are later in the birth order-variables which are correlated with education, IQ, and earnings. Hence DZ twins need not be a random drawing of the population either with respect to environment or genetic endowment.[15] However, if DZ twins are drawn from a different genetic or environmental pool, we would expect to observe different means and/or variances for the individuals in the DZ group than in either the U.S. white male population or the MZ group when we separate the sample into

[14]For example, DZs are more likely to occur among blacks and less likely to occur among orientals. Our study is limited to whites, but ethnic differences may remain.
[15]Lower socioeconomic status women may have a different gene pool than the population as a whole.

MZ and DZ subgroups.[16] The empirical evidence is assessed more fully in Chapter 5, but it seems that the individuals in the MZ and DZ portions of the sample have quite similar means and variances for education, occupational status, and earnings even though the DZs in our sample come from larger families and have more older siblings.

A second reason that twins might not be representative of the population is if "twinness" has important effects on the pairs. Twinness effects may arise for physiological and psychological reasons and may cause twins to differ from the population on some characteristic. For example, left-handedness is two or three times more prevalent among twins than in the total population.[17] Moreover, a number of writers have suggested that (especially for MZ siblings) there are substantial personality identity crises and frequent periods in which one twin becomes the dominant member.[18] However, there is evidence that mental and personality disorders occur no more frequently among MZ twins than in the population.[19] Also, it has been argued that twins may be harmed in their development in the womb because they must share the space and perhaps the nutrition normally available to a single fetus. For this reason some people have argued that twins should average lower on IQ tests. Mittler's (1971, p. 30) summary of the then available evidence on this subject concluded that twins scored an average of 5 points less than the population. However, he also observed that the standard deviation for twins and non-twins did not differ significantly.[20] Vandenberg (1968) has concluded that twins do less well only on the verbal portion of IQ tests. He raises the question of whether twins when young do not practise verbal skills as much as nontwins because the twins can communicate better nonverbally.

[16]The MZ comparison would be more relevant if response bias affects sample/population comparisons.
[17]See Cavalli-Sforza and Bodmer (1971, p. 586). There is a possibility that this occurs because of the position in the womb.
[18]See Mittler (1971, p. 51).
[19]See, for example, Allen et al. (1972).
[20]However, the distribution of SES scores of twins in this sample is higher than for the nontwins.

Most of the evidence on the average IQ of twins is from tests given when the twins were 11 years old or younger. The disadvantage of twins may change if twins and the population were tested at a later age. Jencks and Brown (1977) report that in the Project Talent tests given to 11th graders, twins have the same average IQ as the population. In our sample we have scores on the General Classification Test (GCT), which is like the verbal part of standardized intelligence tests, for those who entered the Navy as enlisted men and whose records still contain this information. We collected this information for all twins where both members were in the Navy, including a random sample of those who did not respond to our questionnaire. The GCT material is discussed in detail in Chapter 5. Briefly there appears to be no difference in the mean and standard deviation for the twins and the Navy as a whole. While the Navy could, to some extent, select its members, as far as we can tell the proportion of twins in the Navy is the same as in the veteran population (see Chapter 5).

Finally, there is a possibility that interactions of family members are an important element of the environment. This can cause two different effects. First, the twins cannot grow up in single-child families which are found in the population. Secondly, if the degree and type of interactions depend on genetic similarity or closeness in age, the distribution of environment for twins would differ from that in the population. Some work on small samples by Jencks and Brown (1977) and by Olneck (1977) suggest that these interactions are not very important.

## 3.5. Reaction functions and interactions

Several geneticists and an astronomer have raised another objection to the use of twins to partition the variance into its genetic and environmental components.[21] The logic of this objection, which has several important implications, is illustrated in fig. 3.2.

---

[21]See Feldman and Lewontin (1975) or Layzer (1974).

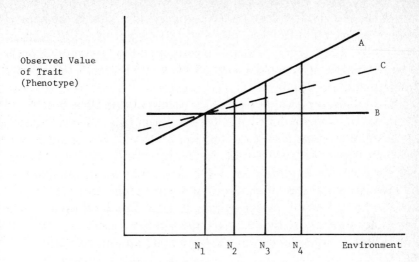

Figure 3.2. Hypothetical reaction functions.

Suppose that genes come in only two forms, $A$ and $B$. In principle it is possible to separate people by genotype and to observe the phenotype of a trait as we vary the environment, i.e. we can plot the reaction functions. The reaction functions for $A$ and $B$ are shown in fig. 3.2. The average phenotype in the population at each value of environment is given by $C$, assuming $G$ and $N$ are uncorrelated. Now suppose the environment is restricted to the range $N_1-N_2$. In this range $A$ and $B$ almost coincide with $C$. Let $N_3-N_4$ be the same length as $N_1-N_2$. In this area $A$ and $B$ are further away from $C$. The variance of the phenotype can be divided into the variance along $C$ (from $N_1$ to $N_2$ or $N_3$ to $N_4$) and the variance around $C$ (from $A$ to $C$ and $C$ to $B$). Assuming that the distribution of environment within $N_1$ to $N_2$ is the same as in $N_3$ to $N_4$, the variance in the phenotype and the proportion due to genetics will be greater the further apart are $A$ and $B$. Thus, genetics has a larger effect in the area $N_3$ to $N_4$.

One implication of fig. 3.2 is that if reaction functions intersect or, more generally, if the effects of genotype vary or interact with the level of environment, there is no unique estimate of the proportion of variance attributable to genetics. This is, of course, a common problem in allocating variances when there is heteroskedasticity. Fortunately, there is a test available (given in Chapter 6) to determine if there are certain types of interaction between genetics and environment.

The second implication of fig. 3.2 is that altering the bounds of the range of environment can alter the proportion of the variance attributable to genetics. If we happen to have a historical period in which we are located on the $N_3$–$N_4$ interval, it does not tell us that variations in environment will not be effective in changing the average level of the phenotype. It merely tells us that in that period the variation in environment was small relative to the variation in genetics. Indeed, as shown in the figure, a shift to $N_1$ will induce a large change in the mean level and in the variance of the phenotype.

In a sense, one implication of the last point is that it is difficult to extrapolate beyond the sample space. While we agree with that sentiment, it is worth noting that in our sample the range of observations in earnings and occupational status cover nearly the full range in the population and, for all practical purposes, cover all the phenotypes we can expect to observe, e.g. annual earnings in 1973 go from $1000 to over $100 000.

The third point is that we often are interested in the level of the phenotype and its responsiveness to changes in environment. Knowledge of the relative size of $\sigma_G^2$ and $\sigma_N^2$ (or $h^2$ and $e^2$) does not convey any information about either $\bar{G}$ or $\bar{N}$ or the change in the phenotype as $N$ varies. For example, suppose everyone had the environment of $N_3$ in fig. 3.2. Then all the variation in the trait would be due to variation in genotype. If everyone suddenly shifted the environment to $N_4$, the level of the phenotype would change though the variation would still be solely genetic in origin. Moreover, the change in the phenotype caused by a change in the environment is given by the slope of $C$ in fig. 3.2. We can rotate $A$, $B$, and $C$ and with an appropriate change in the range in environments can keep constant the variance contributions. But the steeper is $C$ the bigger is the effect of an environmental change on the mean level of the phenotype.

## 3.6. Similarity of environment for MZs and DZs

In section 3.3 we noted that people reared in the same household must surely share some environment. Twins not only are reared in the same household but also share some of the same prenatal conditions.[22] Suppose we denote the correlation in twins environment as $\rho$. A major issue in the study of twins is whether the expected value of $\rho$ is likely to differ for MZ and DZ pairs.

Besides certain technical arguments associated with prenatal development, the major arguments advanced for expecting $\rho$ to be greater for MZs than DZs are that parents tend to provide more similar environments for MZs and that MZ twins choose more similar environments inside and outside the home. There is evidence in Koch (1966) and elsewhere that parents dress and treat MZs more alike on a day-to-day basis than they do DZs. The MZ twins are also more likely to have the same friends and participate in the same activities.

There are, however, several other aspects to this problem. First, day-to-day treatment may be irrelevant. A more meaningful concept would seem to be annual or average childhood quantity and quality of clothes and treatment. Similarly, the average characteristics of friends and activities would seem to be the more relevant aspect. As far as we are aware, no one has studied these questions directly – unless studies of schooling and cognitive ability are so construed.

Secondly, assuming that the previous assertions are correct, it is necessary to ask why parents provide or MZ twins choose a more common environment. One obvious answer is that in their decisions parents or twins react to the needs and requirements of the child. Since the MZ twins are genetically more alike, their needs and requirements are also more alike.[23] This possibility is

[22]The prenatal conditions need not be identical, even for MZ twins. One can be in a better position in the womb, receive more nutrition, or be subjected to different injuries. Indeed, several studies discussed by Vandenberg (1968; p. 31) argue that prenatal environment is more alike for DZs than MZs.

[23]That is, parents reinforce genetic differences. One can construct models where parents provide environments to compensate for genetic differences, e.g. by buying medicines. Cf. Becker and Tomes (1976).

embodied in eqs. (2.7) and (3.1). Another possible answer is that parents "feel" that the MZ but not DZ twins should be assisted in being as alike as possible. Scarr-Salapatek (1975) has tested these two propositions by examining the parental treatment of twins some of whose parents are mistaken as to their twins zygosity. She finds that parents of MZs treat their offspring as alike regardless of whether the parents believe them to be MZs or DZs. They also treat DZs as alike regardless of their zygosity beliefs. Hence she argues that any greater similarity of common environment for twins than for other siblings arises because of their genetic differences.

In eq. (2.7) we distinguish between $\hat{N}$ and $N$, where $\hat{N} - N = fG$. Environment in eq. (3.1) and subsequent equations refers to $N$ which depends upon prices, interest rates, family income, and tastes. The common environment for twins occurs in this model because the twins or their parents face the same prices and have the same family income. We also assume, for the most part, that parents do not prefer one progeny over another.

## 3.7. Genes and human behavior

The reader will no doubt realize that we take the trouble to introduce and discuss in detail the material on biology and MZ and DZ twins because it is important to our study. Indeed, the distinction between MZ and DZ pairs is crucial to the methodology we present in Chapter 4.

The description in section 3.2 of how genes are passed on from one generation to another is a valid representation of modern theory in biology or genetics.[24] There are, however, some distinguished scientists who, while accepting the biological description, seem to maintain that genes do not control, influence or affect human behavior.[25] The last sentence should be qualified in

[24]In fact, it is nearly a quote from a letter to one of the authors from Professor Crow, a geneticist, in which he was kind enough to correct some nonstandard usage in a previous paper.
[25]See, for example, Kamin (1974).

several respects. First, there are a variety of diseases which are known to be caused by a particular, identified genetic combination. Some of these diseases are very rare; but more widely known, although still infrequently occurring ones, are phenylketonuria (PKU) and sickle-cell anemia. Some of these genetically caused diseases result in mental retardation or other severe physical disabilities which are surely related to skills, earnings, and some aspects of human behavior. Since the critics of the nexus between genes and human behavior are aware of these severe debilitating effects, they presumably restrict their comments to the so-called "normal" ranges. But the resulting definition of "normal" seems tautologic. Secondly, the phrase "seem to maintain" was used because it is not clear whether or not this position is taken as a debating stance by individuals who wish to emphasize the importance of environment in training people to overcome genetic defects.[26]

As the reader may be aware, the cross-twin correlation – the covariance in any variable calculated across brothers divided by the variance calculated across individuals – is higher for MZ than DZ twins for intelligence measures and a variety of diseases. This study finds that the greater similarity of MZ brothers persists for schooling, initial and late career occupational status, and earnings at about age 50. Those who reject the idea that genes help produce skills and behavior argue that the greater similarity for MZ pairs occurs because MZ pairs share a more common environment, an argument we have just discussed.

The genetics versus environment or the nature versus nurture debate over intelligence has stirred up much emotion. The debate has become so emotional in part because those who think environment can be used to train or educate people, also believe that their "opponents", i.e. those who argue that genetics plays a role, either wish to maintain the *status quo* or to believe that a large figure for heritability indicates that changes in environment are ineffective. A conclusion that part of the distribution of

[26]In his review of Kamin's book, Goldberger (1976a) wonders if Kamin adopted his stand of no evidence of genetic effects on IQ as a debating ploy.

income occurs because of genetic differences does not require th value judgement that the existing distribution is right. The conclusion that high heritability implies that environmental changes are ineffective is logically incorrect, as is shown in section 3.5.

As we indicated in section 3.5, a finding that any variable has a large genetics component never indicates that the level or distribution of the variable cannot be changed by some appropriate environment.[27] Often there is a problem in specifying the appropriate environment, but in the case of after-tax income we can affect the distribution by using tax and transfer mechanisms. Similarly, wage supplements can be used to alter pretax earnings.

Much of the emotion in the nature–nurture debate also has arisen because the estimates on heritability have been used to make pronouncements on the average genotypic value by race, i.e. on $\bar{G}$. As we stated earlier, information on variances contains no information on means. In section 3.5 we indicated that if everyone had the same environment, genetics would account for all the variation in pheno-type. Thus, if all whites were at $N_4$ and all blacks at $N_3$ phenotypic variation within a race would be entirely accounted for by genes, but if the distribution of $A$ and $B$ were the same for the two groups the mean difference in phenotype would be attributable solely to environmental differences.

Estimates of genetic effects do tell us some things that are of interest. First, they are indicative of why earnings vary, which some people find an interesting intellectual question. Secondly, in judging the fairness of the income distribution, some people want to know why and how people are more and less skilled. Some people have pointed out to us that in terms of judging fairness, family effects (the sum of genetic and family environmental effects) would seem more relevant. Since our data and methods provide a much sharper estimate of such family effects than of its two components of genetics and family environment, it might be asked what extra information is obtained from the separation? 

The answer to this query is two-fold. First, nearly all discussion

---

[27]For example, PKU, which is genetically caused, can be treated by a very special diet. If so treated, no mental retardation occurs.

of equality of opportunity programs are phrased in terms of compensating for poor family environment.[28] The maximum effect of such programs can be gauged by estimates of the effect of family environment. Thus, we can ask: what would occur if prices, family income, and tastes were equalized across families? Secondly, models of the type we are using can be used to examine intergenerational mobility. The effectiveness of a once-and-for-all redistribution of family income or environment differs depending on whether the family effects are genetic or environmental.

[28]See Becker (1967), Okun (1975) and Tawney (1961).

# CHAPTER 4

# STATISTICAL METHODOLOGY

## 4.1. Introduction

The model investigated in this chapter was presented in Chapter 2. We estimate parts of such a system using various techniques. We consider first the question of what estimates can be obtained using single equation ordinary least squares (OLS). Clearly this technique does not provide information about the latent variable coefficients, but can yield estimates of the recursive parameters. We then turn to the latent variable techniques with which we can obtain estimates of the coefficients of the unobserved variables.

## 4.2. Ordinary least squares regressions

Suppose for simplicity that we consider the logarithm of earnings, $Y$, to be a linear function of schooling, $S$, of one unobserved genetic and one unobserved environmental index, $G$ and $N$, and a random disturbance, $u$, uncorrelated with the right-hand variables:

$$Y = \alpha_1 S + \alpha_2 G + \alpha_3 N + u. \tag{4.1}$$

Since (4.1) holds for every individual we can write the difference in the logarithm of earnings, $\Delta Y$, between each individual and his twin as

$$\Delta Y = \alpha_1 \Delta S + \alpha_2 \Delta G + \alpha_3 \Delta N + \Delta u. \tag{4.2}$$

We refer to eq. (4.1) as the "individual" equations and to (4.2) as the within MZ and within DZ equations. There is of course a different equation for MZ and DZ twins.

Let us consider the effects of omitting $G$, $N$, $\Delta G$, and $\Delta N$. Denote the OLS estimate of $\alpha_1$ obtained from (4.1) as $\hat{\alpha}_1$ and that from (4.2) as $\tilde{\alpha}_1$. Then, as is well known, we may write

$$E(\hat{\alpha}_1) = \alpha_1 + \alpha_2\hat{\delta}_2 + \alpha_3\hat{\delta}_3 \tag{4.3}$$

$$E(\tilde{\alpha}_1) = \alpha_1 + \alpha_2\tilde{\delta}_2 + \alpha_3\tilde{\delta}_3, \tag{4.4}$$

where E denotes the expectations operator, $\hat{\delta}_2$ is the OLS estimate obtained by regressing $G$ on $S$, $\hat{\delta}_3$ is the OLS estimate from regressing $N$ on $S$, and $\tilde{\delta}_2$ and $\tilde{\delta}_3$ are defined analogously in terms of $\Delta G$, $\Delta N$, and $\Delta S$. If, as seems likely and is assumed in our larger model, $G$ and $S$ and $N$ and $S$ are correlated, and if at least one of $\alpha_2$ or $\alpha_3$ is nonzero, then $\hat{\alpha}_1$ yields a biased estimate of $\alpha_1$. On the other hand, since for MZ twins $\Delta G$ is identically zero, the bias in $\tilde{\alpha}_1$ reduces to $\alpha_3\tilde{\delta}_3$, and there will be no bias if either $\alpha_3 = 0$ or $\tilde{\delta}_3 = 0$. The former condition would hold if MZ brothers' environment had no *direct* effect on earnings (although it could affect schooling). The second condition would hold if the differences in MZ brothers' environments that directly affect earnings were uncorrelated with schooling differences. This is not likely if $N$ represents environmental influences for childhood years, but might prevail if $N$ were to represent adult influences such as on-the-job training. Alternatively, there would be no bias if the twins shared a completely common environment, since then $\Delta N$ would be zero.[1] For DZ twins $\Delta G$ is not zero and the bias is given by $\alpha_2\tilde{\delta}_2 + \alpha_3\tilde{\delta}_3$.

Griliches (1978) provides an equivalent way of examining these same issues that may be more informative for some readers:

$$Y_{ij} = \alpha_1 S_{ij} + \beta_1 A_{ij} + u_{ij}, \tag{4.5}$$

$$S_{ij} = \beta_2 A_{ij} + H_{ij} + v_{ij}, \tag{4.6}$$

---

[1]We can also think of $u$ as containing the specific environment of each twin that affects earnings.

$$A_{ij} = F_i + a_{ij}, \tag{4.7}$$

$$H_{ij} = L_i + h_{ij}. \tag{4.8}$$

In his formulation there is an unobserved "ability" variable, $A_{ij}$, that has direct effects on both $Y$ and $S$ and on another unobserved "background" variable, $H_{ij}$, that has direct effects on $S$ alone. Here $i$ refers to family and $j$ to the individual. As is shown in (4.7) and (4.8) both $A$ and $H$ have a "familial structure" given by $F_i$ and $L_i$, but also within-family variations represented by $a_{ij}$ and $h_{ij}$. He shows that using data on individuals and within pairs the expected value of the estimates of $\alpha$ are

$$E(\alpha) = \alpha + B_1/(1 + \lambda), \tag{4.9a}$$

$$E(\alpha_w) = \alpha + B_1(1 - \rho_A)/[(1 - \rho_A) + \lambda(1 - \rho_H)], \tag{4.9b}$$

where $\lambda = \sigma_H^2/\sigma_A^2$ is the ratio of the variance in background to the variance in ability, $\rho_A = \sigma_F^2/\sigma_A^2$ is the proportion of the total variance in ability that is familial, $\rho_H = \sigma_L^2/\sigma_H^2$ is the proportion of the total variance in background that is familial, and $\alpha_w$ is the within pair estimate. Thus, if and only if the proportion of total variance that is familial is greater for ability than for background ($\rho_A > \rho_H$), is the expected value of the schooling coefficient greater in the individual than in the family estimate ($E(\alpha) > E(\alpha_w)$). Also, if and only if all variance in ability is familial ($\rho_A = 1$) and some variance in background is not familial ($\rho_H \neq 1$) is the within-family estimate of the schooling coefficient unbiased ($E(\alpha_w) = \alpha$).

In Griliches's model, both $F_i$ and $L_i$ contain a pair's common genotype and common environment, and $a_{ij}$ and $h_{ij}$ contain the within-pair variation in genotype and environment. Since at a minimum common genetic environment is greater for MZ than for DZ twins, $\rho_A$ probably is greater for MZs than DZs, and within-pair equations for the two groups need not be equally efficient in eliminating bias. If $\rho_H$ and $\lambda$ are the same for the two twin types, the bias is smaller for the MZ twins.

In the Stanford–Binet tests, the raw cross-twin correlations for MZ twins reared together exceed 0.85 and, adjusted for test-

retest measurement error, exceed 0.95.[2] The calculated MZ correlation for education in our sample is smaller at about 0.75 or
probably about 0.83 when corrected for measurement error. If $A$
corresponds to IQ, then $\rho_A$ probably exceeds $\rho_H$ for MZs in our
sample, so the bias is smaller in the MZ within pair than in the
individual estimates. Also, that $\rho_A$ is close to one while $\rho_H$
probably is not means that the bias in the within-pair estimates for
MZs probably is small. For DZ twins it is less obvious what the
relationship between $\rho_A$ and $\rho_H$ is. See Griliches (1978) and
Taubman (1978) for available estimates. Therefore it is not clear *a
priori* if the bias is greater in the individual or in the within-pair
estimates for DZs. However, since $\rho_A$ is smaller for DZs than for
MZs, the bias in the within-pair estimates for DZs is greater than
for MZs for given values of $\rho_H$ and $\lambda$.

   The possibility of obtaining an unbiased estimate of $\alpha_1$ from the
OLS estimates of the within MZ equations also rests on two
additional assumptions: no measurement error in the schooling
variable and no interaction term between $G$ and $N$ in (4.1). We
now consider these two assumptions. Then we turn to the question of how to interpret the testing of whether the MZ and DZ
between twins regression relations are significantly different.

### 4.2.1. Measurement error

If $S$ is measured with error then the asymptotic bias in the
estimated schooling coefficient obtained from the within MZ
equation may be serious. Assuming that the true schooling level,
$S$, is measured with error, $w$, as $T$, where $T = S + w$, and that $w$ is
uncorrelated with $S$, then the asymptotic bias in the estimate of $\alpha_1$
obtained from the within MZ equation is $-\alpha_1\mu/[(1+\mu)(1-r)]$,
where $\mu$ is the ratio of the variance of $w$ to the variance of $S$, and

---

[2]See Jencks et al. (1972, pp. 284–285). Our cross-twin correlation using the
General Classification Test reported in Chapter 5 is a bit lower than 0.85 but we
may have more measurement error since two different forms of the tests with
different distributions had to be merged and there are some cases where we
cannot be certain which form was used.

$r$ is the correlation between schooling for an individual and his twin. Hence if $\mu$ were about 0.1 and $r$ were about 0.8 this would bias the estimate of $\alpha_1$ downward by about 50%.

In the individual equation (4.1) the asymptotic bias due to measurement error of course is in addition to that due to omitting unobservables. Since the latter likely biases the coefficient upward while the former biases it downwards, the direction of overall bias is not clear. It is worth noting, however, that the asymptotic bias due to measurement error alone is not as severe in the individual equation as in the within MZ equation since it is given by the expression $-\alpha_1\mu/(1+\mu)$ which is less (in absolute terms) than the corresponding expression for the MZ case given above if $r$ is positive.

The discussion to this point assumes that measurement error is uncorrelated across brothers, as would likely be the case if the respondent gave the wrong number of years of schooling, or errors were made in coding the data. However, if the measurement error arises because years of schooling are not appropriately adjusted for quality of schooling then the errors are likely to be correlated across brothers. In this case the asymptotic bias in the within MZ equation becomes $-\alpha_1\mu(1-r_1)/[(1+\mu)(1-r)]$, where $r_1$ is the cross-twin correlation in the measurement error. If $r$ and $r_1$ are the same order of magnitude, which seems plausible since siblings tend to go to the same school, this reduces to $-\alpha_1\mu/(1+\mu)$. Thus, the bias in measurement error would be the same in the individual and between twin equations. In this case it would take a $\mu$ greater than 0.66 to result in a downward bias of more than 40%.

In principle the measurement error problem can be handled in the context of our latent variable model, as is discussed below.

### 4.2.2. Interactions between G and N

Differencing across MZ brothers eliminates genetic indices when they do not interact with environmental variables. An alternative formulation of our model would include an interaction such as

*GN*. Consider for example the addition of such a term to the reduced form version of (4.1):

$$Y = G + N + \alpha_4 GN + u', \tag{4.1a}$$

where we have renormalized the reduced form coefficients on $G$ and $N$ and represent the composite disturbance term by $u'$. Taking within-pair differences, we have approximately

$$\Delta Y = \Delta G + \Delta N + \alpha_4 N \Delta G + \alpha_4 G \Delta N + \alpha_4 \Delta G \Delta N + \Delta u'. \tag{4.2a}$$

For MZ twins $\Delta G$ is zero, so (4.2a) reduces to

$$\Delta Y = \Delta N + \alpha_4 G \Delta N + \Delta u'. \tag{4.2b}$$

In this case the variance of the difference in earnings within twins is

$$\sigma_{\Delta Y}^2 = \sigma_{\Delta N}^2 + \alpha_4^2 \sigma_{G \Delta N}^2 + 2\alpha_4 \sigma_{\Delta N} \sigma_{G \Delta N} + \sigma_{u'}^2. \tag{4.10}$$

If $\alpha_4$ is zero and if $\Delta N$ is distributed the same at all levels of $G$, the expected value of the variance of $\Delta Y$ (conditional on $G$) is constant at all levels of $G$. If $\alpha_4$ is nonzero and if $\Delta N$ is distributed the same at all levels of $G$, the contribution of $\Delta N$ to $\Delta Y$ is scaled by $G$ and the expected value of the variance of $\Delta Y$ is not constant. If $\Delta N$ is not distributed the same at all levels of $G$, the expected value of the variance of $\Delta Y$ is not constant (except in the unlikely case in which the effects of the nonzero $\alpha_4$ and the nonconstant $\Delta N$ just cancel each other out).

To test the existence of an interaction term we would like to test to see if $\alpha_4$ is significantly different from zero. If we had observations on $G$ and $N$, we could use regression analysis and the data on monozygotic twins to estimate whether or not $\alpha_4$ is significantly different from zero in relation (4.1a). However, if $\sigma_{\Delta N}^2 + \Delta u'$ is a constant for all levels of $N$ and $G$, then in (4.10) $\sigma_{\Delta Y}^2$ will be homoskedastic if and only if $\alpha_4 = 0$. Of course, we do not have direct observations on $G$ or $N$, but we can use as an estimate of $G$ and $N$ the average earnings of the two monozygotic twins.

Following Jinks and Fulker (1970) we can make use of the fact that absolute differences are like standard deviations and estimate

$$|\Delta Y| = a + b(Y_1 + Y_2)/2, \qquad (4.11)$$

where the subscripts refer to the first and second brother in each monozygotic pair. An estimate of $b$ which is significantly nonzero is consistent with a significant interaction effect since the absolute differences or the standard error vary with the level of $G$ and $N$. Jinks and Fulker (1970) also shows that this test is appropriate when the interaction term is of the more general form of $\alpha_4 G^\beta N^\lambda$.

### 4.2.3. Interpretation of the test that the MZ and DZ equations are significantly different

A major advantage of using MZ twins is that it is possible to control for genetic endowments and similarity in family environments. Samples of MZ twins are not easily obtainable. If it were not necessary to control for genes but only for family environment, more readily available samples of ordinary siblings could be employed.

It is possible to use an analysis of covariance or Chow test to determine if the estimates of eq. (4.2) are significantly different for MZ and DZ twins. The null hypothesis is that the expected value of $\alpha_3 \tilde{\delta}_3$ in (4.4) for MZ twins is not significantly different from $\alpha_2 \tilde{\delta}_2 + \alpha_3 \tilde{\delta}_3$ in (4.4) for DZ twins. If $\tilde{\delta}_3$ is the same for the twin types, then the null hypothesis is that $\alpha_2 \tilde{\delta}_2$ is zero and it is not necessary to control for genetic endowments.

This is also a crude test of the hypothesis that there is no direct effect of genetics on income, i.e. that $\alpha_2 = 0$. Obviously, however, this is not a completely satisfactory test for this hypothesis for two reasons. First, we are really testing whether $\alpha_2 \tilde{\delta}_2 = 0$ which would be true if either $\alpha_2 = 0$ or $\tilde{\delta}_2 = 0$. That is to say, genes may affect earnings ($\alpha_2 > 0$) even though $S$ and $G$ are uncorrelated ($\tilde{\delta}_2 = 0$). Secondly, the test includes as part of the maintained hypothesis the assumption that $\tilde{\delta}_3$ is the same for both MZ and DZ twins. Differences in $\tilde{\delta}_3$ could be a cause for rejection of the null hypothesis.

The first of these two problems can be examined within the context of our latent variable models. We turn now to a simplified discussion of latent variable analysis to familiarize the reader with the basic principles involved.

### 4.3. Latent variable analysis

Latent variables are unobserved constructs which are hypothesized to be related to certain observed variables. If there are enough observed variables in the system, it is possible both to control for the latent variables and to estimate the relative variance of the latent and the observed variables.[3] The latter may be either "indicators" or "causes" of the latent variables. The following simple examples illustrate the nature of latent variable problems and particularly the question of the identification of parameters in such models.

Assume that $Y_i$ are observed variables, $Z$ is an unobserved (latent) variable, and $\epsilon_i$ are random disturbance terms uncorrelated with each other and with $Z$. Since $Z$ is not observed we can arbitrarily normalize it by setting its variance equal to unity. Suppose now that there is only one structural equation:

$$Y_1 = \alpha_1 Z + \epsilon_1, \tag{4.12}$$

with unknowns $\alpha_1$ and $\sigma_1^2$ the variance of $\epsilon_1$. We are interested in estimating the separate contributions of $Z$ and $\epsilon_1$ to the variance of $Y_1$. We can calculate $\sigma_{Y_1}^2$ and express its expected value in terms of unknowns as

$$\sigma_{Y_1}^2 = \alpha_1^2 + \sigma_1^2. \tag{4.12a}$$

Not surprisingly since there is only one observable moment ($\sigma_{Y_1}^2$), the model is not identified. However, when there is more than one indicator (equation) available the situation, which is recorded in table 4.1, differs drastically. With three indicators, for example,

---

[3]For early work on latent variables in the economics literature see Zellner (1970) and Goldberger (1972, 1973).

Table 4.1
Identification with indicators alone.

| | Equations | Unknowns | Observable moments | Identification |
|---|---|---|---|---|
| | $Y_1 = \alpha_1 Z + \epsilon_1$ | $\alpha_1, \sigma_1^2 = 2$ | 1 | under |
| add | $Y_2 = \alpha_2 Z + \epsilon_2$ | $\alpha_2, \sigma_2^2 = 4$ | 3 | under |
| add | $Y_3 = \alpha_3 Z + \epsilon_3$ | $\alpha_3, \sigma_3^2 = 6$ | 6 | exact |
| add | $Y_4 = \alpha_4 Z + \epsilon_4$ | $\alpha_4, \sigma_4^2 = 8$ | 10 | over |
| | Normalization: $\sigma_Z^2 = 1$ | | | |

the model is exactly identified; with four or more it is over-identified.

It should be noted that the entire procedure relies crucially on the assumption that the $\epsilon$ values are uncorrelated with each other. Clearly, if a full covariance matrix of $\epsilon$'s had to be estimated, this would exhaust all the information in the observable covariance matrix of the $Y$'s, leaving the model underidentified.

It is also important to note that any nonlinear transformation of an unobserved variable creates a new latent variable and makes identification more difficult. Thus, it is helpful to structure the model to minimize nonlinear transformations of latent variables in reduced form equations. In other types of models, in contrast, nonlinear transforms often aid in identification (Fisher, 1966).

It is also of interest to note that the two-equation model may be interpreted in terms of the usual errors in variables problem. Suppose, for example, that $Z$ represents permanent income, $Y_2$ observed income, and $Y_1$ consumption, and that instead of setting $\sigma_Z^2 = 1$, we set $\alpha_2 = 1$, so that the model becomes

$$Y_1 = \alpha_1 Z + \epsilon_1; \qquad Y_2 = Z + \epsilon_2, \tag{4.13}$$

with the interpretation that permanent income is measured by actual income but with an error $\epsilon_2$. Clearly the model is not identified, as is indicated in table 4.1.[4] However, as was men-

---

[4]However, if the permanent income hypothesis also includes the condition that $Y_1 = \alpha \bar{Y}_2$, the model is identified.

tioned above, latent variables may also be assumed to be caused
by observable variables. In his pathbreaking article Zellner (1970)
investigates this simple two-equation model supplemented by the
additional assumption that $Z$ is related to a set of observable
variables (causes). The latter assumption is enough to identify the
model.

In order to study the identification of these models when both
indicators and causes are present, we assume that the structural
equations are the same as those in table 4.1, but that $Z$ is now
related to a single variable $X$, and a disturbance $u''$ that is
independent of $X$ and of the $\epsilon_i$:

$$Z = \beta X + u'', \tag{4.14}$$

with the arbitrary normalization that $\sigma_{u''}^2 = 1$. From table 4.2 it is
clear that although the model is not identified with one indicator,
it is with two or more indicators. Thus, relating the latent variable
to a cause as well as to indicators has aided in identifying the
system. In the analysis below we assume that family income
adjusted for tastes is the cause that determines the latent
environment variables.

Estimation of these types of models has been discussed by
Zellner (1970), Goldberger (1972, 1973), Jöreskog and Goldberger
(1975), Robinson (1974), Chamberlain (1977a, 1977b) and others.
Briefly, if the model is exactly identified the sample moments can
be equated to expressions for them in terms of the unknown
parameters and the resulting system of equations can be solved

Table 4.2
Identification with indicators and one cause.

|  | Equations | | Unknowns | Observable moments | Identification |
|---|---|---|---|---|---|
|  | $Y_1 = \alpha_1 Z + \epsilon_1$ | | $\alpha_1, \sigma_1^2, \beta = 3$ | 2 | under |
| add | $Y_2 = \alpha_2 Z + \epsilon_2$ | + | $\alpha_2, \sigma_2^2 = 5$ | 5 | exact |
| add | $Y_3 = \alpha_3 Z + \epsilon_3$ | + | $\alpha_3, \sigma_3^2 = 7$ | 9 | over |
|  | $Z = \beta X + u''$ | | | | |
|  | Normalization: $\sigma_{u''}^2 = 1$ | | | | |

for the unknowns. This is the standard "method of moments" technique. If the model is overidentified this same procedure could be used but it would result in more equations than unknowns, and hence multiple solutions. However, if the disturbances are assumed to be independently normally distributed, then it is a simple matter to write out the likelihood function and obtain maximum likelihood estimates of the parameters.

For example, in the four-indicator model in table 4.1 denote $Y = (Y_1, Y_2, Y_3, Y_4)^T$ and $E(YY^T) = \Omega$, where the superscript T indicates transpose. Then if $W$ represents the sample covariance matrix of the $Y$'s and if the $\epsilon_i$ are assumed to be independently normally distributed, the log likelihood of a sample of size $N$ is proportional to:[5]

$$-\frac{N}{2}(\log|\Omega| + \text{tr}(\Omega^{-1}W)).$$

Since $\Omega$ can be expressed in terms of the unknowns, as given by the right-hand sides of the equations in table 4.1, and since the elements of $W$ are observed, the likelihood function can be maximized with respect to the unknown parameters.

Generalization of these models to include more than one latent variable is straightforward. For example, if there are $M$ observable variables, $Y_i$, determined by $K$ latent variables, $Z_i$, and $M$ independent disturbances, $u_i$, then in matrix terms

$$Y = AZ + u, \ E(uu^T) = \theta, \qquad E(Zu^T) = 0, \tag{4.15}$$

where $\theta$ is diagonal and $A$ is an $M \times K$ matrix to be estimated

---

[5]The likelihood function (aside from an irrelevant constant) is given by

$$L = \sum_{t=1}^{N} |\Omega| - \tfrac{1}{2}\exp(-Y'_t\Omega^{-1}Y_t/2)$$

$$= |\Omega| - (N/2)\exp\left(-\sum Y'_t\Omega^{-1}Y_t/2\right)$$

and the log likelihood by

$$\log L = -(N/2)\log|\Omega| - \sum Y'_t\Omega^{-1}Y_t/2$$

$$= -(N/2)\log|\Omega| - (N/2)\text{tr}(\Omega^{-1}W).$$

along with the elements of $\theta$. With a sufficient number of constraints imposed on $E(ZZ^T)$ and on $A$, the parameters of the
model can be estimated. Of course this is almost the standard
factor analysis model that psychologists and sociologists have
worked with for years, where the latent variables are referred to
as the common factors, and the disturbances as the unique
factors. However, the information obtained from the covariances
of the observed variables requires that fewer restrictions be
imposed in the latent variable model.

### 4.3.1. Models with siblings

This latent variable technique can be augmented to handle situa-
tions where information is available not just on individuals, but
also on siblings. Chamberlain and Griliches (1975, 1976), for
example, have used this type of analysis to study the labor market
success of brothers. The advantage is that an additional set of
observable moments is obtained from cross-sibling covariances.
This aids in identification of the model if it is assumed that the
disturbance terms are uncorrelated across brothers. Chamberlain
(1977a) uses an instrumental variable framework to clarify how
and why identification is achieved.

For example, consider the models in table 4.1 and denote by
primes the information on an individual's sibling, thus giving

$$Y'_i = \alpha_i Z' + \epsilon'_i \tag{4.16}$$

Now form cross-sibling covariances, defined as $\sigma_{Y_i Y_j}$. If we
assume that $E(\epsilon_i \epsilon_j{}') = 0$ for all $i$ and $j$, then the situation is as
recorded in table 4.3, where the two indicator model with one
latent variable is in fact overidentified. This result relies on the
assumption that $E(\epsilon_i \epsilon_i{}') = 0$ for all $i$, i.e. there is no correlation
across siblings in the random disturbance. However, such a
correlation, if permitted, would only add $M$ unknowns to the $M$
indicator model. Hence, as is evident from table 4.3, the two-
indicator model would not be identified but the three-indicator
model would be overidentified. It should be noted that all of these

Table 4.3
Identification with indicators alone – but with information on brothers.

| | Equations | Unknowns | Observable moments | Identification |
|---|---|---|---|---|
| | $Y_1 = \alpha_1 Z + \epsilon_1$ | $\alpha_1, \sigma_1^2$ | | |
| | $Y_1' = \alpha_1 Z' + \epsilon_1'$ | $\sigma_{ZZ'} = 3$ | 2 | under |
| add | $Y_2 = \alpha_2 Z + \epsilon_2$ | $\alpha_1, \alpha_2, \sigma_1^2$ | | |
| | $Y_2' = \alpha_2 Z' + \epsilon_2'$ | $\sigma_2^2, \sigma_{ZZ'} = 5$ | 6 | over |
| add | $Y_3 = \alpha_3 Z + \epsilon_3$ | $\alpha_1, \alpha_2, \alpha_3, \sigma_1^2$ | | |
| | $Y_3' = \alpha_3 Z' + \epsilon_3'$ | $\sigma_2^2, \sigma_2^3, \sigma_{ZZ'} = 7$ | 12 | over |
| | Normalization: $\sigma_Z^2 = 1$ | | | |

results also rely on the assumption that $\sigma_{ZZ'} \neq 0$, i.e. the latent variable must be correlated across siblings.

Maximum likelihood estimation of this type of model is again straightforward if the unit of observation is considered to be an individual and his brother, since this allows the observations to be treated as independent.[6] On the other hand, complications arise when information is available on more than one brother for particular individuals, as is discussed in Chamberlain and Griliches (1975). It should be mentioned that this "brothers model" is also suited to analyzing cases in which it is assumed that the latent variable is composed of a family and of an individual effect, although of course the family effect cannot be decomposed into genetic and environmental components. The model by Griliches that is presented in eqs. (4.5)–(4.9) above is an example of this genre.

### 4.3.2. The special case of twins

Just as the latent variable technique can be usefully augmented when information is available on siblings, additional questions can be resolved when information is available on identical and fraternal twins, assuming that we are willing to make certain

---

[6]This is discussed in detail below for the models that we estimate.

assumptions, as discussed below. The importance of information on the two types of twins lies in the known differences in genetic factors between them.

This may be illustrated by the following simple example. Suppose, as in table 4.1, we assume that

$$Y_1 = \alpha_1 Z + \epsilon_1, \tag{4.17}$$

but now interpret $Z$ as being solely genetically determined. For MZ twins we have

$$Y_1^* = \alpha_1 Z^* + \epsilon_1^* \tag{4.18}$$

with $Z^* = Z$, and for DZ twins[7]

$$Y_1' = \alpha_1 Z' + \epsilon_1'. \tag{4.19}$$

Assuming that $\epsilon_1$, $\epsilon_1^*$, and $\epsilon_1'$ are uncorrelated, we have three observable moments and three unknowns, $\alpha_1$, $\sigma_1^2$, and $\sigma_{ZZ'}$, since we can normalize $\sigma_{ZZ^*} = \sigma_{ZZ} = \sigma_Z^2 = 1$. Therefore in this very simple and unrealistic model we need only one indicator to estimate the effect of the latent variable on $Y_1$.[8]

The problem with such a simple model, of course, is that any environmental effects that influence $Y_1$ will appear in $\epsilon_1$ which makes unreasonable the assumption that $\epsilon_1$, $\epsilon_1^*$, and $\epsilon_1'$ are uncorrelated. Hence in our analysis of twins we introduce one or more latent variable to reflect genetic effects and one or more to reflect common environmental effects, in which case we need at least two indicators in order to identify the model.

Indeed, with one genetic and one environmental index (which includes also random events), the one-indicator model reduces to the "conventional twins model", variations of which have been studied extensively in the psychological, medical literature.

---

[7]From now on we use an asterisk to denote an MZ twin and a prime to denote a DZ twin.

[8]As is discussed below the identification problem in larger models when using information on twins is more complicated than simply counting the number of unknown parameters and the number of moments because a distinction must be made between identifying parameters of observable variables and those related to unobservable variables.

(Cavalli-Sforza and Bodmer, 1971, and Mittler, 1971, provide extensive examples and references.) We consider this model briefly. However, it should be recognized that the primary objective of such twins models is to estimate the extent to which variations in a single observed variable can be accounted for by variation in genetic and environmental variables. The estimated ratio of variance of the genetic index to that of the observable is referred to as the "broad heritability" of the observable. This concept was defined and examined in Chapter 3. As mentioned there we believe it is related to certain limited issues in income distribution and social mobility.

On the other hand, the main objective of our analysis is to obtain estimates of a structural model, including the effects of schooling on occupation and earnings, and the effects of occupation on earnings. In the process we are involved with what might be called an extended twins model in that we have a number of equations involving several genetic and environmental indices. We use these constructs in an attempt to control for the unmeasured aspects of genetic endowments and family environment. Alternatively, as is discussed above, our analysis falls under the heading of the latent variable technique since the genetic and environmental indices are not observed, yet are hypothesized to affect several different observables.

Briefly the conventional twins model assumes that an observable, $Y$, is a linear function of a genetic index, $G$, and an environmental index, $N$, normalized so that their coefficients are unity

$$Y = G + N. \tag{4.20}$$

For MZ twins this gives

$$Y^* = G^* + N^*, \tag{4.21}$$

and for DZ twins

$$Y' = G' + N'. \tag{4.22}$$

With three observable moments we can only estimate three parameters out of a list that ideally would include the following:

$\sigma_G^2$, $\sigma_N^2$, $\sigma_{GN}$, $\sigma_{GN'}$, $\sigma_{NN'}$, $\sigma_{NN*}$, and $\sigma_{GG'}$. Since the model is seriously underidentified, past investigators have assumed certain values for some of these parameters (aside from $\sigma_G^2$ and $\sigma_N^2$) and have then produced conditional estimates of the others.

For example, if it is assumed that $\sigma_{GN'} = \sigma_{GN} = 0$, that $\sigma_{NN'} = \sigma_{NN*}$, and that $\sigma_{GG'} = \sigma_G^2/2$, then estimates of $\sigma_{NN'}$, $\sigma_G^2$, and $\sigma_N^2$ can be obtained. Or if it is assumed that $\sigma_{GN'} = \sigma_{GN} = 0$, and that $\sigma_{NN} = \sigma_{NN*}$, then assigning different values to $\sigma_{GG'}$ provides a range of conditional estimates for the other parameters (see, for example, Jensen, 1967).

A variation due to Taubman (1976) sets $\sigma_{GG'} = \sigma_G^2/2$, $\sigma_{NN'} = \sigma_{NN*}$, and $\sigma_{GN'} = \sigma_{GN}(\sigma_{NN'}/\sigma_N^2)$ which leaves $\sigma_G^2$, $\sigma_N^2$, $\sigma_{NN'}$, and $\sigma_{GN}$ to be estimated, conditional on assumed values for $\sigma_{NN'}/\sigma_N^2$, the correlation between brothers' environments.

As Goldberger (1977) points out, the main problems with all variations of the conventional twins model are that too many arbitrary assumptions must be made in order to identify the model and that the results are sensitive to the particular assumptions chosen. We turn now to a consideration of the identification and estimation problems involved in our extended-twin, latent variable model.

### 4.3.3. Identification and estimation of the extended-twin, latent variable model

In its most general form our model, which was given in table 2.1, consists of a four-equation, fully recursive system involving the dependent variables schooling, $Y_1$, initial occupation, $Y_2$, current occupation, $Y_3$, and the logarithm of earnings, $Y_4$. The exogenous variables are all unobserved and consist of four genetic and four environmental indices entering the equations in a triangular manner as follows:[9]

---

[9]We discuss the reasons for including four genetic and four environmental indices and for this triangularity in subsection 2.4.2.

$$Y_1 = \alpha_1 N_1 + \beta_1 G_1 \qquad\qquad\qquad + u_1,$$

$$Y_2 = \gamma_1 Y_1 + \alpha_2 N_1 + \beta_2 G_1 + \delta_1 G_2 + \mu_1 N_2 \qquad\qquad + u_2,$$

$$Y_3 = \gamma_2 Y_2 + \gamma_3 Y_1 + \alpha_3 N_1 + \beta_3 G_1 + \delta_2 G_2 \qquad\qquad (4.23)$$
$$+ \mu_2 N_2 + \theta_1 G_3 + \psi_1 N_3 + u_3,$$

$$Y_4 = \gamma_4 Y_3 + \gamma_5 Y_2 + \gamma_6 Y_1 + \alpha_4 N_1 + \beta_4 G_1$$
$$+ \delta_3 G_2 + \mu_3 N_2 + \theta_2 G_3 + \psi_2 N_3 + \eta G_4 + \epsilon N_4 + u_4.$$

In order to analyze this model we solve for the reduced form

$$Y = \begin{pmatrix} Y_1 \\ Y_2 \\ Y_3 \\ Y_4 \end{pmatrix} = (k_1 \ldots k_4 d_1 \ldots d_4) \begin{pmatrix} N_1 \\ N_2 \\ N_3 \\ N_4 \\ G_1 \\ G_2 \\ G_3 \\ G_4 \end{pmatrix} + \begin{pmatrix} v_1 \\ v_2 \\ v_3 \\ v_4 \end{pmatrix}, \qquad (4.24)$$

where the $k_i$ and $d_i$ are $4 \times 1$ vectors defined in terms of the original parameters. Owing to the manner in which the $N$ and $G$ indices enter the structural equations, the $4 \times 4$ matrices formed as $(k_1, k_2, k_3, k_4)$ and $(d_1, d_2, d_3, d_4)$ are lower triangular. The $v_i$'s take the form

$$v = \begin{pmatrix} v_1 \\ v_2 \\ v_3 \\ v_4 \end{pmatrix} = \begin{pmatrix} u_1 \\ u_2 + \gamma_1 u_1 \\ u_3 + \gamma_2(u_2 + \gamma_1 u_1) + \gamma_3 u_1 \\ u_4 + \gamma_4[u_3 + \gamma_2(u_2 + \gamma_1 u_1) + \gamma_3 u_1] \\ \qquad + \gamma_5(u_2 + \gamma_1 u_1) + \gamma_6 u \end{pmatrix} \qquad (4.25)$$

In order to express the observed moment matrices of the $Y$'s for individuals and across twins in terms of the unknown parameters, it is necessary to make some assumptions about the relationships between the $G$'s, $N$'s, and $u$'s. We initially assume the following:

(a) $E(uu^T) = \text{diagonal}(\sigma_{u_i}^2)$;

(b) $E(uu^{*T}) = 0$;

(c) $E(uu'^T) = 0$;

(d) $E(G_iG_j^*) = \sigma_{G_i}^2 = 1, \qquad i = j,$
$\qquad\qquad = 0, \qquad\qquad i \neq j$;

(e) $E(G_iG_j') = \lambda\sigma_{G_i}^2, \qquad i = j$
$\qquad\qquad = 0, \qquad\qquad i \neq j$;

(f) $E(G_iG_j) = \sigma_{G_i}^2 = 1, \qquad i = j,$
$\qquad\qquad = 0; \qquad\qquad i \neq j$;

(g) $E(N_iN_j^*) = \sigma_{N_iN_i^*}, \qquad i = j,$
$\qquad\qquad = 0, \qquad\qquad i \neq j$;

(h) $E(N_iN_j') = \sigma_{N_iN_i'}, \qquad i = j,$
$\qquad\qquad = 0, \qquad\qquad i \neq j$;

(i) $E(N_iN_j) = \sigma_{N_i}^2 = 1, \qquad i = j,$
$\qquad\qquad = 0, \qquad\qquad i \neq j$;

(j) $E(N_iG_j) = \sigma_{N_iG_i}, \qquad i = j,$
$\qquad\qquad = 0, \qquad\qquad i \neq j$;

(k) $E(N_iG_j^*) = \sigma_{N_iG_i}, \qquad i = j,$
$\qquad\qquad = 0, \qquad\qquad i \neq j$;

(l) $E(N_iG_j') = \sigma_{N_iG_i'}, \qquad i = j,$
$\qquad\qquad = 0, \qquad\qquad i \neq j$;

$$(4.26)$$

where as before an asterisk denotes an MZ twin and a prime denotes a DZ twin and a superscript T denotes the transpose of a matrix.

Under (a)–(c) the structural disturbances are mutually orthogonal for individuals and are uncorrelated across twins. In addition it is assumed that they are uncorrelated with all the $G_i$'s and $N_i$'s. According to (d)–(f) the genetic indices are uncorrelated with each other for any individual, while the correlation between

MZ twins for a particular index by definition equals $\sigma_{G_i}^2$ and the correlation across DZ twins is assumed to be the same fraction $\lambda$ of $\sigma_{G_i}^2$ for all $i$. More generally $\lambda$ could vary with $i$. As was discussed in Chapter 3, if there is random mating and additive gene effects, we would expect $\lambda$ to be one-half. Assumptions (g)–(i) indicate that the $N$ indices are mutually uncorrelated for individuals, while across twins the correlation for a specific index is allowed to be nonzero and to differ for MZ and DZ twins. Finally, according to (j)–(l) for both individuals and for twins, the $i$th genetic index is correlated only with the $i$th environmental index. Since the $N_i$'s and $G_i$'s are unobserved, their variances have been arbitrarily normalized to unity. This implies of course that all the estimated $\sigma$'s can be interpreted as correlation coefficients. With these assumptions we can write out the expressions for the sample moments as follows:

$$E(YY^{\mathrm{T}}) = \Omega_0 = \sum k_i k_i^{\mathrm{T}} + \sum d_i d_i^{\mathrm{T}}$$
$$+ \sum (k_i d_i^{\mathrm{T}} + d_i k_i^{\mathrm{T}})\sigma_{N_i G_i} + V, \qquad (4.27)$$

$$E(YY^{*\mathrm{T}}) = \Omega_{\mathrm{M}} = \sum k_i k_i^{\mathrm{T}}\sigma_{N_i N_i^*} + \sum d_i d_i^{\mathrm{T}}$$
$$+ \sum (k_i d_i^{\mathrm{T}} + d_i k_i^{\mathrm{T}})\sigma_{N_i G_i'}, \qquad (4.28)$$

$$E(YY'^{\mathrm{T}}) = \Omega_{\mathrm{D}} = \sum k_i k_i^{\mathrm{T}}\sigma_{N_i N_i'} + \lambda \sum d_i d_i^{\mathrm{T}}$$
$$+ \sum (k_i d_i^{\mathrm{T}} + d_i k_i^{\mathrm{T}})\sigma_{N_i G_i'}, \qquad (4.29)$$

where the summations in each case are from 1 to 4 and $V$ is defined as $E(vv^{\mathrm{T}}) = V$. For the analysis which follows, it is useful to define new matrices:

$$\phi_{\mathrm{M}} = \Omega_0 - \Omega_{\mathrm{M}} = \sum k_i k_i^{\mathrm{T}}(1 - \sigma_{N_i N_i^*}) + V, \qquad (4.30)$$

$$\phi_{\mathrm{D}} = \Omega_0 - \Omega_{\mathrm{D}} = \sum k_i k_i^{\mathrm{T}}(1 - \sigma_{N_i N_i'}) + (1 - \lambda) \sum d_i d_i^{\mathrm{T}}$$
$$+ \sum (k_i d_i^{\mathrm{T}} + d_i k_i^{\mathrm{T}})(\sigma_{N_i G_i} - \sigma_{N_i G_i'}) + V. \qquad (4.31)$$

We consider now the question of identification of the model.[10]
A count of unknown parameters indicates that there are 47: six
$\gamma$'s, ten $k$'s, ten $d$'s, four each of $\sigma_{N_iG_i}$, $\sigma_{N_iG'_i}$, $\sigma_{N_iN^*_i}$, $\sigma_{N_iN'_i}$, the four
$\sigma^2_{u_i}$'s and one $\lambda$. Yet there are only 30 observable moments with
which to estimate these parameters. Although this model is
heavily underidentified it serves as a base to consider the various
alternative models that could be estimated.

To identify the model we make two key assumptions about the
various $N$ indices. In Chapter 2 we argued that the deterministic
investment function for each of the $j$ skills could be written as

$$I_j = \sum a_{kj}P_k + b_jr + c_j(Y_F + T).$$

We further argue that for those investments made in childhood
the prices, $P$'s, and interest rate, $r$, are the same for the twins in a
family. Of course different families can face different $P$'s and $r$,
and some investments are made after childhood. Our first
assumption is that it is a reasonable approximation to ignore price
and interest rate effects and to have within- and across-family
variation in the $I_j$'s to be a function of family income and tastes
$(Y_F + T)$. But if the same variable affects all the skills, then each
of the $N_i$ will be proportional to one other and only a single
unobserved environmental variable need be included in the
analysis. It is possible, moreover, to test to see if a second such
index is needed.

The reader should note the contrast between our approach and
that of Chamberlain and Griliches. (See eqs. (4.5)–(4.9) for an
example of their type of model.) They assume that the latent
variables are unobserved skills which need not have proportional
impacts across various indicators. In our model we disaggregate
each of the latent skills into an investment component and a
genotypic component. Each investment component is proportional to adjusted family income and thus proportional across
indicators. The genotypic component of each skill need not be
proportional across indicators.

[10]For a general analysis of the identification problem in variance components
model the reader is referred to Chamberlain (1977a). We are indebted to Chamberlain for correcting an error in an earlier version of our model.

Secondly, we assume below that $\sigma_{NN*} = \sigma_{NN'}$ or that the cross-twin correlation in environment is the same. To see the consequences of this assumption, for the moment we continue not to impose it. We remind the reader that our justification for this assumption is that any greater similarity of MZ environment that occurs because investments in human capital depend on genetic endowments is treated as genetic. This is a reduced form interpretation and, as is generally the case with reduced form estimates, it need not yield appropriate estimates when structural parameters are needed.

For ease of presentation, we also temporarily assume that the $E(\sigma_{G_1 N_1}) = E(\sigma_{G_1 N_1'}) = 0$. The first and third new assumptions together reduce the number of parameters to be estimated by 20, leaving 25 to be estimated from the 30 observable variances and covariances.

Taking into account the assumptions up to this point, we have

$$\Omega_M = kk^T \sigma_{N_1 N_1^*} + \sum d_i d_i^T, \tag{4.28a}$$

$$\Omega_D = kk^T \sigma_{N_1 N_1'} \lambda \sum d_i d_i^T, \tag{4.29a}$$

$$\phi_M = kk^T (1 - \sigma_{N_1 N_1^*}) + V. \tag{4.30a}$$

In expression (4.30a) there are ten observed moments on the left-hand side. The right hand side has 15 unknown coefficients, six $\lambda$'s, four $\sigma_{u_i}^2$'s, $\sigma_{N_1 N_1^*}$, and four $k$'s. If $\sigma_{NN*} = 1$, $\phi_M$ reduces to $V$. The unknowns in $V$ are the coefficients on the observed variables and the variances of the $u_i$'s. Note further that each element in $\phi_M$ is one-half of the corresponding element in the variance matrix calculated from within MZ pair data. For example, $\sigma_{\Delta S}^2 = 2(\sigma_S^2 - \sigma_{SS*})$ while the 1, 1 element in $\phi_M$ is $(\sigma_S^2 - \sigma_{SS*})$. If we restrict $\sigma_{NN*}$ to equal 1, we can reproduce the within MZ results if our model in terms of the observed variables were fully triangular.

The coefficients of the observable variables (i.e. the six $\lambda$'s) and the variances of the disturbance terms (i.e. the four $\sigma_{u_i}^2$) must be obtained from $\phi_M$. This is so because $V$ does not appear in either $\Omega_M$ or $\Omega_D$, the $\sigma_{u_i}^2$'s appear only in $V$, and the $\gamma$'s – although they appear in the $d$'s and $k$'s – cannot be unscrambled from estimates of them. The estimates of these ten parameters would exhaust the information in $\phi_M$ since it only contains ten elements.

Note further that each element in $\phi_M$ is one-half of the corresponding element in the variance matrix calculated from within MZ pair data. For example, $\sigma^2_{\Delta S} = 2(\sigma^2_S - \sigma_{SS*})$ while the 1, 1 element in $\phi_M$ is $(\sigma^2_S - \sigma_{SS*})$. If we restrict $\sigma_{NN*}$ to equal 1, we can reproduce the within MZ results if our model were fully triangular in the observed variables.

As discussed in subsection 2.4.2 above, however, we feel justified in assuming that our model is not fully triangular in the observed variables. In particular we assume that initial occupation, $Y_2$, does not directly affect the logarithm of current earnings, $Y_4$, but only does so indirectly through the mature occupation, $Y_3$, in which case $\gamma_5 = 0$. This results in an additional degree of freedom in $\phi_M$, which can be used to obtain an estimate, of $\sigma_{N_1N_1^*}$.

It must be emphasized that the identification of the $\gamma$'s, $\sigma^2_{u_i}$'s and $\sigma_{N_1N_1^*}$ is accomplished solely in terms of $\phi_M$ and does not depend on the restrictions made in the rest of the system. However, since $kk$ multiplies $\sigma_{N_1N_1^*}$, the numerical estimates of these parameters may be affected by the restrictions imposed upon the rest of the system.

To examine the identification of the remaining parameters we form the expression $\lambda\Omega_M - \Omega_D$ which we denote as $\theta_1$:

$$\theta_1 = (\lambda\sigma_{N_1N_1^*} - \sigma_{N_1N_1'})kk^T. \tag{4.32}$$

Similarly we form $\sigma_{N_1N_1^*}\Omega_D - \sigma_{N_1N_1'}\Omega_M$ in $\Omega_D$ which we denote as $\theta_2$:

$$\theta_2 = (\lambda\sigma_{N_1N_1^*} - \sigma_{N_1N_1'}) \sum d_i d_i^T. \tag{4.33}$$

Consider the equations sets (4.32) and (4.33); (4.33) must be used to obtain the ten $d$'s since the $d$'s appear nowhere else. This leaves (4.32) to solve for the four $k$'s, $\lambda$, $\sigma_{N_1N_1^*}$ and $\sigma_{N_1N_1'}$.[11] But it is

---

[11]Bock and Vandenberg (1967) used a particular form of $\theta_2$ to estimate the number of genetic indices that determine a set of different tests. They assume that $\lambda = \frac{1}{2}$ and $\sigma_{NN*} = \sigma_{NN'}$.

impossible to solve (4.32) for the four $k$'s, $\lambda$, $\sigma_{N_1N_1^*}$ and $\sigma_{N_1N_1'}$ since even if $\lambda$ were known ($\frac{1}{2}$ for example) we still could not distinguish between $k$ and $\lambda\sigma_{N_1N_1^*} - \sigma_{N_1N_1'}$. To identify the model there are two obvious choices. First we can assume that $\sigma_{N_1N_1^*} = \sigma_{N_1N_1'} = \rho$, that is the correlation between brothers' environments is the same for MZ and DZ twins. In this case (4.32) can be used to obtain the four $k$ values and $\lambda$, since $\lambda$ appears on the left-hand side (4.32) as well as on the right. Secondly, we can allow $\sigma_{N_1N_1^*}$ and $\sigma_{N_1N_1'}$ to differ by reducing the number of genetic indices, thereby allowing (4.33) to aid in solving for $\lambda$ and $\sigma_{NN'}$.

We make the first of these assumptions in our basic model. With this assumption any systematic differences in the correlations across environments of DZ versus MZ twins due to greater genetic similarity in the latter is captured by the $G_i$ terms.

To see the consequence of this assumption suppose that we were to vary $\sigma_{N_1N_1'}/\sigma_{N_1N_1^*}$. The value of $\theta_2$ in (4.33) depends on this ratio. There is always a ratio such that an element in $\theta_2$ is zero. Alternatively, there is a ratio such that $\theta_2$ is close to zero for all elements. If we allow for four $N$ variables there would be a set of ratios such that all the elements in $\theta_2$ would be zero. If $\theta_2$ contains only zeros, the $d$'s will also be estimated at zero, provided $(\lambda\sigma_{N_1N_1^*} - \sigma_{N_1N_1'})$ does not equal zero. Thus, it is possible to make assumptions in which the estimates of the genetic effects are zero.

In the appendix to this chapter we consider the identification issues of some extensions and modifications of this model. Two extensions which are of enough importance that we will examine them here are measurement error and a nonzero covariance of $G_1$ and $N_1$. We noted earlier that measurement error would be of more importance in the MZ within pair equations than in equations based on individuals because the noise to signal ratio would be greater in the within pair equations. Since we show above that the coefficients of the observed variables use essentially the same information as in the MZ equations, measurement error may be very important here too. However, under some circumstances it is possible to estimate the variance of the measurement error in the latent variable model.[12]

Consider again equation (4.30a) for $\theta_M$. If we assume that $\gamma_S = 0$ and that $\sigma_{NN^*} = 1$, we are using the ten elements in $\phi_M$ to estimate nine coefficients. If, as in section 4.2.1, measured schooling, $S$, equals true schooling $T$, plus measurement error, $w$, and if $E(w_{ij}, w_{2j}) = E(T_{ij}, w_{ij})$, then

$$\sigma_S^2 = \sigma_T^2 + \sigma_w^2.$$

It is true schooling that determines occupational status and earnings. Therefore eqs. (4.27) are modified by replacing $\sigma_S^2$ with $\sigma_T^2$ and eq. (4.5) is modified by replacing $\sigma_S^2$ by $\sigma_T^2 + \sigma_w^2$. With these modifications the expected value of the 1, 1 element in $V$ becomes $\sigma_{u_1}^2 + \sigma_w^2$ while all other elements are unchanged. Since $\sigma_{u_1}^2$ appears elsewhere in $V$ we can identify $\sigma_w^2$.

To simplify the exposition we assume above that genotype and environment are uncorrelated. At this point we demonstrate that it is possible to identify the model even if this correlation is not restricted to zero. To keep the issues simple we consider a model in which $\sigma_{N_1 N_1^*} = \sigma_{N_1 N_1'} = 1$, in which the coefficient on the genetic twins in the DZ equations $(\lambda) = \frac{1}{2}$, and in which $N_1$ is correlated only with the genetic index that can have direct effects on all the indicators, $G_1$.

Imposing all the other restrictions we are using we obtain

$$\Omega_M = kk^T + \sum d_i d_i^T + (kd_1^T + d_1 k^T)\sigma_{N_1 G_1}, \tag{4.28b}$$

$$\Omega_D = kk^T + \tfrac{1}{2} \sum d_i d_i^T + (kd_1^T + d_1 k^T)\sigma_{N_1 G_1}, \tag{4.29b}$$

$$\phi_M = V, \tag{4.30c}$$

where we make use of the fact that if $\sigma_{NN^*} = \sigma_{NN'} = 1$, $N = N'$ and $\sigma_{N_1 G_1'} = \sigma_{N_1 G_1}$. Similarly, we can express $\theta_1$ and $\theta_2$ as

---

[12]This is discussed in more detail in Chapter 7.

$$\theta_1 = -\tfrac{1}{2}kk^{\mathrm{T}} - \tfrac{1}{2}(kd^{\mathrm{T}} + dk^{\mathrm{T}})\sigma_{N_1G_1}, \tag{4.32b}$$

$$\theta_2 = -\tfrac{1}{2} \sum d_i d_i^{\mathrm{T}}. \tag{4.33b}$$

The model would thus consist of (4.30c), (4.32b), and (4.33b). However, only (4.32b) differs from the corresponding ones in the basic model.

In (4.32b) there is enough information to identify the four elements in $k$ and $\sigma_{N_1G_1}$ because $d$ enters into the expression by which $\sigma_{N_1G_1}$ is multiplied. The parameters other than $k$ are not only identified using the same arguements as above, but in a just identified model their estimates are unchanged.

It is worth noting that in our empirical work we have not been able to obtain convergence for the above model because the likelihood function is very flat. We suspect that the problem arises for the following reason. The estimate of $\sigma_{N_1G_1}$ affects the goodness with which we fit $\theta_1$. While the algorithm does not work this way we could fit perfectly the diagonal elements in $\theta_1$ by choosing the $k_1, \ldots, k_4$ as the square roots of the corresponding diagonal elements while letting the off-diagonal elements not fit perfectly. In a sense then the improvement in the likelihood function occurs as $\sigma_{N_1G_1}$ lets us improve the fit in these off-diagonal elements. Apparently, different $\sigma_{N_1G_1}$ improve the fit of different elements.

We consider now the derivation of maximum likelihood estimators for our models.[13] For simplicity we work with the reduced form rather than the structural equations. Since the right-hand side of each reduced form equation in (4.24) contains only unobservable $G$ and $N$ indices and structural disturbances, we can consider the entire right-hand side as a set of reduced form residuals. The covariance matrices of these residuals are given in eqs. (4.27), (4.28), and (4.29) above.

For estimation purposes we assume that the unit of observation is an individual and his twin brother. The corresponding $8 \times 1$

---

[13]See, for example, Goldberger (1972) for a discussion of different estimation methods, including maximum likelihood, in latent variable models not involving twins.

vectors of reduced form residuals for the individual and his twin
$\begin{pmatrix} Y \\ Y' \end{pmatrix}$ and $\begin{pmatrix} Y \\ Y^* \end{pmatrix}$ are denoted as $Y'$ and $Y^*$ for DZ and MZ twins,
respectively. Treating a twin pair as a unit of observation is
convenient since it allows us to assume that the observations are
independently distributed. We define the corresponding $8 \times 8$
covariance matrices $\Omega'$ and $\Omega^*$ for DZ and MZ twin observations,
respectively, as:

$$E(Y'Y'^T) = \Omega' = \begin{pmatrix} \Omega_0 & \Omega_D \\ \Omega_D & \Omega_0 \end{pmatrix},$$

$$E(Y^*Y^{*T}) = \Omega^* = \begin{pmatrix} \Omega_0 & \Omega_M \\ \Omega_M & \Omega_0 \end{pmatrix}. \tag{4.34}$$

Assuming now that the structural residuals ($u_i$) are independently
normally distributed and treating the $G$ and $N$ indices as non-
stochastic, the log-likelihood function of the reduced form for a
sample with $(T' + 1)$ and $(T^* + 1)$ DZ and MZ twins, respectively,
is given by (aside from a constant):[14]

$$L = -\frac{T'}{2}(\log|\Omega'| + \mathrm{tr}[\Omega'^{-1}W']) - \frac{T^*}{2}(\log|\Omega^*| + \mathrm{tr}[\Omega^{*-1}W^*]),$$
$$\tag{4.35}$$

where $W'$ and $W^*$ are defined analogously to $\Omega'$ and $\Omega^*$, except
that their elements are the observed sample covariances of the
four dependent variables.[15]

This likelihood function can be maximized with respect to the
unknowns that appear in eqs. (4.27)–(4.29) if the model is
identified. It should be noted that although the likelihood function
involves nonlinearities, it does have the advantage that the sample
information is contained in the moment matrices $W'$ and $W^*$.

[14]This derivation is of course the same as that given earlier for the standard
latent variable problem except that the distinction is made here between MZ and
DZ twins.

[15]$W'$ and $W^*$ are in turn defined in terms of $W_0$, $W_D$, and $W_M$ which
correspond to $\Omega_0$, $\Omega_D$, and $\Omega_M$. However, we do not restrict $W_0$ to be the same
for MZ and DZ twins, but use instead the actual sample covariance, which we
denote as $W_0^M$ and $W_0^D$.

This differs from most nonlinear regression problems, in which each sample point must be dealt with on every iteration. One obvious implication is that the convergence speed of the algorithm does not depend on the sample size, which is advantageous in view of our large sample. It is possible, however, that at some iteration the predicted $\Omega'$ or $\Omega^*$ matrices will not be positive definite, in which case the logarithm of their determinant is undefined. This difficulty does not arise in the standard nonlinear regression problem involving minimization of the determinant of the covariance matrix of residuals because the predicted covariance matrix is positive definite regardless of the values of the unknown parameters.[16]

As mentioned above we wish to estimate alternative models involving different parameters. In order to test the significance of adding one or more parameters to a particular version of our model we use a likelihood ratio test. That is, we maximize the likelihood function both before and after adding say $K$ variables. Since twice the (positive) difference in the log likelihood is distributed as chi-square with $K$ degrees of freedom we can determine whether the null hypothesis, that the $K$ variables have no affect, should be rejected at a prespecified confidence level. Of course this test is only valid when the hypotheses are "nested", i.e. one model is a subset of the other. Unfortunately, owing to the identification problems discussed above, it is not always possible to test hypotheses of interest because the larger models are not identified.[17]

---

[16]It should be mentioned that the type of model in which we are interested probably could be estimated by LISREL, a computer program developed by Jöreskog and M. van Thillo. They develop a very general covariance structure model for a multivariate normal vector. Although their program is not set up to analyze twin problems in particular, it is possible that with an appropriate choice of parameter matrices the twin problem could fit into the Jöreskog–van Thillo scheme. The advantage of the program we use is that it is written specifically for the twin problem, and thus allows us readily to test different models.

[17]Also the estimates of $\Omega_0$ can vary since the latent variable model uses data from both MZs and DZs.

### 4.4. Qualifications

Although the extended-twin latent variable approach discussed in
this chapter is a powerful tool for use in analyzing information on
twins, it is well to keep in mind the various assumptions it
necessitates. Perhaps the most serious problem is that the model
which we would ideally like to estimate is heavily underidentified.[18] This is evident from the discussion above. Even after
making a large number of arbitrary assumptions concerning correlations [(a)–(l) in (4.26)] we are left with 47 parameters to be
estimated from 30 sample moments. Perhaps the most serious in
this list of assumptions is the one specifying that the structural
disturbances ($u_i$) are uncorrelated across equations for individuals
and completely uncorrelated across twins. This assumption is
violated for example if there are omitted variables influencing
both earnings and occupational choice, for individuals, or if there
are omitted variables that affect one of the dependent variables
for both the individual and his twin.[19] Hopefully of course the
inclusion of the $G_i$ and $N_i$ indices reduces the importance of such
omitted variables.

The peculiar nature of the model's underidentification creates
further difficulties in that it is not possible to trade-off between
certain sets of parameters, holding the total number fixed. For
example, as is discussed in the appendix, if more than one
environmental index is included, some prior restrictions must be
imposed on the correlations of such indices between brothers,
regardless of the other variables included. Hence, a very general
environmental model cannot be estimated. Similarly given that we
wish to include four genetic indices, it is not possible to estimate
different correlations across MZ and across DZ twins for the
environmental indices.

Unfortunately underidentification of the large model implies
that tests of some hypotheses are ruled out. In particular, in view

[18]For a good summary of this line of criticism see Goldberger (1976).
[19]Of course to the extent that such variables can be incorporated into the $N$
indices as noncommon environmental effects, there is no problem.

of "traditional twins model" attempts to determine the importance of environmental and genetic effects, it would be interesting to test the significance of adding four environmental indices to a model containing four genetic indices, or vice versa. Clearly, even our extended-twins model suffers, although to a lesser degree, from the same type of underidentification problem as does the standard twins model in this respect. We can compare likelihood function values for models with just genetic indices included with those containing only environmental indices. But since such models are not nested we cannot test the significance of the observed likelihood differences. On the other hand, to the extent that these genetic and environmental indices standardize for the unobserved influences in our structural equations, we obtain appropriate estimates of the structural parameters using our extended-twin, latent variable technique.

A final comment on the identification problem concerns an important recent paper by Chamberlain (1977b) in which he shows that with a symmetric treatment of genes and environment, a twin model is identified only if the corresponding model for ordinary siblings is identified. Basically, in his model the unobservables are decomposed into $n$ genetic and $n$ environmental indices. Although the MZ twins can then be used to estimate the genetic aspects, this leaves $n$ unrestricted environmental indices, each of which has a within- and between-family component, as in (4.7) and (4.8). If $\sigma_{N_iN_i^*}$, $i = 1, \ldots, 4$, are unrestricted, our model is not identified unless additional restrictions are imposed on the $V$ matrix. The same restrictions also identify the same model with data on siblings.

There are, however, several instances in which models are identified using data on MZ and DZ twins, but not with ordinary siblings. One trivial case is when the latent variable is based solely on genetic endowments. A second more interesting case is when there are genetic effects and when $\alpha_{N_iN_i^*} = \sigma_{N_iN_i^*} = 1$ for all $i$, as can be seen by referring back to (4.30). In this case $\phi_M$ reduces to $V$ from which we can obtain the parameter estimates for a fully recursive model while controlling for individual differences in unobserved ability. With data on siblings, if genetic endow-

ments influence ability a fully recursive model cannot be estimated.


**Appendix**

In section 4.3.2 we initially proposed a model with four latent
genetic and four latent environmental variables. We show that if
we only impose the weak restrictions in eq. (4.26) we have an
underidentified system with 30 observed variances whose expected values can be expressed in terms of 47 unknown parameters.
To identify the model, we assume in part that only adjusted
family income determines investments in various skills.

However, in general the various investment equations depend
on prices and other variables which could vary within and across
families. It is of some interest, therefore, to re-examine the
identification issue when there are four unobserved environmental
variables. For the reader's convenience we repeat eqs. (4.28),
(4.29), and (4.30) which summarize the general model:

$$E(YY^{*T}) = \Omega_M = \sum k_i k_i^T \sigma_{N_i N_i^*} + \sum d_i d_i^T$$

$$+ \sum (k_i d_i^T + d_i k_i^T)\sigma_{N_i G_i}, \tag{4.28}$$

$$E(YY'^T) = \Omega_D = \sum k_i k_i^T \sigma_{N_i N_i'} + \lambda \sum d_i d_i^T$$

$$+ \sum (k_i d_i^T + d_i k_i^T)\sigma_{N_i G_i'}, \tag{4.29}$$

$$\phi_M = \Omega_0 - \Omega_M = \sum k_i k_i^T (1 - \sigma_{N_i N_i^*}) + V. \tag{4.30}$$

Equation (4.30) now contains 24 unknown parameters – ten $k_i$'s,
four $\sigma_{N_i N_i^*}$, and the ten elements in $V$. If we assume that $\sigma_{N_i N_i^*} = 1$
for all $i$, then we can use the information in $\phi_M$ to estimate the ten
parameters in $V$. If the system were fully triangular in the
observed variables, the estimates in $V$ would be those obtained
from the within MZ equations estimated by OLS. However, even
if we assume that for all $i$, $\sigma_{N_i N_i^*} = \sigma_{N_i N_i'} = 1$, which also implies

that $\sigma_{N_iG_i} = \sigma_{N_iG_i'}$, only eight unknown parameters have been eliminated and some other coefficients must not be identified.

In the main text we showed that when there is only one $N$ we can estimate $\sigma_{N_1N_1^*}$ if we set $\gamma_5$ (one of the unknown parameters in $V$) to zero and set $\sigma_{N_1N_1^*} = \sigma_{N_1N_1'}$. When $\sigma_{N_iN_i^*} = \sigma_{N_iN_i'} \neq 1$, the information in $\phi_M$ can only be used to estimate $\sigma_{N_iN_i^*}$, $i = 1, \ldots, 4$ if further restrictions are placed on $V$ or if some of the parameters in $\phi_M$ can be estimated elsewhere. But since $V$ appears nowhere else, its parameters cannot be estimated elsewhere. Even if $\sigma_{N_iG_i} = \sigma_{N_iG_i'} = 0$ for all $i$ and the $d_i$'s were known, the items left in (4.28) would be of the form $k_1^2 \sigma_{N_1N_1^*}$ and it would not be possible to obtain separate estimates of the $k_i$'s or of the $\sigma_{N_1N_1^*}$.

To estimate models with more than one environmental variable, we must either restrict its $\sigma_{N_iN_i^*}$ to be one, or assume that $\sigma_{N_iN_i^*}$ is the same for all $i$ included or impose additional restrictions on $V$. Chamberlain and Griliches (1977) demonstrate how this can be done in their sibling models.

# CHAPTER 5

# THE DATA

## 5.1. Introduction

The methods described in Chapter 4 have been applied to a wealth of information obtained on adult twin subjects over a period of almost 35 years by the Twin Registry, Medical Follow-up Agency, National Academy of Sciences–National Research Council (NAS-NRC). This information was made available to the University of Pennsylvania for the study reported here. The twin subjects themselves provided most of the information through questionnaires. With the help of the National Archives and Records Service of the General Services Administration, information has been obtained from the subjects' military records; the Veterans Administration (VA) provided data on medical experience after separation from military service, and the Social Security Administration provided information on current and past earnings. In all communication between these organizations substantive study information was scrupulously deleted if identifiers were provided to outside agencies; and all identifiers, except for arbitrarily assigned numbers by which the final linkages were accomplished, were deleted if substantive information was being exchanged. The privacy of the subjects has thus been fully preserved. Only in the files of the NAS–NRC, that provided the original roster for the study, is it possible to relate some, but not all, of the individual's data to his name.

The systems of birth and VA records through which the study

sample was created and that pertain to it, are unlike any previously used in behavior genetics research. One of the great advantages of using birth certificates in compiling the sample is that it arises from a segment of the U.S. population clearly defined demographically, geographically, and in time. Basic descriptive information is available for this population and for every member of the study group. Both members of the twin pairs studied have been in military service. That part of their experience has been documented fully in standardized formats, and they can be compared to all veterans. The military information had been collected for administrative purposes long before this study was conceived so that the specific study objectives could introduce no artifacts into that information. The military data have been used directly and they also provide meaningful baselines against which the observations obtained in this investigation can be compared.

Although the information compiled is unique in the extent and time covered, it has been obtained from the many different sources with various degrees of "completeness" (Hrubec and Neel, 1977). Reasons for missing data depend on the specific nature of the data, their source, method of collection, and sometimes on particular characteristics of the subject. Of particular interest is whether the relationships observed in the study apply more generally to veterans and to U.S. males. This is a complex question that, to some extent, will remain open to individual interpretation. To help answer it, this chapter gives a detailed description of how the study sample is constructed, its characteristics, how the study data have been collected, how the zygosity of the subjects has been determined, and how those on whom data are available compare to all members of the NRC Twin Registry and to veterans in general.

## 5.2. Sample construction

Subjects for the study were chosen from the Twin Registry of the NRC. The Registry maintains a twin panel that constitutes a scientific resource for a wide variety of medical–genetic investigations. Since the methods used to construct the panel and to diagnose zygosity of the twins have been described in detail (Hrubec and Neel, 1977; Jablon et al., 1967), only the more salient points will be discussed here. Certificates of live white male multiple births occurring during the years 1917–1927 provided the starting point in assembling the panel.[1] These were obtained from Vital Statistics Offices of the various continental United States. Of the then 48 states, all cooperated except Arizona, Delaware, Georgia, Maine, Missouri, New Hampshire, Utah, Vermont, and the city of New Orleans, Louisiana. Certificates were obtained from Connecticut only recently, and this state has not been included in the present study.

The search of birth certificates yielded 54 000 sets that met the search criteria with respect to sex, race, and year of birth. These were matched against the Master Index File of the Veterans Administration (VAMI), and slightly more than 16 000 twin pairs were identified as having both members who entered military service. Service was generally during the Second World War because of the years of birth chosen.[2] No subsequent work was carried out on the approximately 15 000 pairs with only one member identified at the VAMI or on the 23 000 pairs with neither member identified there. For the pairs with both members found at the VAMI, military and VA records were reviewed and abstracted to document the medical experiences of the twins during military service and as veterans, and to obtain information that would be helpful in diagnosing their zygosity. A few identification errors were discovered through the review of records and of the questionnaire replies described below. These were excluded, and at the present the panel consists of 15 924 twin pairs.

[1] At present there are 24 pairs in the panel that originate from triplet births. The two members with military service and the most complete information on file have been selected for inclusion in the twin panel. The number of triplet sets originally identified has not been determined.
[2] The years of birth and veteran status were chosen so as to identify living twins on whom medical information could be obtained through the military services and the VA and who could be followed because generally their survival and address could be determined.

## 5.3. Sources and characteristics of the main sample data

Not all of the 15 924 pairs in the Twin Registry could be included in this study. A mail questionnaire was the primary data collection instrument. Excluded from mailing were those who died prior to the time of the questionnaire, those for whom no valid address was available, and those who had previously returned statements indicating a refusal to cooperate or who had requested removal from the mailing list. The validity of an address was determined through previous mailings, including two questionnaires that also provided data for the present study. Thus, there is an association in the availability of data from several of the sources. To clarify it, the questionnaire data collection process of the Registry is described below in detail.

### 5.3.1. Medical history and zygosity questionnaire (Q1)

At the time the survey for this study was to be mailed it had been possible to obtain addresses for about 27 300 individuals among the 31 848 in the panel. The sources of the addresses were the VA and the military records, the twin brothers reached in previous questionnaire mailings; and occasionally other sources. From 1965 to the start of the present study in 1974, whenever the first address was accessioned, a questionnaire (Q1) was sent out routinely that verified eligibility of the man for the panel, provided a means of determining the zygosity of the twin pair, ascertained the medical history of the respondent since his separation from service, and asked for his twin brother's address. This and the other relevant questionnaires can be found in the appendix (see pp. 255–265). Reports from this questionnaire together with the medical information abstracted from military and VA records have been evaluated for a number of specific diseases (Pollin et al., 1969).

The outcome of mailings of the Q1 medical history questionnaire are shown cumulatively by year in table 5.1. By 1974 replies to this questionnaire had been received from 20 494 individuals,

Table 5.1

Number of twin individuals by status in mailing of medical history questionnaire (Q1) and cumulative percent by year of mailing or death.

| Status in Q1 mailing | Calendar year of mailing or death | | | | | | | | | | Total |
|---|---|---|---|---|---|---|---|---|---|---|---|
| | <1965 | 1965 | 1966 | 1967 | 1968 | 1969 | 1970 | 1971 | 1972 | 1973 | (1/1/74) |
| Eligible and alive at beginning of year or prior contact | 31 848 | 29 829 | 29 726 | 29 665 | 29 618 | 29 570 | 29 523 | 29 471 | 29 442 | 29 397 | 29 359 |
| *Events during year* | | | | | | | | | | | |
| Deaths among eligible[a] | 2019 | 103 | 61 | 47 | 48 | 47 | 52 | 29 | 45 | 38 | 2489 |
| Total contacts | – | 8352 | 10 570 | 1190 | 782 | 440 | 0 | 8 | 705 | 1476 | 23 523 |
| Replies | – | 7947 | 9247 | 839 | 616 | 293 | 0 | 8 | 517 | 1027 | 20 494 |
| Refusals | – | 403 | 1315 | 349 | 165 | 147 | 0 | 0 | 184 | 448 | 3011 |
| Alive, unable to reply | – | 2 | 8 | 2 | 1 | 0 | 0 | 0 | 4 | 1 | 18 |
| *Status at end of year* | | | | | | | | | | | |
| Mail returned as undeliverable[b] | – | 501 | 2675 | 2715 | 2832 | 2847 | 2820 | 2810 | 3091 | 3224 | 3224 |
| Remaining eligible[c] | 29 829 | 21 374 | 10 743 | 9506 | 8676 | 8189 | 8137 | 8100 | 7350 | 5836 | 5836 |
| Percent remaining eligible | 100.0 | 71.7 | 36.0 | 31.9 | 29.1 | 27.5 | 27.3 | 27.2 | 24.6 | 19.6 | 19.6 |
| Percent replies among eligible or prior contact | 0.0 | 26.6 | 57.8 | 60.8 | 63.0 | 64.1 | 64.2 | 64.3 | 66.1 | 69.7 | 69.8 |

[a] Deaths among those contacted in the questionnaire mailing are not included.
[b] Included among eligible. Counted in each year shown are those then alive and with no subsequent address that led to contact before 1/1/74. Deaths are subtracted in year in which they occurred and lead to decreases in 1970 and 1971.
[c] Eligible at beginning of year minus deaths and contacts during year.

who represented 69.8% of those alive and eligible or previously contacted, and 87.1% of those probably reached by the mailings. This last group includes the 23 523 individuals who either replied, or who overtly indicated an unwillingness to cooperate, or to whom three unsuccessful requests for cooperation were mailed without indication that they could not be reached at the address used, or whose letters were returned with evidence that they were under institutional care and unable to reply. In the entire panel there were 2 175 individuals who were alive in 1974 but for whom no address had ever been obtained, and 437 with a valid address and otherwise eligible to whom no Q1 had yet been sent.

### 5.3.2. Epidemiologic questionnaire (Q2)

Individuals who replied to the Q1 medical history and zygosity questionnaire constituted a sample for a more detailed epidemiologic questionnaire that included information on occupation and family background (Q2, see appendix). This second questionnaire was designed to control heredity and environmental variables in evaluating the epidemiologic factors of symptoms of angina pectoris and of chronic obstructive pulmonary disease (Cederlof et al., 1969; Hrubec et al., 1976; Hrubec et al., 1973), but some of the data collected through it have also been used in the present study of factors affecting earnings. Q2 was mailed following receipt of a reply to Q1. As table 5.2 shows, 14 707 replies to the second questionnaire had been received at the beginning of the present study. These represented 72.6% of those alive and eligible or previously contacted, and 81.4% of those probably reached by the mailings. There were 1007 individuals who were eligible for a Q2 mailing to whom the questionnaire had not yet been mailed in 1974.

### 5.3.3. Education, occupation, and earnings questionnaire (Q3)

The main questionnaire of this study (Q3) was mailed to 12 640 individuals in twin pairs with a valid address on file for both

Table 5.2
Number of twin individuals by status in mailing of epidemiologic questionnaire (Q2) and cumulative percent by year of mailing or death.

| Status in Q2 mailing | Calendar year of mailing or death | | | | Total |
|---|---|---|---|---|---|
| | < 1967 | 1967 | 1968–72 | 1973 | (1/1/74) |
| Eligible and alive at beginning of year or prior contact | 17 194 | 17 146 | 17 946 | 19 258 | 20 255 |
| *Events during year* | | | | | |
| Deaths during year among eligible[a] | 48 | 39 | 122 | 30 | 239 |
| Total contacts | – | 13 851 | 221 | 3993 | 18 065 |
| Replies | – | 11 614 | 220 | 2873 | 14 707 |
| Refusals | – | 2226 | 0 | 1109 | 3335 |
| Alive, unable to reply | – | 11 | 1 | 11 | 23 |
| *Status at end of year* | | | | | |
| Mail returned as undeliverable[b] | – | 197 | 197 | 1183 | 1183 |
| Remaining eligible[c] | 17 146 | 3292 | 3752 | 1163 | 1951 |
| Percent remaining eligible | 100.0 | 19.2 | 21.9 | 6.8 | 11.4 |
| Percent replies among eligible or prior contact | – | 67.7 | 65.9 | 76.4 | 72.6 |

[a,b]See footnotes to table 5.1.
[c]Eligible at beginning of year, plus becoming eligible during year minus deaths and contacts during year.

members as determined by previous mailings, both alive as determined by search of the VAMI,[3] and neither requesting removal from the Registry mailing list prior to that time. A second mailing was made if the first request did not produce a definite reply or refusal, and a third mailing by certified mail was made to men whose twin brothers had already replied. A copy of the questionnaire is included in the appendix. Information has been obtained on current marital status, year of marriage, current age of wife, number and sex of children, number of living siblings, birth order of respondent among them, church attendance,

[3]Because the VA extends burial benefits to veterans who survived any period of military action, the fact of death is recorded with great accuracy (Beebe and Simon, 1969). Ascertainment of deaths in the twin panel was made through the VAMI until 1971 when the computerized Beneficiary Identification and Records Locator Subsystem (BIRLS) became operational and has been used for that purpose since then.

education of respondent and members of his family and types of schools attended by them, initial occupation of subject and other family members, employment status, earnings of respondent and wife, job satisfactions and preferences, employment history of wife, factors affecting choice of career, education of parents and inlaws, the level of health care, and the Social Security number of subject and wife.

The distribution of responses to the questionnaire mailings for the two members of each twin pair is shown in table 5.3. Of all the individuals in the sample, 53.6% replied and 39.1% of them were in pairs with both members having replied. There are 2469 twin pairs with replies from both members. The rate of replies was 72.8% among men whose brothers also replied. Table 5.4 gives the distribution of replies to Q1 by the distribution of replies to Q3. Of 121 refusals to Q1, who were included in the Q3 mailing, 100 also refused Q3; however, most Q1 refusals did not receive Q3. They were excluded from the mailing if on the last previous mailing they directly expressed an unwillingness to cooperate.[4]

## 5.4. Data editing, coding, storage, and retrieval

Standard procedures have been followed in processing the data which is mostly machine compatible and generally stored in hardcopy as well as coded form. Generally information was coded for individuals, without reference to the twin brother's records and missing data were specified by distinct codes. Information on date and place of birth was obtained from birth certificates. Dates of birth of members of twin pairs rarely differ by one day, and greater differences were reviewed and corrected. Service records were used to obtain information on date of first entry into service, address at

[4]Included in the Q3 mailing were individuals who did not reply to the last previous request for cooperation, sent by regular first-class mail, but who were thought to have been reached because their letter had not been returned as undeliverable. Generally the latter are also considered as refusals in the definitions usually used by the Registry along with subjects who indicate their refusal by a written statement or fail to reply to a letter for which they signed a receipt.

Table 5.3

Distribution of outcome of mailing earnings study questionnaire (Q3) to 12 640 twin individuals in sample by outcome status of twin brother.

| Man's status, Q3 | Twin brother's status, Q3 | | | | | |
|---|---|---|---|---|---|---|
| | Replied | Alive, unable to reply | Refusal, no reply | Mail returned[a] | Death ascertained through mailing | Total number |
| Replied | 4938 | 2 | 1640 | 183 | 18 | 6781 |
| Alive, unable to reply | 2 | 0 | 1 | 0 | 0 | 3 |
| Refusal, no reply | 1640 | 1 | 3186 | 371 | 20 | 5218 |
| Mail returned | 183 | 0 | 371 | 44 | 1 | 599 |
| Death ascertained through mailing[b] | 18 | 0 | 20 | 1 | 0 | 39 |
| Total | 6781 | 3 | 5218 | 599 | 39 | 12 640 |
| Percent replied | 72.8 | 66.7 | 31.1 | 30.6 | 46.2 | 53.6 |

[a]Post Office indicated addressee not at the address used.
[b]VA information on death is updated routinely, but at irregular intervals.

Table 5.4

Number of twin individuals by status in mailing of earnings study questionnaire (Q3) and status in mailing of medical history of questionnaire (Q1).

| Status in Q3 mailing | Status in Q1 mailing | | | | | |
|---|---|---|---|---|---|---|
| | Replies | Refusals | Mail returned[a,b] | Deaths ascertained through mailing or alive, unable to reply | Not in mailing | Total |
| *In mailing* | | | | | | |
| Replies | 6761 | 16 | 0 | 0 | 4 | 6781 |
| Refusals | 5100 | 100 | 3 | 0 | 15 | 5218 |
| Mail returned[a] or unable to reply | 596 | 4 | 0 | 0 | 2 | 602 |
| Addressee deceased | 38 | 1 | 0 | 0 | 0 | 39 |
| Total in mailing | 12 495 | 121 | 3 | 0 | 21 | 12 640 |
| *Not in mailing* | | | | | | |
| Subject deceased | 634 | 148 | 203 | 99 | 2185 | 3269 |
| Subject alive, brother deceased | 1639 | 280 | 413 | 4 | 329 | 2665 |
| Both alive, last mail contact with subject not successful | 3064 | 2354 | 2804 | 12 | 2198 | 10 432 |
| Both alive, last mail contact with brother not successful | 2662 | 108 | 3 | 1 | 68 | 2842 |
| Total not in mailing | 7999 | 2890 | 3423 | 116 | 4780 | 19 208 |
| Total | 20 494 | 3011 | 3426 | 116 | 4801 | 31 848 |

[a] Post Office indicated addressee not at the address used.
[b] Includes deaths 1965–74 excluded from Q3 mailing.

entry, branches of service, date of last separation from service at the time of review in 1960–62, and date, place, and diagnoses on hospital admission or restriction to quarters of outpatients. The diagnoses were coded according to the 1962 edition of the International Classification of Diseases, Adapted for Indexing of Hospital Records, i.e. except in details, comparable to the seventh, or 1955, Revision of the World Health Organization's International Statistical Classification of Diseases. A major (eighth) revision of both of these classifications was made in 1965 and diagnoses coded up to that time were converted to the new codes, mostly by mechanical means. However, about 3000 hard-copy records were reviewed to code diagnoses in categories not directly comparable between the two classifications.

The VA provided current address, if one was available, information, including diagnoses, on medical pension and compensation claims and on VA hospitalizations, and for the deceased members of the panel information on date, place, and often cause of death. The VA diagnoses as well as those obtained on the medical history questionnaire (Q1) and from death certificates were processed as described above for the military service diagnoses. Microfilm images of fingerprints, provided by the Federal Bureau of Investigation, were coded and scored.

The various questionnaires were edited and coded according to procedures specific to each questionnaire. On Q1, from which eligibility for the twin panel was confirmed, men whose twin brother was deceased sometimes indicated that they were not twins. All file information was reviewed before a decision was made to exclude these and other men because they did not meet the eligibility criteria for the twin panel. The epidemiologic questionnaire (Q2) is complex, and an attempt was made in coding not to interpret responses extensively. Internal inconsistencies were found such as the respondent indicating on a general item that he never drank alcohol, but subsequently answering detailed questions indicating appreciable alcohol use. Such information was not discarded but was assigned special codes that would allow determining the effect of excluding or including such records in particular analyses. The characteristics of these data are described by Hrubec et al. (1976, 1973). The questionnaires of this study, Q3, were coded only for twin pairs with both members responding. For individuals with successive marriages information relating to the first wife or marriage was coded for all items except income, for which that of the current wife was used. Data on all children were retained when reported, but adopted children, and step- and half-siblings were identified by separate codes.

The variety of educational experiences reported on Q3 for the various family members required a special coding procedure. Actual number of years of completed education were recorded with the value of 19 assigned to the PH.D. or equivalent degree and 20 assigned to M.D. or D.D.S. Individuals currently undergoing education were coded on different scales in the 30–39 range of codes, those with advanced technical or vocational education (nurses, laboratory technicians) in the 40–49 range, persons with special education for handicapped in the 50–59 range, and education of step-parents was coded by adding 60 to the proper code values. Appropriate adjustments on these higher-range values were made in processing the data by treating as high school graduates those with vocational training and by converting education of step-parents back to the same codes as were used for parents. Occupation was evaluated according to both the socioeconomic classification of the Bureau of the Census (U.S. Department of Commerce, 1963) to determine a socioeconomic index (SEI), and the Duncan scale. The empirical work in Chapters 6 and 7 uses the Duncan scale version. If more than one occupation was recorded the average value of all was coded. In uninformative occupation descriptions (e.g. government employee) the coding was based on the years of schooling reported. Earnings before deductions were reported either as hourly, weekly, monthly, or yearly. Machine conversion to annual amounts was made.

Coded data were punched onto cards and transferred to magnetic tape for storage and further processing. All items were checked for valid data ranges and internal consistency checks were made, as described in Taubman (1976a). Processing of the data tapes was carried out primarily through a wide variety of standard computer programs.

## 5.5. Classification of zygosity

### 5.5.1. Methods

Zygosity of the twin pairs in the panel is shown by single years of birth in table 5.5. It has been determined using various methods, depending on the information available for the pair. About 806 twin pairs have been classified using blood-group typing that almost always included the ABO, MN, S, P, Rh, Kell, and Duffy systems. Those not classified by laboratory methods, who answered Q1, have been classified by answers to the questions: "As children were you and your brother as alike as two peas in a pod or of ordinary family resemblance?" and "In childhood, did your parents, brothers and sisters, or teachers have trouble telling you apart?". Several investigations indicate that among twin pairs

Table 5.5
Year of birth by zygosity classification of twins in NRC twin panel.

| Year of birth | Zygosity | | | | |
|---|---|---|---|---|---|
| | MZ | DZ | Unknown | Total | Percent MZ |
| 1917 | 426 | 634 | 190 | 1250 | 40.2 |
| 1918 | 672 | 792 | 274 | 1738 | 45.9 |
| 1919 | 704 | 990 | 366 | 2060 | 41.6 |
| 1920 | 994 | 1274 | 386 | 2654 | 43.8 |
| 1921 | 1094 | 1454 | 462 | 3010 | 42.9 |
| 1922 | 1140 | 1460 | 516 | 3116 | 43.8 |
| 1923 | 1262 | 1614 | 478 | 3354 | 43.9 |
| 1924 | 1258 | 1742 | 492 | 3492 | 41.9 |
| 1925 | 1340 | 1638 | 578 | 3556 | 45.0 |
| 1926 | 1452 | 1734 | 620 | 3806 | 45.6 |
| 1927 | 1442 | 1684 | 686 | 3812 | 46.1 |
| Total | 11 784 | 15 016 | 5048 | 31 848 | 44.0 |

whose zygosity is determined by rigorous laboratory procedures about 95% of the pairs can make a correct independent self-classification (Jablon et al., 1967; Cederlof et al., 1961; Nichols and Bilbro, 1966). In the entire file of 15 924 twin pairs, for 2054 pairs the only information available from which to determine zygosity was fingerprints and anthropometric measurements. The methods used have been described (Jablon et al., 1967),[5] although additional data have been obtained since that report (Hrubec and Neel, 1977). There are 2524 pairs whose zygosity could not be determined either because there was no information on them (1423 pairs) or because of contradictions in the available data (1101 pairs). By the methods described above, in the entire panel 5892 pairs have been classified as monozygotic (MZ) and 7508 as dizygotic (DZ). These and the zygosity unknown group are shown by source of classification, Q3 response, and year of birth in table 5.6. Among 2401 pairs with classified zygosity who completed Q3, 51.4% are monozygotic compared to 44.0% in the entire panel, and this difference is almost constant with age.

## 5.5.2. *Effects of misclassification of twin types*

In this sample twins are classified as to twin-type information on blood type, answers to the peas-in-a-pod question, and fingerprints (see subsection 5.5.1 for details). The results of Jablon et al. (1967) and the fact that we do not use certain pairs where the information is ambiguous ensure that about 95% of the pairs are

[5]In principle, a discriminant score was developed by determining the greatest variance in intrapair differences obtainable on a criterion variable under different groupings, transformations and weightings of the dependent variables. The procedure was circular, in that intrapair differences in eye color and hair color were first evaluated against differences in height and weight to determine an appropriate anthropometric discriminant score. By evaluating the fingerprint data on patterns and ridge counts against the anthropometric score, a fingerprint discriminant score was developed. Ultimately, for each pair with fingerprint data for both twins, all available information on eye color, hair color, height, weight, and fingerprints was assembled into a final score. This was validated on a sample of 310 pairs classified by blood typing and found to be reliably accurate (Jablon et al., 1967).

## Table 5.6

Percent classified as monozygotic and total number of pairs classified by source of zygosity classification, in specified group by age at Q3.

| Age at Q3 (1974) | Source of zygosity classification | | | | | | | | | |
|---|---|---|---|---|---|---|---|---|---|---|
| | Respondents, completed pairs | | | | | NRC twin panel | | | | |
| | Blood grouping[a] | Questionnaire (Q1)[b] | Finger-print score only[c] | Total classified | Unclassified | Blood grouping[a] | Questionnaire (Q1)[b] | Finger-print score only[c] | Total classified | Unclassified |
| **47–49** | | | | | | | | | | |
| Percent MZ | 50.7 | 51.9 | 70.0 | 51.9 | – | 47.8 | 45.8 | 43.6 | 45.6 | – |
| Total pairs | 146 | 688 | 10 | 844 | 23 | 293 | 3583 | 769 | 4645 | 942 |
| **50–54** | | | | | | | | | | |
| Percent MZ | 50.5 | 51.5 | 50.0 | 51.3 | – | 45.1 | 43.1 | 43.5 | 43.2 | – |
| Total pairs | 194 | 963 | 18 | 1175 | 39 | 390 | 5294 | 962 | 6646 | 1167 |
| **55–57** | | | | | | | | | | |
| Percent MZ | 59.4 | 48.4 | 75.0 | 50.8 | – | 56.1 | 42.2 | 40.6 | 42.7 | – |
| Total pairs | 74 | 304 | 4 | 382 | 6 | 123 | 1663 | 323 | 2109 | 415 |
| **All ages** | | | | | | | | | | |
| Percent MZ | 52.2 | 51.2 | 59.4 | 51.4 | – | 47.8 | 43.9 | 43.0 | 44.0 | – |
| Total pairs | 414 | 1955 | 32 | 2401 | 68 | 806 | 10 540 | 2054 | 13 400 | 2524 |

[a]Among twins in clinical examination programs or in Michigan State.
[b]Not contradicted by fingerprint scores when these were available.
[c]Combined with anthropometric data when available.

properly classified. While a 5% misclassification error is not large, it is necessary to consider its implications on our estimates of the coefficients of the observed and latent variables.

Consider first the effects of misclassification on estimates of intrapair correlations. For simplicity, assume the misclassification proportion is the same for both twin types, namely 0.05. Then if misclassification is random we have:

$$\hat{c}^* = 0.95c^* + 0.05c',$$
$$\hat{c}' = 0.05c^* + 0.95c',$$

where $\hat{c}^*$ and $\hat{c}'$ are the intrapair correlations for MZs and DZs as calculated from the data and include the misclassified pairs, and $c^*$ and $c'$ are the corresponding true estimates if there were no misclassification. We can solve these two equations for $c^*$ and $c'$ by

$$0.95\hat{c}^* - 0.05\hat{c}' = 0.9025c^* - 0.0025c^*,$$
$$0.05\hat{c}^* - 0.95\hat{c}' = 0.0025c' - 0.9025c',$$

and then

$$c^* = \frac{0.95\hat{c}^* - 0.05\hat{c}'}{0.9},$$

$$c' = \frac{0.95\hat{c}' - 0.05\hat{c}^*}{0.9}.$$

In table 5.7 we present estimates for the $\hat{c}$ and $c'$ values. The estimates of $c^*$ exceed those of $\hat{c}^*$ by about 0.012 while the estimates of $c'$ are less than those of $\hat{c}'$ by about 0.012. To a first approximation our estimates of genetic contributions are twice the difference in intrapair correlations. Thus, using the unadjusted data will cause us to understate the genetic effects by roughly 0.05. Since the adjustment is nearly the same for the four indicators, we will continue to use the unadjusted data and when appropriate refer back to this adjustment.

Misclassification will also affect the within-pair regressions. Briefly, some pairs classified as MZs are DZs for whom genes differ. Thus, in the equations for the so-called MZs, some 5% of

Table 5.7

Estimates for MZ and DZ intrapair correlations on selected variables before and after adjustment for 5% misclassification error.

| Variable | Unadjusted | | Adjusted | |
|---|---|---|---|---|
| | $\hat{c}^*$-MZ | $\hat{c}'$-DZ | $c^*$-MZ | $c'$-DZ |
| Years of schooling ($S$) | 0.764 | 0.545 | 0.776 | 0.533 |
| First occupation[a] ($OC_i$) | 0.525 | 0.333 | 0.536 | 0.322 |
| Occupation in 1967[a] ($OC67$) | 0.429 | 0.205 | 0.441 | 0.193 |
| ln earnings in 1973 (ln $Y_{73}$) | 0.545 | 0.295 | 0.559 | 0.281 |

[a]Socioeconomic index scores as described in U.S. Department of Commerce (1959).

the pairs do not have $\Delta G = 0$. If the pseudo MZs are a random drawing from the DZ population, we would expect there to be a small upward bias in the MZ equations. Similarly, in the DZ equations the bias from not holding genetic endowments constant will be diluted. A correction similar to that for the $\hat{c}$'s can be applied here.

## 5.6. Characteristics of respondents to Q3

### 5.6.1. General considerations

The objectives of this research include generalizing the conclusions beyond the particular subjects studied. The groups to which generalization might reasonably be attempted are all NRC twins whether or not they participated in Q3, all white male Second World War veterans, and all U.S. white males. It is not a necessary condition that the Q3 respondents in all respects represent these populations; it is necessary only that about the same relationships between the study variables prevail among these successively nested groups. Thus, for example, if among U.S. males a year of additional education provides the same increase in earnings (or a transformation thereof) at the lower as at the higher education levels, a good estimate of this increase can

be obtained even though sample information is more often unavailable for subjects with less education than for subjects with
more education. On the other hand, demonstrating comparability
on many variables, while reassuring, does not prove conclusively
that generalization is correct. Unsuspected interactions may prevail. The assessment of whether generalization is justified from
observational studies is necessary, but complex. While it cannot
be fully conclusive, it is facilitated by a careful examination of
methodologic issues pertaining to the study. Such an evaluation is
attempted in this section.

Very many selective processes affect the ultimate acquisition
and full use of data from the main questionnaire of this study
(Q3). Some relate to the mechanisms of twinning described in
Chapter 3. The more important ones are listed below and subsequently evaluated.

• Birth as a twin.
• Survival of *both* pair members through childhood to the age of
  military service.
• *Both* pair members passing the selective screening of the military
  induction physical examination by meeting the specified medical
  and mental criteria.
• Availability of birth certificates to the NRC and inclusion in the
  NRC twin panel.
• Survival of *both* pair members through military service to the
  time of the questionnaire mailing.
• The availability of an effective mailing address for *both* pair
  members.
• *Both* pair members adequately completing the questionnaire and
  returning it to the NRC.

It is generally appreciated that the gestational and birth
experience of members of twin pairs differentiates them from the
single-born and sometimes from each other in important respects
(Price, 1950). Twins tend to be smaller at birth than the single-
born, at greater risk of neonatal medical complications, and they
have a somewhat higher early mortality rate (Peller, 1944; Hendricks, 1966; Gittelsohn and Milham, 1965). The mothers of DZ

twins tend to be older than mothers of single births and perhaps more likely to conceive (Enders and Stern, 1948; Eriksson and Fellman, 1967). Thus, high DZ twinning rates and limited use of birth control in the lowest socioeconomic groups may be associated (Allen and Schachter, 1970). Twins would tend to be selected by that mechanism and as a group would have a somewhat lower socioeconomic status.

Survival and medical experience of twins in later childhood and adult life seems to be comparable to that of the single born, but systematic data to support this view are not available. However, even if such comparability is assumed, selection for health among members of the twin panel probably took place. Owing to shared environment or genetic factors, the medical experience of twin pair members probably tended to be similar. The requirement that each man and also his twin brother survive until the military induction examination and meet the examination standards may have selected a healthier and perhaps a more mentally capable group than if selection criteria had been imposed only on individuals.

The NRC Twin Registry represents a nearly complete roster of all twins that met the selection criteria as to race, year of birth, and military service. The states that cooperated in the search for the multiple births in the years 1917–1927 contained 93% of the white U.S. population in the year 1920, while in 1940 93% of all U.S. births also occurred in these states (U.S. Department of Health, Education, and Welfare, 1950–1975). Undoubtedly some eligible births were missed due to clerical error; the identification of individuals as veterans in the VA Master Index File could not always be positively accomplished, and the VA had no record of a small fraction of veterans. However, it is likely that, overall, clerical errors or failures of identification were rare and mostly random events and not strongly related to socioeconomic characteristics. In comparison with the other mechanisms that produce selective effects on the study data, the operational procedures used to compile the Registry are probably not important sources of selective bias.

The questions of selection during the military and veteran

periods are similar to those of selection during childhood and early adult years; however, more information on mortality and morbidity is available for the veteran population and for the members of the panel. Studies of veterans by Myers and Pitts (1977) indicate a favorable survival of veterans compared to nonveterans, and of officers compared to enlisted men (Seltzer and Jablon, 1977). Table 5.8 shows the 1970 life-table functions $l_x$ as the number expected to live to age $x$ among 100 000 alive at age 20 and, in another comparison, at age 47. The function is given for U.S. white males, white male veterans, all 31 848 NRC twins, and members of pairs with both twins answering Q3. It appears that the improvement in survival of the NRC twins occurs only at the older ages and, compared to U.S. white males, the improvement is slight. Questionnaire respondents had to be alive at the time of

Table 5.8
Number surviving at specified age among 100 000 alive at start by group and beginning year of age.

| Beginning year of age | Respondents, completed pairs[a] | NRC twin panel[a] | White male veterans[b] | U.S. white males[c] |
|---|---|---|---|---|
| *Starting age 20* | | | | |
| 20 | 100 000 | 100 000 | 100 000 | 100 000 |
| 25 | 100 000 | 98 880 | 99 165 | 99 012 |
| 30 | 100 000 | 98 130 | 98 752 | 98 157 |
| 35 | 100 000 | 97 530 | 98 041 | 97 264 |
| 40 | 100 000 | 96 510 | 97 845 | 96 045 |
| 45 | 100 000 | 94 760 | 96 576 | 94 168 |
| 50 | 99 910 | 92 120 | 92 087 | 91 105 |
| 55 | 99 580 | 88 620 | 86 072 | 86 562 |
| *Starting age 47* | | | | |
| 47 | 100 000 | 100 000 | 100 000 | 100 000 |
| 50 | 99 910 | 98 104 | 96 905 | 97 859 |
| 55 | 99 580 | 94 377 | 90 575 | 92 980 |

[a]Based on mortality through 31 December 1975 excluding military action deaths. For respondents only the time period after June 1974 is considered.
[b]Myers and Pitts (1977, variant 5).
[c]U.S. Department of Health, Education, and Welfare (1973), Life Tables for 1973.

the mailing in 1974, when the youngest were 47 years old. They have not been followed long enough to experience any appreciable mortality.

The availability of an effective address is determined by the individual's contacts with the VA, the extent to which he seeks benefits for which he may be eligible, his mobility, his relationship to his twin brother and by the personal, social, and economic traits that are related to these factors. Selective processes are affected further by differential questionnaire responses. Since these responses are voluntary, the respondents are in that sense a self-selected group.

## 5.6.2. Comparison of distributions of relevant variables with other data

The different selective factors discussed in subsection 5.6.1 most probably interact in complex ways. The specific nature of these interactions is not of concern here, but rather their combined effect on the parameters being estimated in this investigation, namely the relationships between the genetic components of education, earnings, intelligence, and the corresponding environmentally determined components of these variables. Two distinct questions are at issue. (1) Are the distributions of the variables of interest among the respondents to the questionnaire similar to other NRC twins, U.S. veterans, and U.S. males? (2) Are the relationships between these variables and their genetic and environmental components representative of those that would be obtained for U.S. veterans and U.S. males? The first of these questions can be treated by a comprehensive comparison of distributions of relevant socioeconomic traits among the respondents with corresponding distributions for the other groups obtained from various sources. The second is more difficult to answer, and it will be dealt with by reference to other studies of socioeconomic factors (Hauser, 1976; Olneck, 1977). The sources of the data are indicated in references or in footnotes to each of the tables introduced in this section.

Table 5.9
Percent distribution of age in 1970 in specified groups.

| Age in 1970 | Respondents, completed pairs | NRC twin panel[a] | Male veterans[b] Second World War | Total | U.S. white males |
|---|---|---|---|---|---|
| ≤24 | | | | 7.6 | 13.0 |
| 25–29 | | | | 9.3 | 11.0 |
| 30–34 | | | | 9.9 | 9.2 |
| 35–39 | | | | 12.5 | 9.0 |
| 40–44 | 24.1 | 23.9 | 19.9 | 15.0 | 9.7 |
| 45–49 | 52.2 | 51.9 | 32.9 | 16.2 | 9.8 |
| 50–54 | 23.7 | 24.2 | 25.4 | 12.3 | 9.1 |
| 55–59 | | | 11.9 | 6.0 | 8.1 |
| 60–64 | | | 6.4 | 3.4 | 6.8 |
| 65+ | | | 3.1 | 7.8 | 14.3 |
| Total | 100.0 | 100.0 | 99.6 | 100.0 | 100.1 |
| Number[d] | 4938 | 31 848 | 12 462 | 28 112 | 53 389 |
| Average age in 1970 | 47.1 | 47.1 | 50.6 | 44.0 | 45.3 |

[a]Alive in 1970.
[b]Pitts et al. (1977, table 1-4, census estimates).
[c]U.S. Department of Health, Education, and Welfare (1970), Vol. I, Natality, Section IV, Table 4-2. Excluding <20 years.
[d]Numbers in the three rightmost columns are in thousands.

Table 5.9 gives the age distributions of the several groups included in the above described comparison. Age in the twin panel is of course restricted by the range of eleven years of birth over which the sample was selected. Responding twin pairs are quite comparable to the entire twin panel. By restriction to the 1917–1927 births the oldest Second World War age groups have been excluded from the panel. All of the veteran groups shown are considerably concentrated between the ages 35–54 compared to the U.S. white male populations enumerated in 1970 (U.S. Department of Health, Education, and Welfare, 1950–1975; Pitts et al., 1977), but the average age of the responding twin pairs is only 1.8 years greater than that of all U.S. white males over 20 years old.

Table 5.10
Percent distribution of period of most recent military service in specified groups by age in 1970.

| Age in 1970 | Period of military service | Respondents, completed pairs | NRC twin panel | Male veterans,[a] total | U.S. males age 20+[b] |
|---|---|---|---|---|---|
| ≤44 | Second World War | 81.4 | 79.0 | 16.5 | 8.6 |
| | Korea | 16.2 | 17.7 | 32.1 | 16.7 |
| | Other or none | 2.4 | 3.3 | 51.4 | 74.8 |
| | Total | 100.0 | 100.0 | 100.0 | 100.1 |
| | Number[c] | 1188 | 7618 | 15 255 | 29 394 |
| 45–49 | Second World War | 86.1 | 87.6 | 90.2 | 70.8 |
| | Korea | 10.2 | 9.3 | 7.2 | 5.7 |
| | Other or none | 3.7 | 3.1 | 2.6 | 23.5 |
| | Total | 100.0 | 100.0 | 100.0 | 100.0 |
| | Number | 2580 | 16 528 | 4552 | 5799 |
| ≥50 | Second World War | 87.6 | 89.1 | 70.3 | 26.6 |
| | Korea | 8.7 | 6.9 | 4.2 | 1.6 |
| | Other or none | 3.7 | 4.0 | 25.5 | 71.8 |
| | Total | 100.0 | 100.0 | 100.0 | 100.0 |
| | Number | 1170 | 7702 | 8306 | 21 934 |
| Total | Second World War | 85.3 | 85.9 | 44.3 | 25.1 |
| | Korea | 11.3 | 10.7 | 19.8 | 7.8 |
| | Other or none | 3.4 | 3.4 | 35.9 | 67.1 |
| | Total | 100.0 | 100.0 | 100.0 | 100.0 |
| | Number | 4938 | 31 848 | 28 112 | 57 128 |

[a]Pitts et al. (1977, table 1-4, census estimates).
[b]Pitts et al. (1977, tables1-4 and 2-1).
[c]Numbers shown in the two rightmost columns are in thousands.

The distribution of periods of service is shown by age in table 5.10. In both the younger and the older age groups the percent of twins with service in the Second World War is greater than among all veterans. For all ages combined, only 10.7% of the twins served during the Korean period and there was no service during the First World War. Responding pairs are quite comparable to the entire panel within age groups and for all ages combined. The age groups ≤44 and ≥50 include, respectively, the ages of 43–44 and 50–53 for the NRC twins.

In table 5.11 the percent distribution of marital status is compared between Q3 respondents, the entire panel, and U.S. white

Table 5.11
Percent distribution of marital status in specified groups by age in 1970.

| Age in 1970 | Marital status | Respondents,[a] completed pairs | NRC twin panel[b] | White[c] male veterans | U.S.[c] white males |
|---|---|---|---|---|---|
| 40–44 | Never married | 6.2 | 7.0 | 6.0 | 6.2 |
| | Married | 91.8 | 89.8 | 88.6 | 88.6 |
| | Separated | | | 1.2 | 1.1 |
| | Divorced | 1.8 | 3.0 | 3.6 | 3.5 |
| | Widowed | 0.3 | 0.2 | 0.7 | 0.7 |
| | Total | 100.1 | 100.0 | 100.1 | 100.1 |
| 45–49 | Never married | 5.7 | 5.3 | 4.0 | 5.1 |
| | Married | 91.3 | 91.1 | 90.3 | 89.1 |
| | Separated | | | 1.3 | 1.4 |
| | Divorced | 2.7 | 3.1 | 3.0 | 3.2 |
| | Widowed | 0.3 | 0.5 | 1.4 | 1.2 |
| | Total | 100.0 | 100.0 | 100.0 | 100.0 |
| 50–54 | Never married | 4.5 | 4.5 | 5.2 | 5.7 |
| | Married | 92.7 | 91.9 | 87.7 | 87.4 |
| | Separated | | | 1.9 | 1.9 |
| | Divorced | 2.3 | 3.0 | 3.5 | 3.3 |
| | Widowed | 0.5 | 0.7 | 1.6 | 1.8 |
| | Total | 100.0 | 100.1 | 99.9 | 100.1 |

[a] Among 4227 Q2 respondents who gave this information.
[b] Among 12 049 Q2 respondents who gave this information.
[c] Pitts et al. (1977, tables 2.1–2.6).

males by age. The percent single and percent married are quite similar between responding twin pairs and the total panel, but the percent divorced is slightly lower among the respondents. The percentage of widowers among the twins is lower than among other veterans or among U.S. white males of the same age.

Compared to all veterans, the responding pairs have a higher mean number of years of school completed, a considerably lower percentage with only eighth grade education or less, and a considerably higher percentage with 16 or more years of school, as is shown in table 5.12. In contrast to that difference, veterans have only a slight educational advantage compared to U.S. white

Table 5.12
Percent distribution and years of school completed in specified group by age in
1970.

| Age in 1970 | Completed years of school | Respondents, completed pairs | NRC twin panel | White male veterans | | U.S. males white | |
|---|---|---|---|---|---|---|---|
| 40–44 | 0–8 | 4.5 | | 13.3[a] | 10.8[b] | 17.8[a] | 15.8[b] |
| | 9–11 | 13.6 | | 17.3 | 15.8 | 17.6 | 16.2 |
| | 12 | 32.3 | –[c] | 34.4 | 37.7 | 32.0 | 36.4 |
| | 13–15 | 15.1 | | 15.0 | 14.0 | 13.3 | 11.9 |
| | ≥ 16 | 34.6 | | 20.0 | 21.6 | 19.3 | 19.7 |
| | Total | 100.1 | | 100.0 | 99.9 | 100.0 | 100.0 |
| | Mean years | 13.5 | – | 12.3 | 12.4 | 11.9 | 11.9 |
| 45–49 | 0–8 | 6.2 | | 15.3 | 14.5 | 20.2 | 18.1 |
| | 9–11 | 13.5 | | 17.1 | 15.6 | 17.0 | 16.1 |
| | 12 | 34.7 | – | 37.8 | 39.5 | 35.7 | 38.0 |
| | 13–15 | 13.5 | | 13.3 | 13.6 | 12.1 | 12.5 |
| | ≥ 16 | 32.1 | | 16.5 | 16.9 | 15.0 | 15.3 |
| | Total | 100.0 | | 100.0 | 100.1 | 100.0 | 100.0 |
| | Mean years | 13.3 | – | 11.9 | 12.0 | 11.5 | 11.7 |
| 50–54 | 0–8 | 9.4 | | 21.1 | 18.7 | 25.3 | 23.3 |
| | 9–11 | 11.5 | | 20.3 | 17.0 | 19.9 | 17.9 |
| | 12 | 39.7 | – | 34.9 | 37.4 | 33.1 | 35.1 |
| | 13–15 | 13.4 | | 10.5 | 13.0 | 9.9 | 11.4 |
| | ≥ 16 | 26.0 | | 13.2 | 13.9 | 11.7 | 12.3 |
| | Total | 100.0 | | 100.0 | 100.0 | 100.0 | 100.0 |
| | Mean years | 12.9 | – | 11.3 | 11.6 | 10.8 | 11.2 |

[a]Pitts et al. (1977, tables 2.9 and 2.1).
[b]Hauser (1977), unpublished tabulations.
[c]Not available.

males. No meaningful comparison of current education between the responding twin pairs and the entire twin panel can be made since this information is available only for questionnaire respondents. However, it is possible to compare education at time of entry into military service between respondents and nonrespondents to Q3 based on the information obtained for twin pairs with Navy service. The details of obtaining this sample and data collection on it are described in section 5.8. In this group, respondents completed on the average 11.5 years of schooling compared to 10.9 years for nonrespondents, a significant difference with $P < 0.001$. The years of schooling completed, shown in table 5.12, also compare data on veterans and U.S. white males obtained by Pitts et al. (1976) with data from Hauser (1977). these distributions are quite similar. Hauser's mean values are only slightly higher than those of Pitts et al., and both are appreciably lower than the values for the responding twin pairs.

Mean 1973 earnings, combined for Q3 respondent and wife, are shown in table 5.13 by age for the 4938 individuals in pairs with both twins replying. Included in the computation are 520 individual respondents with zero earnings, and the means have been adjusted for comparison with the Pitts et al. (1976) data for 1970. The latter values are somewhat higher than values of individual earnings reported for 1973 by Hauser (1976) among native white men age $46 - 56$ and among veterans in that group. Hauser's values are 12 290 and 12 780 in these two respective samples, with a standard deviation of about 9400 in both groups. The distributions of earnings among twin respondents and in a tabulation provided by Hauser (1977) are shown in table 5.14. Compared to white male veterans or U.S. white males in this age range, the "none or not reported" category occurs more frequently among NRC twins in responding pairs, but this reflects primarily the apparent exclusion of the "not reported" group from Hauser's tabulation. In subsequent analyses of the NRC twin data the zero

Table 5.13
Mean 1970 family income in specified group by age.

| Age in 1970 | Respondents,[a] completed pairs | NRC twin panel[b] | White male[c] veterans | U.S. white[c] males |
|---|---|---|---|---|
| 40–44 | 14 675 | – | 13 216 | 13 113 |
| 45–49 | 14 539 | – | 13 638 | 12 998 |
| 50–54 | 14 104 | – | 12 658 | 12 322 |

[a]Adjusted to 1970 values by taking 0.78 of combined earnings of husband and wife reported on study questionnaire (Q3), zero values included.
[b]Not available.
[c]Pitts et al. (1977, table 2.8).

Table 5.14
Percent distribution of annual earnings in specified group by age in 1970.

| Age in 1970 | Annual earnings | Respondents, completed pairs[a] | NRC twin panel[b] | White male veterans[c] | U.S. white males[c] |
|---|---|---|---|---|---|
| 40–44 | None or not reported | 10.4[d] | – | 3.3 | 3.9 |
| | 1–9999 | 8.5 | – | 34.2 | 36.0 |
| | 10 000–11 999 | 10.8 | – | 16.4 | 16.6 |
| | 12 000–13 999 | 14.6 | – | 12.4 | 12.3 |
| | 14 000–15 999 | 12.0 | – | 9.5 | 9.1 |
| | 16 000–19 999 | 14.5 | – | 10.3 | 9.3 |
| | 20 000–25 999 | 16.0 | – | 7.3 | 6.8 |
| | ≥ 26 000 | 13.3 | – | 6.5 | 6.0 |
| | Total | 100.1 | – | 99.9 | 100.0 |
| 45–49 | None or not reported | 10.0[d] | – | 4.7 | 5.3 |
| | 1–9999 | 12.5 | – | 36.2 | 39.0 |
| | 10 000–11 999 | 13.4 | – | 16.5 | 15.8 |
| | 12 000–13 999 | 12.7 | – | 11.9 | 11.2 |
| | 14 000–15 999 | 11.8 | – | 9.4 | 9.2 |
| | 16 000–19 999 | 13.8 | – | 9.1 | 8.4 |
| | 20 000–25 999 | 12.2 | – | 6.4 | 5.9 |
| | ≥ 26 000 | 13.5 | – | 5.8 | 5.2 |
| | Total | 99.9 | – | 100.0 | 100.0 |
| 50–54 | None or not reported | 11.6[d] | – | 7.8 | 8.3 |
| | 1–9999 | 13.8 | – | 41.2 | 43.5 |
| | 10 000–11 999 | 12.1 | – | 14.2 | 13.7 |
| | 12 000–13 999 | 16.3 | – | 11.9 | 11.0 |
| | 14 000–15 999 | 10.9 | – | 8.1 | 7.5 |
| | 16 000–19 999 | 11.8 | – | 6.8 | 6.7 |
| | 20 000–25 999 | 11.9 | – | 5.2 | 5.0 |
| | ≥ 26 000 | 11.5 | – | 4.7 | 4.2 |
| | Total | 99.9 | – | 99.9 | 99.9 |

[a]Earnings in 1973.
[b]Not available.
[c]Hauser (1977), unpublished tabulation of earnings for 1972.
[d]Includes "not reported".

earnings values have not been used. Twin respondents were twice as likely to report incomes exceeding $20 000 as veterans or U.S. males, and only about 12% of the twin respondents had incomes under $10 000 compared to over one-third of the subjects in Hauser's tabulation. Earnings distributions of veterans and U.S.

Table 5.15
Percent distribution of mother's completed years of school in specified group by
age in 1970.

| Age in 1970 | Mother's completed years of school | Respondents, completed pairs | NRC twin panel[a] | White male veterans[b] | U.S. white males[b] |
|---|---|---|---|---|---|
| 40–44 | 0–8 | 53.8 | – | 51.8 | 54.8 |
|  | 9–11 | 8.6 | – | 12.6 | 12.5 |
|  | 12 | 24.7 | – | 25.9 | 23.5 |
|  | 13–15 | 6.6 | – | 6.6 | 6.0 |
|  | ≥ 16 | 6.3 | – | 3.1 | 3.1 |
|  | Total | 100.0 | – | 100.0 | 99.9 |
| 45–49 | 0–8 | 56.2 | – | 59.4 | 61.6 |
|  | 9–11 | 6.8 | – | 10.7 | 10.2 |
|  | 12 | 24.1 | – | 20.8 | 19.3 |
|  | 13–15 | 7.0 | – | 6.2 | 6.0 |
|  | ≥ 16 | 5.9 | – | 3.0 | 2.9 |
|  | Total | 100.0 | – | 100.1 | 100.0 |
| 50–54 | 0–8 | 62.0 | – | 65.9 | 68.4 |
|  | 9–11 | 5.6 | – | 8.7 | 9.0 |
|  | 12 | 20.3 | – | 18.8 | 16.8 |
|  | 13–15 | 5.9 | – | 4.4 | 3.7 |
|  | ≥ 16 | 6.3 | – | 2.1 | 1.9 |
|  | Total | 100.1 | – | 99.9 | 99.8 |

[a]Not available.
[b]Hauser (1977), unpublished tabulations.

males appear similar, although veterans do have a slight earnings advantage.

The distribution of mother's years of schooling is compared among the NRC responding twin pairs, veterans, and U.S. males in table 5.15 by age in 1970. The distributions of all three groups are similar, but the NRC twins about twice as often have mothers who completed college as do the other two groups. Likewise, father's years of schooling are compared among these samples in table 5.16 with results similar to those noted for mother's education.

In table 5.17 is shown the percent distribution of number of

Table 5.16
Percent distribution of father's completed years of school in specified group by age in 1970.

| Age in 1970 | Father's completed years of school | Respondents, completed pairs | NRC twin panel[a] | White male veterans[b] | U.S. white males[b] |
|---|---|---|---|---|---|
| 40–44 | 0–8 | 62.5 | – | 63.8 | 65.9 |
| | 9–11 | 7.0 | – | 10.7 | 10.9 |
| | 12 | 15.2 | – | 15.5 | 14.1 |
| | 13–15 | 5.5 | – | 5.6 | 5.0 |
| | ≥16 | 9.8 | – | 4.3 | 4.1 |
| | Total | 100.0 | – | 99.9 | 100.0 |
| 45–49 | 0–8 | 65.7 | – | 68.2 | 70.0 |
| | 9–11 | 5.5 | – | 8.7 | 8.5 |
| | 12 | 15.2 | – | 13.8 | 12.6 |
| | 13–15 | 4.8 | – | 4.7 | 4.6 |
| | ≥16 | 8.8 | – | 4.5 | 4.3 |
| | Total | 100.0 | – | 99.9 | 100.0 |
| 50–54 | 0–8 | 68.1 | – | 72.1 | 74.4 |
| | 9–11 | 3.4 | – | 7.1 | 6.8 |
| | 12 | 15.8 | – | 11.5 | 10.6 |
| | 13–15 | 4.5 | – | 4.7 | 4.4 |
| | ≥16 | 8.1 | – | 4.5 | 3.8 |
| | Total | 99.9 | – | 99.9 | 100.0 |

[a]Not available.
[b]Hauser (1977), unpublished tabulations.

siblings. For the NRC twins only siblings alive in 1940 are counted, at which time the respondents were between 13 and 23 years old. The co-twins are not included in the count of siblings shown in the stub of the percent distribution. There is an appreciably greater proportion of twins than of veterans or of U.S. males in families with only one birth. However, when all children are considered, the proportion of two-child families is greater for veterans and for U.S. males than for twins. The mean number and standard deviation of *all siblings*, including the co-twin of the twin respondent, are also shown in table 5.17. Even though in these large samples some of the differences between group means are

Table 5.17
Percent distribution and mean ± standard deviation of number of siblings in specified group by age in 1970.

| Age in 1970 | Number of siblings | Respondents, completed pairs[a] | NRC twin panel[b] | White male veterans[c] | U.S. white males[c] |
|---|---|---|---|---|---|
| 40–44 | 0 | 11.4 | – | 7.5 | 7.7 |
| | 1 | 24.3 | – | 18.6 | 16.7 |
| | 2 | 20.4 | – | 17.1 | 17.0 |
| | 3 | 12.9 | – | 13.7 | 13.7 |
| | 4 | 10.7 | – | 11.6 | 11.0 |
| | 5 | 5.5 | – | 7.8 | 8.1 |
| | 6 | 5.4 | – | 7.0 | 7.0 |
| | ≥ 7 | 9.4 | – | 16.7 | 18.7 |
| | Total | 100.0 | – | 100.0 | 99.9 |
| | Mean ± SD | 3.86 ± 2.43 | | 3.65 ± 2.79 | 3.78 ± 2.87 |
| | Number of respondents | 1174 | | 1610 | 2109 |
| 45–49 | 0 | 11.0 | – | 6.1 | 6.3 |
| | 1 | 23.3 | – | 15.5 | 14.6 |
| | 2 | 20.6 | – | 17.3 | 16.6 |
| | 3 | 13.6 | – | 14.7 | 14.5 |
| | 4 | 10.8 | – | 11.5 | 11.6 |
| | 5 | 6.8 | – | 8.8 | 9.2 |
| | 6 | 4.9 | – | 7.1 | 7.2 |
| | ≥ 7 | 8.9 | – | 19.0 | 20.0 |
| | Total | 99.9 | – | 100.0 | 100.0 |
| | Mean ± SD | 3.88 ± 2.42 | – | 3.91 ± 2.82 | 3.99 ± 2.86 |
| | Number of respondents | 2550 | | 1750 | 2171 |
| 50–54 | 0 | 8.4 | – | 6.3 | 6.2 |
| | 1 | 21.4 | – | 13.2 | 12.3 |
| | 2 | 19.0 | – | 16.6 | 15.8 |
| | 3 | 12.9 | – | 12.7 | 12.9 |
| | 4 | 11.6 | – | 10.5 | 10.9 |
| | 5 | 8.5 | – | 10.6 | 10.7 |
| | 6 | 4.7 | – | 7.3 | 7.5 |
| | ≥ 7 | 13.5 | – | 22.8 | 23.7 |
| | Total | 100.0 | – | 100.0 | 100.0 |
| | Mean ± SD | 4.27 ± 2.57 | – | 4.22 ± 2.97 | 4.32 ± 2.99 |
| | Number of respondents | 1151 | | 1252 | 1928 |

[a]Number of siblings is number, other than co-twin, alive in 1940; but co-twin is included in mean ± S.D.
[b,c]See footnotes a and b in table 5.15.

significant on statistical testing, differences between the samples are small and not consistent for all three age groups.

The·diagnosis of chronic obstructive pulmonary disease in the twin panel was made through information supplied on a mailed questionnaire (Q2) according to criteria developed by the British Medical Research Council (1960). Data on chronic respiratory disease for veterans and U.S. white males have been obtained from the Health Interview Survey of the National Center for Health Statistics and have been reported (Wilder, 1973). The different methodologies make the comparisons of the two types of estimates in table 5.18 questionable, particularly since the Health Interview Survey is a more inclusive classification. However, the percent of all veterans or U.S. white males reporting chronic respiratory disease is slightly greater only in the oldest age groups than the percent of all twins reporting chronic obstructive pulmonary disease. The percent for U.S. white males is quite comparable to that of white male veterans over the ages represented in the twin panel. The percent for responding twin pairs is somewhat lower than the percent in the entire twin panel, especially in the youngest age group.

The percent receiving VA disability has been reported by age and war as of June 1968 (Administrator of Veterans Affairs, 1969). To preserve age comparability, the same age groups as were used in the 1968 report have been established for pension and compensation status among the NRC twins in 1970 and the com-

Table 5.18
Percent with 1970 chronic respiratory disease in specified group by age in 1970.

| Age in 1970 | Respondents, completed pairs | NRC twin panel[a] | White male veterans[b] | U.S. white males[b] |
|---|---|---|---|---|
| 40–44 | 4.7 | 6.2 | 5.1 | 4.9 |
| 45–49 | 4.3 | 5.5 | 5.6 | 5.6 |
| 50–54 | 4.3 | 5.3 | 6.3 | 7.1 |
| 55–59 | – | – | 8.9 | 9.3 |

[a]Among 12 785 respondents to Q2 whose replies were coded.
[b]Pitts et al. (1977, tables 3.26 and 3.1).

Table 5.19
Percent receiving VA disability pension or compensation by age in
1970.

| Age group in 1970 | Respondents, completed pairs | NRC twin panel | Male veterans[a] | | U.S. males[b] |
|---|---|---|---|---|---|
| | | | World War II | Total | |
| 40–44 | 5.5 | 6.5 | 7.3 | 8.0 | 6.1 |
| 45–49 | 12.5 | 12.5 | 11.7 | 12.3 | 10.5 |
| 50–54 | 14.3 | 14.3 | 13.4 | 14.2 | 8.4 |

[a]Administrator of Veteran Affairs (1969, tables 44 and 77), ages and status as of June 1968.
[b]As footnote [a] and U.S. Department of Health, Education, and Welfare (1968, Vol. I, Natality, 1968, section III, table 3-2).

parison is presented in table 5.19. Second World War veterans and the NRC twins are quite similar. Among responding pairs fewer are compensated in the youngest groups, and the same proportions in the oldest age groups, as among veterans in general.

Information on the distribution of veterans by branch of service has not been published. Data on branch of service distribution for Second World War veterans presented in table 5.20 have been obtained from a 2% stratified random sample of premium records of the National Service Life Insurance program. About 98% of military personnel serving in the Second World War participated in this program. Women and nonwhites are included. For all ages combined, a somewhat higher percentage of twins in pairs responding to Q3 served in the Navy than of all military personnel, but this tendency almost vanishes when age-specific comparisons are made. There is virtually no difference in branch of service distributions between twins in responding pairs and the entire NRC panel for all ages combined and within age groups.

As mentioned in the first paragraph of this subsection and in subsection 5.6.1, the primary question in evaluating the generality of our findings is a comparison of the relationships between the major study variables to these relationships observed among all

Table 5.20
Percent distribution of branch of military service in specified group by age in 1970.

| Age in 1970 | Branch of service | Respondents, completed pairs | NRC twin panel | WW II[a] veterans |
|---|---|---|---|---|
| ≤ 44 | Army | 52.2 | 48.4 | 51.7 |
| | Navy | 43.7 | 45.9 | 42.1 |
| | Marines | 3.3 | 4.5 | 5.1 |
| | Coast Guard | 0.8 | 1.1 | 1.1 |
| | Total | 100.0 | 99.9 | 100.0 |
| 45–49 | Army | 64.7 | 64.1 | 65.8 |
| | Navy | 29.0 | 28.8 | 27.2 |
| | Marines | 4.8 | 5.4 | 5.5 |
| | Coast Guard | 1.6 | 1.7 | 1.5 |
| | Total | 100.1 | 100.0 | 100.0 |
| ≥ 50 | Army | 74.7 | 77.6 | 78.0 |
| | Navy | 20.3 | 18.0 | 18.4 |
| | Marines | 3.0 | 2.9 | 2.6 |
| | Coast Guard | 2.1 | 1.5 | 1.0 |
| | Total | 100.1 | 100.0 | 100.0 |
| Total | Army | 64.0 | 63.6 | 70.0 |
| | Navy | 30.5 | 30.3 | 24.8 |
| | Marines | 4.0 | 4.6 | 4.0 |
| | Coast Guard | 1.5 | 1.5 | 1.2 |
| | Total | 100.0 | 100.0 | 100.0 |

[a]Estimated from a 2% stratified random sample of National Service Life Insurance premium records.

veterans and among U.S. males. Such a comparison is possible using data presented by Hauser (1976) and summarized in table 5.21. Correlations between schooling and occupation socio-economic index (SEI) are somewhat lower among NRC twin respondents to Q3 than among veterans or U.S. males, as are correlations between first and current occupation SEI. Correlations between the natural logarithm (ln) of earnings and the other variables are higher among NRC twin respondents than among veterans or U.S. males. The differences between cor-

Table 5.21

Selected correlation coefficients among schooling, occupation socioeconomic index (SEI) and ln of earnings for NRC twin individuals in pairs of Q3 respondents,[a] white male veterans[b] and U.S. white males[b].

| | Schooling | First occupation SEI | Current occupation, 1962, 1967 SEI | Current occupation 1973 SEI | ln earnings |
|---|---|---|---|---|---|
| *Schooling* | | | | | |
| NRC twin respondents | 1.00 | 0.53 | 0.53 | – | 0.44 |
| Veterans | 1.00 | 0.69 | 0.61 | 0.59 | 0.19 |
| U.S. males | 1.00 | 0.65 | 0.61 | 0.59 | 0.22 |
| *First occupation SEI* | | | | | |
| NRC twin respondents | – | 1.00 | 0.44 | – | 0.35 |
| Veterans | – | 1.00 | 0.64 | 0.59 | 0.19 |
| U.S. males | – | 1.00 | 0.64 | 0.59 | 0.19 |
| *Current occupation, 1962, 1967 SEI* | | | | | |
| NRC twin respondents, 1967 | – | – | 1.00 | – | 0.35 |
| Veterans, 1962 | – | – | 1.00 | 0.75 | 0.25 |
| U.S. males, 1962 | – | – | 1.00 | 0.74 | 0.24 |
| *Current occupation, 1973 SEI* | | | | | |
| Veterans | – | – | – | 1.00 | 0.22 |
| U.S. males | – | – | – | 1.00 | 0.28 |

[a] Among 4938 respondents 4301 were in pairs of known zygosity with both members having reported earnings greater than zero. Correlations are based on all of the 4301. If one twin did not answer he is given twin brother's answer. If neither answered, mean of values reported by all respondents is used.
[b] For 4836 white males, and 3676 veterans among them, ages 46 to 56 in 1973, data from Hauser (1977).

relation coefficients of NRC twins and those of veterans and of U.S. males are statistically significant, but they are based on very large samples. The results of statistical testing may indicate only that the two studies were carried out using different methodologies.

Another comparison can be made that takes advantage of the genetic equivalence between DZ twins and siblings discussed in Chapter 3. Except for being of the same age, DZ twins are in fact siblings. A comparison of within DZ pair correlations with cross-sibling correlations obtained by Olneck (1977) is presented in table 5.22. These intraclass correlations of schooling and of first occupation have almost the same value for the two samples. There is somewhat less within-pair similarity in current occupation status for the NRC twins than for the Kalamazoo brothers, but the opposite relationship is seen for ln of earnings in these two groups. Only the difference between the correlation coefficients for current occupation is statistically significant.

Table 5.22

Correlation coefficients between members of DZ twin pairs and between siblings for schooling, first occupation, current occupation and ln earnings for NRC DZ twin respondents to Q3 and for the Kalamazoo brothers sample ($N =$ 346 weighted pairs).

| Variable | NRC DZ twins[a] | Kalamazoo brothers[b] |
|---|---|---|
| Schooling | 0.54 | 0.55 |
| First occupation | 0.33 | 0.39 |
| Current occupation | 0.20 | 0.31 |
| ln earnings | 0.30 | 0.22 |

[a]See footnote a to table 5.21. Among DZ twins 2068 individuals reported earnings.
[b]Olneck (1977).

## 5.7. Comparisons of monozygotic (MZ) and dizygotic (DZ) twins

Models for analyzing twin data generally assume that the mean values of observations on MZ twins equal those of DZ twins. The same assumption may be made with respect to total variances of MZ and DZ measurements. Contradictions of these assumptions call for a statistical assessment of the possibility of random sampling artifacts. If errors of sampling can be ruled out, these inequalities may provide valuable insights into the subject being studied, even though the applicability of specific models may become questionable (Nance, 1976).

In table 5.23 are presented mean values and variances of the

Table 5.23
Some summary statistics for individuals in the NAS–NRC sample (calculated separately for MZs and DZs).

|  | MZs | | DZs | |
|---|---|---|---|---|
|  | Mean | Variance | Mean | Variance |
| 1973 annual earnings | 18.4[a] | 150[b] | 18.1[a] | 166[b] |
| ln 1973 annual earnings | 9.67[a] | 0.28 | 9.64[a] | 0.32 |
| 1967 or 1972 occupational score | 50.4 | 472 | 49.8 | 445 |
| Years of schooling | 13.5 | 9.1 | 13.3 | 9.8 |
| Initial full time civilian occupation[c] | 36.7 | 610 | 35.0 | 590 |
| Age | 51.0 | 8.4 | 51.2 | 8.8 |
| Mother's education years | 10.0 | 9.6 | 9.7 | 11.9 |
| Father's education years | 9.3 | 12.6 | 9.1 | 14.8 |
| Father's occupational status | 29.6 | 532 | 28.6 | 503 |
| % Catholic | 26 | 19 | 23 | 18 |
| % Jewish | 4 | 4 | 5 | 5 |
| % Other non-Protestant | 2 | 2 | 3 | 3 |
| Number of siblings alive 1940 | 2.6 | 4.9 | 3.0 | 5.6 |
| Number of older siblings alive 1940 | 1.6 | 3.3 | 2.1 | 3.7 |
| Number of pairs | 1019 | | 907 | |

Note: Calculations are for those for whom earnings are nonzero for both brothers. For other variables, if one brother answered and the other did not, nonrespondent is set equal to his brother. If both did not answer, both are set at mean or put in "other category". For mother and father data, if brothers' answers differ, mean of responses is used.

[a]Thousands of dollars.
[b]Millions of dollars.
[c]As recalled in 1974.

more important observations in this study. These data have been published (Taubman, 1976). The only statistically significant differences of means are in number of siblings alive in 1940, the number of older siblings alive in 1940, and mother's education. Even these differences are slight. They can be explained by the increase in the DZ twinning rate with maternal age and the relationship with social class. Proportionately more of DZ than of MZ twins are born to older women of higher parity. The differences of variance are also slight, and even though several of them are significant in this large sample, they are not likely to produce serious distortions in the analysis. The computations in table 5.23 are based on twin pairs with nonzero earnings for both members. Other computations, based on 2236 MZ individuals and 2068 DZ individuals with 1973 earnings reported and greater than zero, yield values that are essentially the same as those in table 5.23. The means of MZ and DZ twins, respectively, are 18.3 and 18.0 thousand dollars of annual 1973 earnings, 9.66 and 9.64 of ln of earnings, and 13.5 and 13.6 of years of schooling.

## 5.8. The Navy twin pair sample

### 5.8.1. Sample selection and collection of data

Military service records, established during 1935–55, but mostly during the Second World War, were accessible for nearly all NRC twins regardless of their participation in current studies. These service records, from which basic information had already been obtained, were available until 1973 when 80% of those of the Army were destroyed in a fire at the Federal Records Center in St. Louis. Thus, for twin pairs with both members in that branch of service, full information is now available for only about 4%. However, Navy and Marine Corps records have been preserved. In the entire twin panel 30.3% of the subjects served in the Navy and only 4.6% in the Marines. The personnel system of the Marine Corps is different from that of the Navy. Therefore only twin pairs with both members in Navy service were included in the Navy record abstracting study.

In the entire panel there were 6710 individuals in 3355 twin pairs with both members ever in the Navy. Zygosity was known for 2755 of these pairs. Of these, in 502 pairs both members returned Q3. All of the latter have been included in the record abstracting study. There remained 2253 pairs of known zygosity with one or both members being nonrespondents to Q3. Of the latter, a 30% systematic sample was selected for inclusion in the Navy record study. Chosen were 1382 individuals in 691 pairs with the digits 1, 2, or 8 in the units position of an arbitrarily assigned pair-number on which the file is sequenced. Together with the 1004 Q3 respondents these make up the sample of the study. The sampling procedure is specified in terms of counts of individuals in table 5.24.

Abstracted from the records of induction was information on education, state of residence at induction, survival and marital status of parents, religion, the Navy job qualifications classification and specific job recommendations, and nature and duration of first full-time civilian occupation. The General Classification Test (GCT) scores and special aptitude test scores were obtained from the induction records and from the service record. All scores found have been recorded. The service record also provided information on military rating and pay grade, proficiency score, Naval training schools attended, and data on unauthorized leave and disciplinary actions including masts and courts-martial. Information usually obtained from the service record was sometimes obtained from records of separation if the service record was unclear, incomplete, or inconsistent. Separation records generally did not contain any test score information, but they did provide a statement of job preference on separation. A copy of the abstracting form is included in the appendix.

The abstracted information was edited, coded, punched on cards, checked for validity, and transferred to magnetic tape for processing with the other information of the study. Several items required special handling. Occupations were sometimes coded in the service record in the Department of Labor's Dictionary of Occupational Titles code. Such coded entries were accepted directly when available. If occupation was recorded but not coded

Table 5.24
Number of individuals in twin pairs with both members having Navy service by status in Navy Record Abstracting Study (R19-41), Q3 response and zygosity.

| Zygosity | Selected for Navy record abstracting | | | Not selected for Navy record abstracting (one or both no Q3) | Total individuals in Navy–Navy pairs |
|---|---|---|---|---|---|
| | Both Q3 respondents | One or both no Q3 | Total selected | | |
| Monozygotic | 596 | 722 | 1318 | 1612 | 2930 |
| Dizygotic | 408 | 660 | 1068 | 1512 | 2580 |
| Unknown | 0 | 0 | 0 | 1200[a] | 1200 |
| Total known | 1004 | 1382 | 2386 | 3124 | 5510 |
| Total | 1004 | 1382 | 2386 | 4324[a] | 6710 |

[a]Includes 28 individuals in 14 pairs where both twins answered Q3 but who were not selected for the Navy record study because zygosity was not determined.

in the service record, it was coded using the 1960 Bureau of Census occupation codes. A conversion of the Department of Labor codes to the Census codes is being undertaken.

## 5.8.2. The general classification test scores

Considerable subsequent processing of the GCT scores was required. The GCT is available only for individuals who entered service as enlisted men. Officers have been tested by special tests, but their scores have not been retained in the records. The GCT is not to be considered an "IQ" test; it measures ability to understand words and ideas. According to Stuit (1947) it is primarily a measure of verbal reasoning abilities. However, such vocabulary tests generally have correlations of about 0.8 with standard intelligence tests. The GCT was used by the Navy to assign personnel to particular jobs and to select them for certain kinds of training.

The Navy GCT scores included in this study are of two different kinds, obtained from different tests. Before July 1943 a test was used that had a maximum score of 100, a mean of about 73, and if overlaid on two normal curves, standard deviations of

10 above and 12 below the mean (U.S. Department of the Navy, personal communication). During mid-year of 1943 a new test was introduced that provided a so-called Navy Standard Score (NSS) with a mean of 50 and a standard deviation of 10. In some Navy records the old scores had been converted to the NSS. These converted scores were sometimes so described and often they could be identified by standard suffixes indicating percentile ranges of the NSS.[6] As is shown in table 5.25, tests dated before July 1943 represent an admixture of converted and unconverted scores. The data in table 5.25 also indicate that a test date after June 1943 is a good indication that a score is an NSS whether or not it has been suffixed. If a date of a test was before July 1943 and the score was not suffixed appropriately, its numeric value could help to determine whether it had been converted. Such scores, if 78 or higher, were almost certainly unconverted. Unconverted scores in the 30–50 range indicated low aptitude, and entries in the record about recommendations regarding the man's career, training, and military assignments would often confirm this. Conversely, an NSS in the 60–70 range indicated high aptitude. In about 7% of the 408 tests shown in table 5.25 as dated before July 1943 a second test score, that appeared to be an NSS, was found in the record. With the above considerations in mind, all scores were reviewed and most could be appropriately converted. When multiple test scores were found, after any necessary conversions, a mean value was used. A memorandum describing the procedure in detail is available on request.

[6]The Navy Standard Score was recorded, for example, as 48-3, the suffix 3 indicating the middle percentile group. The relationship of suffixes, scores, and percentile ranges was as follows:

| Suffix | Score range | Percentile range |
|--------|-------------|------------------|
| −5     | ≤34         | 0–7              |
| −4     | 35–44       | 8–31             |
| −3     | 45–54       | 32–69            |
| −2     | 55–64       | 70–93            |
| −1     | ≥65         | 94–100           |

Table 5.25
Mean, standard deviation of first recorded general classification test (GCT) score[a] and number of individuals scored by Q3 response and by time of test and score format.

| | Tests after June 1943 with suffix[b] | Tests after June 1943 without suffix | Tests before July 1943 without suffix | All first recorded scores |
|---|---|---|---|---|
| **Q3 Respondents** | | | | |
| Mean | 52.37 | 52.88 | 69.44 | 57.26 |
| SD | 10.58 | 10.01 | 15.63 | 14.10 |
| Number with score | 203 | 229 | 162 | 689 |
| **Q3 Nonrespondents** | | | | |
| Mean | 49.43 | 48.41 | 68.24 | 54.19 |
| SD | 10.28 | 10.58 | 16.67 | 15.11 |
| Number with score | 287 | 371 | 246 | 1024 |
| **Total** | | | | |
| Mean | 50.65 | 50.12 | 68.72 | 55.42 |
| SD | 10.50 | 10.58 | 16.25 | 14.78 |
| Number with score | 490 | 600 | 408 | 1713 |
| **Weighted total[c]** | | | | |
| Mean | 49.94 | 49.11 | 68.44 | 54.71 |
| SD | 10.33 | 10.49 | 16.50 | 14.94 |

[a]The individual's GCT score first recorded on abstracting form, generally the earliest.
[b]The suffix is a digit appended to the score that indicates a percentile range of a Navy standard GCT score, see footnote 6 (p. 150).
[c]Weighted so as to represent 100% of Navy–Navy pairs from the sample of Q3 respondent pairs and 30% of pairs with one or both nonrespondents to Q3.

Some indications of the extent to which the review and conversion of GCT scores succeeded are as follows. Of 1713 valid GCT scores in the first coded field, all were either accepted, converted, or the final value was taken from the second field. One additional score was accepted from the second field, so that 1714 individuals have been assigned scores. The mean of scores in the first field before review or conversion was 55.4 with a standard deviation (SD) of 14.8. The mean of the reviewed and, where necessary, converted scores used in this study is 50.1 with an SD

of 10.3, very close to the standard values for the test. For men
who provided earnings data on Q3 the mean and SD of the
reviewed scores are respectively 52.5 and 9.9, nearly the same as
the respective values of 52.6 and 10.3 for Q3 respondents' first
recorded scores dated after June 1943. For those who did not
provide earnings data on Q3, the mean of converted scores is 48.9
and the SD 10.2, again very close to the respective first recorded
values for Q3 nonrespondents tested after June 1943, namely 48.9
and 10.5.

### 5.8.3. Characteristics of the Navy sample

Considerations of selection effects, similar to those discussed for
all questionnaire respondents in section 5.6, also apply to twins in
the study of Navy records. In table 5.26 are presented, for several
Q3 variables, mean values for individuals not included in the
Navy record abstracting study and mean values for groups of
individuals in pairs with both twins having had Navy service and
in the record study. Only Q3 respondents who reported 1973
earnings have been included in the first two columns, and only
twin pairs with 1973 earnings reported for both twins have been
included in the last two columns. Compared in table 5.26 are all
those meeting the above criteria and not selected for the Navy
record study, those selected for the study, those selected for the
study for whom GCT scores have been obtained, and all pairs in
the study that remained complete after the selection criteria were
imposed regarding Navy service and availability of data on
zygosity and earnings.

Compared to other Q3 respondents, those selected for the Navy
records study were less often of rural place of birth ($P \leq 0.001$),
had higher earnings ($P \leq 0.01$), had a higher SEI score ($P < 0.05$),
were younger ($P \leq 0.001$), had fewer siblings living in 1940 ($P < 0.001$), and had mothers with more education ($P \leq 0.01$). These
differences, though statistically significant, are not large. They
become statistically negligible when individuals in the Navy study
with GCT scores are compared to those not in the Navy study,

## Table 5.26
Comparison of Q3 respondents who supplied 1973 earnings by status in Navy study sample.

| Variable[a] | With Q3 earnings Not in Navy sample (3531 individuals) | | With Q3 earnings, in pairs with both twins in Navy sample | | | | | |
|---|---|---|---|---|---|---|---|---|
| | | | All individuals (893 individuals)[b] | | All individuals with GCT (609 individuals)[b,c] | | All pairs, MZ or DZ (404 pairs)[b,c] | |
| | Mean | Variance | Mean | Variance | Mean | Variance | Mean | Variance[d] |
| Catholic | 0.26 | 0.19 | 0.25 | 0.19 | 0.26 | 0.19 | 0.24 | 0.18 |
| Born rural | 0.37 | 0.23 | 0.31 | 0.21 | 0.32 | 0.22 | 0.25 | 0.19 |
| Raised in south | 0.18 | 0.15 | 0.19 | 0.15 | 0.19 | 0.15 | 0.18 | 0.15 |
| ln Y73 | 9.63 | 0.31 | 9.69 | 0.28 | 9.64 | 0.25 | 9.69 | 0.20 |
| OCC67 | 49.1 | 459.8 | 51.0 | 434.9 | 50.0 | 406.0 | 50.7 | 373.0 |
| EDMAS | 13.3 | 9.5 | 13.5 | 9.1 | 13.2 | 8.8 | 13.6 | 7.8 |
| Age | 51.5 | 8.3 | 49.7 | 6.9 | 49.5 | 5.9 | 49.7 | 6.9 |
| No. siblings alive, 1940 | 3.0 | 5.6 | 2.6 | 5.2 | 2.8 | 5.7 | 2.6 | 4.9 |
| ED mother | 10.1 | 8.2 | 10.4 | 9.0 | 10.2 | 7.6 | 10.4 | 8.5 |
| ED father | 9.6 | 12.5 | 9.7 | 11.7 | 9.6 | 10.7 | 9.7 | 12.1 |
| OCC father | 26.9 | 582.4 | 28.8 | 585.1 | 27.0 | 566.3 | 32.0 | 510.5 |

[a]For all variables, individual excluded if no 1973 earnings given. On variables referring to parents, twin pair responses averaged or, if no answer from either twin, set equal to mean of nonzero answers. For other variables, except ln '73 earnings, if one twin did not answer he is given twin brother's answer, if neither answered, mean of nonzero responses.
[b]Only with known zygosity.
[c]Only with 1973 earnings known for both pair members.
[d]Variance of pair average which does not include within pair variation.

except that the GCT score group is less often of rural place of birth ($P \leq 0.05$) and even younger than those in the above comparison ($P < 0.001$). The age range of the sample is restricted to eleven years and the age differences are small. Except for age, those in the Navy study with GCT scores are very similar to those not in the Navy study.

In table 5.23 were presented means and variances for MZ and DZ questionnaire respondents. Means of some of the variables given there are shown in table 5.27 to contrast this comparison with a comparison of MZ and DZ twins in the Navy records study. In the Navy study as well as among all respondents the MZ twins are slightly younger than the DZ twins, and they have somewhat greater earnings, occupational SEI, and education than the DZ twins. Variances of these variables among twins in the Navy study are within 20% of those among all questionnaire respondents in the same zygosity group, except that for years of schooling of DZ Navy study twins the variance is 12.6, 29% higher than the 9.8 value for all DZ questionnaire respondents.

Within the Navy record study sample, as shown above, the MZ twins had slightly greater earnings ($P \leq 0.01$) and occupation SEI ($P \leq 0.05$) than DZ twins, but education and age did not differ significantly between zygosity groups. Earnings, occupation, and education information was obtained by questionnaire and the Navy study MZ–DZ comparisons of these variables include only questionnaire respondents. GCT data were obtained in the Navy

Table 5.27

| Variable | All Q3 respondents | | Navy records study | |
|---|---|---|---|---|
| | MZ | DZ | MZ | DZ |
| ln 1973 earnings | 9.67 | 9.64 | 9.73 | 9.62 |
| Occupation SEI | 50.4 | 49.8 | 52.3 | 48.6 |
| Years of schooling | 13.5 | 13.3 | 13.6 | 13.4 |
| Age in 1974 | 51.0 | 51.2 | 49.7 | 49.8 |
| Number of observations | 2038 | 1814 | 534 | 359 |

study regardless of questionnaire response. Altogether there are 946 MZ individuals and 768 DZ individuals with GCT scores, and there are 395 MZ pairs and 294 DZ pairs with scores available for both twins. The means ± standard deviations for individuals in the two zygosity groups are, respectively, $50.43 \pm 10.41$ and $49.75 \pm 10.12$. This difference in means is not significant. The correlations between pair members are $+0.76$ for the MZ and $+0.49$ for the DZ twins. Most of the within twin pair correlations of intelligence test scores reported in the literature have been somewhat higher than these values, but these other studies were generally done on subjects younger than men entering the Navy, mostly during the Second World War.

# CHAPTER 6

# ORDINARY LEAST SQUARES REGRESSION ESTIMATES OF THE MODEL

## 6.1. Introduction

We now present estimates of the determinates of socioeconomic success as represented by the four indicators discussed above in Chapters 1 and 2: educational attainment, initial occupational status, mature occupational status, and mature earnings. We utilize the recursive model presented in Chapter 2, the statistical methodologies discussed in Chapter 4, and the data described in Chapter 5 and in the appendix. In the present chapter we explore ordinary least squares regression estimates of this system. In the next chapter we consider the maximum likelihood estimates of the latent variable model.

In this chapter we first consider questions related to the appropriate functional form for the relations in the model. We next examine ordinary least squares estimates of the model for individuals in the data set (i.e. without utilizing our knowledge about relations between twin brothers). Then we look at ordinary least squares estimates of differences between monozygotic and dizygotic twin brothers. Finally, we consider the implications of including a measure of cognitive ability in regressions for individuals from a subset of the sample.

Our estimates of the relations for all individuals in the sample generally are in accord with the other studies which are reviewed in Chapter 1. They are consistent with the hypothesized recursive structure: years of schooling and the occupational status measures have significant roles in determining subsequent socioeconomic indicators. Even with this recursive structure included, several background variables remain significant, which suggests the existence of family effects beyond those captured by the basic recursive schooling and occupational status measures. The estimated total return to schooling in earnings is about 8% when no other variables are in the equation, but this drops by 0.9% when we control for measured background variables. All in all these estimates leave very substantial portions of the variances in the four socioeconomic variables unexplained, which suggest that there may be major excluded variables. If these excluded variables are correlated with the included variables, the estimated coefficients of the latter group are biased.

Our estimates based on differences between twins suggest that general practice may result in substantial biases in the estimation of important coefficients. For example, the failure to control for characteristics related to genetics and common (largely home) environment may cause biases of the order of magnitude of 50% in the coefficient of years of schooling in the determination of initial occupation and of 70% in the coefficient of years of schooling in the earnings relation! These biases are quite large. The returns to schooling may be greatly overstated by most previous studies. The policy implications of such possible biases are enormous.

Measurement error may account for part of these differences. Under plausible assumptions about the nature of measurement error in our MZ within pair regressions, up to half of the bias referred to in the previous paragraph may be accounted for. However, this still leaves substantial differences.

We have re-estimated the equations for four socioeconomic indicators for a subset of our sample for which we have a measure of cognitive ability. The measure of cognitive ability has a significant positive impact for each of our four basic indicators. For example, earnings are 13% higher for each increase in cognitive ability score of one standard deviation. While not controlling for cognitive ability does not appear to cause widespread biases coefficients in the occupational status equations, it does seem to cause a bias of 30–35% in the coefficient of most interest to us – the returns to schooling in terms of earnings. A comparison of the MZ within-pair equations and the equations for individuals in which we control for measured background and cognitive skills suggests that including cognitive ability and observable background measures (and not correcting for measurement error in schooling) may suffice to avoid large biases in the schooling coefficient in the earnings relation. Still, a comparison of our results from this chapter with those from the next suggests that there are unmeasured family determinants of socioeconomic success which are quite important, although their exclusion may not be causing large biases in the estimated coefficients of the observable variables.

Our results for individuals are in accord with most other studies for white men with substantial amount of labor force experience.[1] Our findings based on within-pair equations for DZ twins are also in rough accord with Olneck's results using his sample of Kalamazoo brothers who are in the 35–60 age interval. Moreover, our results based on within-pair equations for MZ yields an estimate of the effects of schooling on earnings that is very close to Olneck's within-sibling equations in which he also controls for cognitive skills. However, our results for individuals are not in accord with the much greater number of studies in which the men had relatively few years of experience. Nor do our within DZ pair regressions results agree with those of Chamberlain and Griliches.

## 6.2. Functional forms

In Chapter 2 we discussed the advantage of using a semilog functional form for the earnings equation to permit easier comparisons with estimates in the human capital tradition (also see subsection 1.2.4). We also note in section 4.3 that it is advantageous to use linear relations for the other indicators to aid in

---

[1] See Fägerlind (1975), Olneck (1977), and Taubman and Wales (1974).

identification in the latent variable methodology. Thus, it is desirable to use linear forms for the other indicators in the OLS estimates to maintain comparability with the latent variable estimates of Chapter 7.

Here we can provide some further insight into the preferred functional forms. First we consider the possibility of interaction terms between genetics and environment as introduced in section 3.6. In subsection 4.2.2 we presented a test, due to Jinks and Fulker (1970), for interactions. Briefly, the test consists of regressing the absolute differences in $Y$ on MZ pairs' average value of $Y$. If the slope coefficient is not statistically significant, the null hypothesis of no interactions cannot be rejected. The test can be repeated for various transforms of $Y$.

Application of this test suggests homoskedasticity for the natural logarithm of earnings, but not for earnings itself. This result supports the use of a semilog or a loglinear earnings function for the estimates reported below. Because the semilog form is more consistent with the variance in the dependent variable in our sample and because its use permits easier comparisons with the other estimates which are reviewed in subsection 1.2.4 above, we focus on this alternative for earnings.

For the other three indicators both the linear and the logarithmic versions display heteroskedasticity, with variance increasing in the dependent variable in the linear version but decreasing in the logarithmic form. In principle it would be possible to find transforms such that the variances of these three indicators are homoskedastic. However, within the latent variable model of the next chapter it is useful to have the same transform of a variable wherever it appears in the model. Moreover, Taubman (1976) reports that the results from analysis of variance, which is related to latent variable analysis, are virtually identical for earnings and the logarithm of earnings even though the former is not distributed homoskedastically. Furthermore, for years of schooling and initial and mature occupational status, the linear regressions seem at least as satisfactory as the semilog and loglinear alternatives. Therefore, we focus on the linear functions for these three indicators in sections 6.3 and 6.4 and in Chapter 7, despite some evidence of significant interaction terms.

Secondly, in the preliminary analysis we also considered the following possible reasons for additional nonlinear relationships between schooling and earnings or other variables. (1) The coefficient on schooling varies continuously with years of schooling. (2) The coefficient on years of schooling is different for M.D.s, LL.B.s and Ph.D.s than for those who have less education. (3) Alternatively, those with M.D.s, LL.B.s and Ph.D.s should be treated as having more than 19 or 20 years of schooling. (4) There is a response bias for those who have less than nine years of schooling such that their average earnings are unrepresentatively high. We found: (a) little evidence to support points 1 and 2; (b) that 22 years for M.D.s, LL.B.s and Ph.D.s gives a higher $\bar{R}^2$ in a semilog earnings equation, but that 19 or 20 years gives a higher $\bar{R}^2$ in the occupational status equations; and (c) that those with less than nine years of schooling received on average about the same earnings as those with a 12th grade education. However, the inclusion of separate dummy variables for those with less than a 9th grade education or M.D.s, etc. causes the coefficient on education in the various equations to change only by small amounts in estimates for individuals or within pairs. Hence, for simplicity and for comparability with other studies we use the standard years of schooling variable.

## 6.3. Regressions for individuals

In sections 1.2, 2.3, and 4.2 above we discuss a number of shortcomings in the literature on regression estimates of the determinants of indicators of socioeconomic success. Many of these also apply to ordinary least squares estimates of such equations for individuals in our data set. Nevertheless, such estimates allow us to compare the results obtained with our data with those obtained by others (see section 1.2). They also provide a basis for comparison with the within-twins estimates which are discussed below in section 6.4 and for comparison with the relations in which we include a measure of cognitive ability which are the subject of section 6.5 below.

Table 6.1 presents ordinary least squares regressions for each

# Table 6.1

Ordinary least squares regression estimates for four indicators of socioeconomic success for individuals.

| | S | $OC_i$ | $OC_{67}$ | Age | Raised rural | Married 1974 | Cath. | Jew | Born South | No. siblings alive, 1940 | $S_F$ | $S_M$ | $OC_F$ | Constant | $\bar{R}^2$ |
|---|---|---|---|---|---|---|---|---|---|---|---|---|---|---|---|
| **Years of schooling** | | | | | | | | | | | | | | | |
| (S-1) $S$ | | | | -0.05 (3.5) | -0.41 (4.3) | 0.23 (1.9) | -0.24 (2.3) | 1.61 (7.8) | -0.01 (0.1) | -0.20 (10.2) | 0.12 (8.1) | 0.10 (6.4) | 0.017 (9.4) | 13.82 (17.7) | 0.19 |
| **Initial occupation** | | | | | | | | | | | | | | | |
| (OCI-1) $OC_i$ | 0.42 (40.8) | | | | | | | | | | | | | -2.01 (14.7) | 0.28 |
| (OCI-2) $OC_i$ | | | | 0.0092 (0.7) | -0.31 (4.0) | 0.08 (0.8) | 0.11 (1.3) | 1.22 (7.2) | 0.46 (4.8) | -0.14 (8.7) | 0.086 (7.0) | 0.066 (4.9) | 0.0095 (6.3) | 1.66 (2.6) | 0.12 |
| (OCI-3) $OC_i$ | 0.37 (33.2) | | | 0.028 (2.6) | -0.15 (2.2) | -0.0030 (0.03) | 0.20 (2.6) | 0.62 (4.1) | 0.46 (5.4) | -0.064 (4.4) | 0.041 (3.6) | 0.027 (2.2) | 0.0030 (2.2) | -3.49 (5.9) | 0.30 |
| **Mature occupation** | | | | | | | | | | | | | | | |
| (OC67-1) $OC_{67}$ | | 0.35 (34.5) | | | | | | | | | | | | 0.79 (5.9) | 0.22 |
| (OC67-2) $OC_{67}$ | 0.26 (22.5) | 0.21 (13.9) | | | | | | | | | | | | 12.0 (8.9) | 0.25 |
| (OC67-3) $OC_{67}$ | | | | -0.022 (1.9) | -1.07 (14.4) | 0.11 (1.2) | -0.12 (1.5) | 0.79 (5.0) | 0.34 (3.7) | -0.067 (4.4) | 0.057 (4.9) | 0.043 (3.4) | 0.0031 (2.2) | 6.08 (9.9) | 0.09 |
| (OC67-4) $OC_{67}$ | 0.26 (22.0) | 0.20 (13.7) | | -0.010 (1.0) | -0.90 (13.7) | 0.037 (0.5) | -0.083 (1.1) | 0.13 (0.9) | 0.25 (3.0) | 0.012 (0.9) | 0.0080 (0.8) | 0.0026 (0.2) | -0.010 (7.2) | 2.12 (3.8) | 0.30 |

| Mature earnings | S | $OC_i$ | $OC_{67}$ | ln $Y_{73}$ | Age | Raised rural | Married 1974 | Catholic | Jewish | Born South | No. Siblings | | constant | $R^2$ |
|---|---|---|---|---|---|---|---|---|---|---|---|---|---|---|
| (Y-1) ln $Y_{73}$ | 0.080 (32.4) | | | | | | | | | | | | 8.58 (262.5) | 0.20 |
| (Y-2) ln $Y_{73}$ | | 0.031 (8.38) | 0.068 (24.9) | | | | | | | | | | 8.56 (262.8) | 0.21 |
| (Y-3) ln $Y_{73}$ | 0.030 (8.0) | −0.011 (4.1) | −0.054 (3.0) | 0.14 (6.6) | 0.032 (1.6) | 0.43 (11.2) | 0.007 (0.3) | −0.021 (5.0) | 0.014 (5.2) | 0.012 (4.0) | 0.0018 (5.3) | | 9.80 (67.5) | 0.11 |
| (Y-4) ln $Y_{73}$ | 0.059 (20.0) | 0.030 (8.0) | −0.0076 (3.0) | 0.0013 (0.1) | 0.14 (5.3) | 0.05 (2.7) | 0.32 (8.8) | −0.0024 (0.1) | −0.0082 (2.4) | 0.0059 (2.3) | 0.0050 (1.8) | −0.00090 (2.8) | 8.85 (63.4) | 0.24 |

*Variable definitions:*

$S$ is years of schooling, reported in 1974  
$OC_i$ is initial full time civilian occupation, reported in 1974, scaled on the Duncan score  
$OC_{67}$ is mature occupation, reported mostly in 1967 but later for some of the sample, scaled on the Duncan score  
ln $Y_{73}$ is the natural log of annual earnings in 1973, reported in 1974  
Age is 1974 minus birth date, taken from birth certificates  
Raised rural is a dummy variable equal to 1 if raised in rural districts, reported in 1967  
Married, 1974 is a dummy variable equal to 1 if married in 1974, reported in 1974  
Catholic is a dummy variable equal to 1 if raised in Catholic religion, reported in 1974  
Jewish is a dummy variable equal to 1 if raised in Jewish religion, reported in 1974  
Born South is a dummy variable equal to 1 if born in the Census defined region of the South, taken from birth certificates  
No. Siblings alive, 1940 is number of sibs alive in 1940, reported in 1974  

$S_F$ is years of schooling of father, reported in 1974  
$S_M$ is years of schooling of mother, reported in 1974  
$OC_F$ is father's occupation, Duncan score, reported in 1967  

The absolute value of *t*-statistics are given in parentheses beneath the point estimates.

of four-indicators for the 3870 individuals in our sample who are classified as MZ or DZ and where both siblings have nonzero earnings in 1973. The indicators are years of schooling, initial full-time civilian occupation, mature occupation (in 1967), and logarithm of mature earnings (in 1973).

For each indicator there is one regression (labelled S-1, OCI-2, OC67-3, Y-3) which includes only ten background variables which represent specific observable channels through which the underlying genetic and environmental influences may be manifested. The $\bar{R}^2$'s range from 9 to 19% and are somewhat greater for the indicators which pertain to the earlier part of the life cycle (i.e. years of schooling and initial occupation) than for those which relate to the later part. Since most of these background variables related to the family in which the child was born and bred, it seems plausible that the indicators earlier in the life cycle have higher $\bar{R}^2$'s. (Fägerlind presents similar findings; Taubman, 1975, presents evidence for religion which may be contrary.) Even for the indicators pertaining to the earlier phase of the life cycle, however, the estimated relations are not consistent with at least four-fifths of the variances in the dependent variables.[2]

The signs of the significant coefficient estimates for these background variables generally are consistent with those obtained in the other studies which are reviewed in section 1.2 above. For all four indicators there are significantly positive estimates for being Jewish, father's and mother's years of schooling, and father's occupational status. These variables all seem to represent family characteristics, both environmental and genetic, which result in attitudes and capacities associated with socioeconomic success.

A comparison of the magnitudes of the estimated coefficients

---

[2]We are not able to include some variables which others have found to be important (e.g. cognitive ability, family income or wealth) because of a lack of data in our entire sample. With such variables included the regression probably would be more consistent with the variations in the four indicators. In section 6.5 below we discuss some estimates for a subset of our sample for which we are able to include a measure of cognitive ability. The impact on $\bar{R}^2$ of including this variable is fairly small (no greater than 0.03).

for the father's and mother's years of schooling, however, does not *prima facie* support Leibowitz's (1974) conjecture that the latter is larger since the mother typically spent more time with the children in the home. On the contrary, the estimates are larger for the coefficients of father's schooling in every relationship even though father's occupational status, which probably mediates part of the influences of father's schooling and reduces the direct effect of schooling, is included. However, some results in section 6.5 are more in conformity with her suggestion. Moreover, it is possible that Leibowitz still is right even for our entire sample. Since we do not have direct measures of father's or of family income, the coefficient of father's years of schooling possibly is higher than it would be if we had such income measures. But a direct measure of parental income is included in Sewell and Hauser (1975), who also find that father's education has a larger coefficient than does mother's.

For all four indicators there are significantly negative effects of having been raised in rural areas and of having more siblings. Such results may reflect the poorer rural environment (in respect to economic and other stimuli) and the increased competition from more siblings for financial resources, and for parental attention and emotion (Lindert, 1976).

For years of schooling, being Catholic has a significantly negative coefficient. This apparently reflects more than the greater competition for resources in the larger Catholic families since the variable still is significant when the number of siblings is included. For the other three indicators, however, being Catholic does not have coefficient estimates significantly different from zero.

Among the background variables obviously associated with childhood family background, the only significantly nonzero estimates which might be surprising are the positive ones for having been born in the South that appear in the initial and mature occupational status regressions. This positive impact is less surprising, however, when one realizes that a number of other negative characteristics associated with the South are being controlled for (i.e. more rural, less parental education, larger families, less occupational status for father, fewer Jews). Moreover, the result is consistent with a model of discrimination as in Becker (1958) in which the South had a greater taste for discrimination.

One background variable not mentioned yet is age. It has a significantly negative coefficient estimate for years of schooling and for earnings (and one bordering on being significant for mature occupation). In these equations we interpret this variable to represent secular business cycle and life cycle effects, as well as the disruptive impact on older individuals of the Second World War. The oldest members of the sample were born in 1917, were of high school age at the depths of the Great Depression, were of college age in the late 1930s before the war-induced recovery, were old enough to be eligible for military service from the start of the war, served in the war in their mid and late twenties, and re-entered civilian life thereafter. In contrast, the youngest members of the sample were born in 1927, were of high school age in the war years, were not eligible for military service until the later part of the war, if not career men were in the service for fewer years, were of normal college age in the postwar boom period, and were easily able to benefit from the G.I. educational support after the war. They also are in a cohort for which average education is higher because of the upward secular trend in years of schooling. Since our respondents were in the 45–56 range in the year for which we have earnings data, for the earnings relation the significantly negative impact of age also may reflect the well-documented peaking of earnings around ages 45–50.[3]

The final background variable is a dummy variable for those married at the time of our survey in 1974. This variable, which does not directly refer to childhood family background, has a positive significant coefficient for mature earnings and one on the borderline of significance for years of schooling. The latter coefficient suggests that this variable is at least partially representing characteristics (e.g. emotional stability) which led to greater earlier as well as later life cycle socioeconomic success. Those who were married in 1974 had no higher occupational

---

[3]This is meant as a descriptive phrase and not as a conclusion about the relative importance of age versus years of work experience.

status, but worked more or selected higher paying jobs for the same status distribution probably in order to support multiperson households in a generation in which wives often were not employed.

A second set of regressions in which the only right-hand side variable is years of schooling is presented in table 6.1 for initial and mature occupation and for earnings (i.e. OCI-1, OC67-1, Y-1). In each case the coefficient estimate is positive and significantly different from zero at least at the 1% level. In each case the relation has a higher $\bar{R}^2$ than the regression with only the ten back-ground variables. The coefficients of determination, increase from 0.12 to 0.28, from 0.09 to 0.22, and from 0.11 to 0.20, respectively. Nevertheless, very considerable variations in the dependent variables are left unexplained. The pattern of higher $\bar{R}^2$ for indicators in the earlier stages of the life cycle also continues. Of particular interest is the size of the coefficient estimate of years of schooling in the semilog earnings function. The value of 0.08 is of the same order of magnitude as is reported by Mincer and others on the basis of census data (see subsection 1.2.4), even though our sample is restricted to veterans most of whom were eligible for G.I. bill benefits which enabled them to invest profitably in more years of schooling for given expected wage differentials. Thus, when we treat our sample as a cross section of individuals, we obtain estimates of about the same magnitude as do others. On the other hand the time spent in the military reduced the expected working life and thus the expected gains from schooling.

Table 6.1 includes a third set of regressions for mature occupation and earnings in which the recursive structure which is discussed in Chapters 2 and 4 alone is used (i.e. OC67-2, Y-2).[4] That is, in addition to years of schooling, initial occupational status is included in the mature occupational status relation and mature occupational status is included in the logarithmic earnings func-

---

[4]The parallel relation for initial occupation includes only years of schooling, which is discussed above (i.e. OCI-1). Note that we exclude $OC_i$ from the earnings equation for reasons discussed in sections 2.4.2 and 4.3.

tion. In both cases the coefficient estimates of the additional variables are significantly positive and the overall consistency with variations in the dependent variable increases somewhat. However, there remain very considerable unexplained variations. Also, the pattern remains of higher $\bar{R}^2$'s for the indicators in the earlier phases of the life cycle.[5] The estimated coefficients of the direct effects of years of schooling decline somewhat from 0.35 to 0.26 for mature occupation and from 0.080 to 0.068 for the logarithm of earnings. Part of the effects of schooling apparently is mediated by the introduction of the recursive occupational status measures. Sewell and Hauser (1972, 1975) report a similar result. The total (i.e. direct plus indirect through the recursive relations) effects, however, remains about the same: 0.35 for mature occupational status and 0.079 for the logarithm of earnings.

The final set of regressions in table 6.1 combines the recursive structure of the third group and the ten background variables of the first group (i.e. OCI-3, OC67-4, Y-4). Included are regressions for initial and mature occupational status and for the logarithm of mature earnings.[6] The combination results in relations which have the highest $\bar{R}^2$'s. The coefficients of determination are 0.30 for initial and mature occupational status and 0.24 for the logarithm of earnings.

In comparison with other studies which are reviewed in subsection 1.2.3 and 1.2.4 above, these $\bar{R}^2$'s are about in the middle of the range for earnings functions, but near the bottom of the range for occupational status. Smaller $\bar{R}^2$'s than in some other studies may be due to our lack of data on cognitive ability, motivational variables, and father's or parents' income. (See section 6.5 for the equations with cognitive ability for a subset of our sample.) Sewell and Hauser (1972, 1975), for example, report significant coefficients for all three of these variables. Bowles and

[5] This observation relates to the recursive structure including the initial occupation. See the previous note.

[6] The regression for years of schooling with the ten background variables included also falls into this category but is discussed above with the first set of regressions (S-1).

Nelson (1974), Leibowitz (1974), Conlisk (1971), Hauser, Sewell and Lutterman (1973), de Wolff and van Slype (1973), Taubman and Wales (1974, 1975), and Taubman (1975) all report significantly nonzero coefficients for at least one of these variables on which we do not have data.

In any case our regressions, as also is true for other studies, leave considerable variations in the indicators of socioeconomic success unexplained. Since important variables apparently are excluded, there may be large biases in the coefficient estimates for the included variables. A comparison of these estimates for individuals with those obtained for the differences within twin pairs, and with those obtained for a subsample, when a cognitive ability measure is added and with those obtained with the latent variable methodology, may provide useful insight into the extent of such biases. We provide such comparisons in the next two sections and in the next chapter.

As is the case in most other studies, the direct effects of the background variables are much less substantial and less significant in many cases once the recursive structure for years of schooling and occupational status is added. Smaller but still significantly positive coefficient estimates remain for the impact of father's and mother's years of schooling on initial occupational status, of father's years of schooling on earnings, of father's occupational status on initial occupational status, of being Jewish on initial occupational status and on earnings, of having been born in the South on initial and mature occupational status, and of being married in 1974 on mature earnings. Smaller (in absolute value), but still significantly negative coefficient estimates remain for having been raised in rural areas (on initial and mature occupational status), of the number of siblings alive in 1940 (on initial occupational status and on earnings), and of age (on earnings). The magnitude of the estimates of the coefficient of father's schooling remains consistently larger than those for mother's schooling. Among these background variables the only sign which possibly is surprising is the positive one for being born in the South (on the attainment of occupational status). The comments made above in the discussion of the regressions with only back-

ground variables included about this and about other variables
(e.g. age, marital state) which remain significantly nonzero with
sign unchanged are still germane here.

There are several cases, however, in which the addition of the
recursive schooling and occupational status variables dramatically
affects the coefficient estimates of the background variables. In
the equation for the initial occupational status, for example, once
years of schooling is controlled for the direct effect of age and of
being Catholic is significantly positive (instead of insignificant).
The total effects i.e. the direct effects plus those transmitted
through the recursive structure), also are positive, although
smaller in magnitude (i.e. 0.010 and 0.112, respectively).

The other interesting cases are the significantly negative estimates of the direct effects of father's occupational status on
mature occupational status and on earnings. This contrasts with
the results in which the recursive variables are excluded, and with
the other studies discussed in subsections 1.2.3 and 1.2.4 above,
which report either positive (e.g. Bowles and Nelson, 1974) or
insignificant effects when other variables are added. The total
effects, however, in both cases are quite small in magnitude
(−0.005 and 0.0003, respectively). One possible interpretation is
that father's status enables offspring to buy more schooling, but
induces them to work less intensely.

With a few exceptions, the impact of the background variables
is generally reduced once the recursive schooling and occupational status variables are added. A comparison of the estimates
for the initial and mature occupational status suggests that in most
cases the absolute value and the significance of these effects
decline over the life cycle. The only exception to this generalization among the estimates in table 6.1 is the apparently increasingly
negative impact over the life cycle of having been raised in a rural
area. The general decline in the influence of these background
variables over the life cycle is plausible since career-related
developments apparently become more important as individuals
grow older (Mincer, 1974). It also is consistent with most of the
findings of Sewell and Hauser (1972, 1975), Featherman (1971b),
Kelley (1973), Fägerlind (1975), and Taubman (1975).

Even though the impact of the background variables is reduced through the intermediation of schooling and occupational status and such effects tend to decline over the life cycle, significant direct influences remain in the estimated relations for the mature occupational status and mature earnings indicators of socio-economic success. Three of the background variables still have significantly nonzero coefficient estimates in the former case and seven do in the latter. Thus, there are direct effects of background variables even after controlling for schooling and occupational status. There may be other important background variables which have significant effects, but for which we do not have obser-vations. Their exclusion may cause significant biases in the esti-mates for the coefficients of the observed variables. We return to this topic in section 6.4 and in Chapter 7.

To this point in our review of the effects of combining the recursive structure of schooling and occupational status with the background variables, we have concentrated on the coefficient estimates of the background variables. Let us now turn to the coefficient estimates of the recursive variables.

The addition of the background variables to the recursive structure has almost no impact on the estimates of the direct effects of occupational status. In the relation for mature occupa-tional status the estimate for the coefficient of initial occupational status drops from 0.21 to 0.20. In the relation for mature earnings the estimate for the coefficient of mature occupational status falls from 0.031 to 0.030. Such differences are not significant. In both cases a strong recursive role for occupational status continues to be supported.

The addition of the background variables also has no significant impact on the estimated direct effect of schooling on mature occupational status. In the other two cases, however, the esti-mated schooling coefficient falls somewhat: from 0.42 to 0.37 for initial occupation and from 0.068 to 0.059 for mature earnings. In these two equations, therefore, the exclusion of the background variables on which we have observations apparently causes a bias of approximately 13–17% in the schooling coefficient. While not insignificant, such an order of magnitude does not seem overwhelming in comparison to the possible size of the biases which are discussed in the next two sections.

The results in table 6.1 seem to support a strong role for schooling in the determination of occupational status and earnings. Under the assumptions necessary for the human capital model to hold (see section 2.3) if there are no further biases in our estimates, the total average rate of return to investment in education is about 6.8% (ignoring G.I. bill benefits). Such numbers are in the same range, although near the lower end of that range, as estimates obtained in other studies (subsection 1.2.4).

### 6.4. Regressions for differences between twins

We discuss the properties of estimates for the differences between twins in detail above in section 4.2. For dizygotic twins differencing between brothers controls for environmental features which are common to the brothers. In substantial part these are due to the influence of the family, including such factors as parental role models and access to capital markets. For monozygotic twins differencing between brothers controls for common environment and for genetics. For monozygotic twins estimates of the schooling coefficients are unbiased if there is no measurement error and if one of the following three conditions hold: (a) environment has no effect on earnings; (b) the differences in siblings' environments which affect earnings are uncorrelated with schooling differences; or (c) there are no differences in siblings' environments.[7]

Of course estimating regressions with the differences between twins as the unit of observation makes sense only if there are differences in the relevant variables for a substantial number of pairs. The variable which *a priori* might seem to be most suspect in this respect is years of schooling, since it might be plausible to

---

[7]In these regression estimates, as contrasted with some of the latent variable estimates of the next chapter, we do not assume that the environmental correlation across brothers are the same for the two types of twins.

assume that parents generally ensured that both brothers in a pair of twins received the same education. But, in our sample 54% of the brothers in the 1022 MZ pairs and 66% of the brothers in the 914 DZ pairs differ in their reported numbers of years of schooling. Of the respective groups, 34 and 50% differ by at least two years. Therefore, we apparently do have enough differences in years of schooling between twins to proceed with using the differences between twin brothers as the unit of observation. The existence of frequent differences in years of schooling for the twins in our sample may not be surprising since in many cases schooling was interrupted by the war and the decision about how many years to continue schooling after the war was made not by the parents but by the individual twins. However, some of these differences are probably attributable to measurement error.

In all of our regressions we chose to use single entry rather than double entry methods. In single entry methods, each pair is one observation (e.g. $Y_2$-$Y_1$). In double entry methods, each pair is entered twice (e.g. $Y_2$-$Y_1$ and $Y_1$-$Y_2$), and weighted regressions are used. Double entry methods force constant terms to zero. The constants in our equations are often statistically significant in our large sample, though small as a percentage of the mean of the variable. For example, about three-tenths of 1%, or $50 in $Y$-4 for MZs. Table 6.2 includes ordinary least squares regressions estimates of the differences between brothers for both monozygotic and dizygotic twins for initial and mature occupational status and for the logarithm of mature earnings. Analysis of covariance (i.e. Chow tests) rejects the null hypothesis that the monozygotic and dizygotic relations are the same for earnings. Under the assumptions that measurement error is not a problem and that the same distributions of structural parameters apply to both types of twins, this result suggests that genetics, which are controlled for only when using the data from the monozygotic twins, are important.

The difference in education is included in every regression. Alternative regressions are presented with and without a dummy variable for marital status in 1974, the only one of the ten background or control variables which may differ between the

Table 6.2

Ordinary least squares regressions of differences within pairs of monozygotic and dizygotic twins.[a]

| | MZ | | | | | | DZ | | | | | |
|---|---|---|---|---|---|---|---|---|---|---|---|---|
| | $\Delta S$ | $\Delta OC_i$ | $\Delta OC_{67}$ | $\Delta$ married | Constant | $\bar{R}^2$ | $\Delta S$ | $\Delta OC_i$ | $\Delta OC_{67}$ | $\Delta$ married | Constant | $\bar{R}^2$ |
| **Initial occupational status ($OC_i$)** | | | | | | | | | | | | |
| (OCI-1) | 0.21 (5.9) | | | −0.17 (1.2) | −0.13 (16.7) | 0.03 | 0.28 (9.5) | | | −0.11 (0.7) | −0.02 (14.5) | 0.09 |
| (OC2-2) | 0.21 (5.9) | | | | −0.13 (82.5) | 0.03 | 0.28 (9.5) | | | | −0.02 (31.3) | 0.09 |
| **Mature occupational status ($OC_{67}$)** | | | | | | | | | | | | |
| (OC67-1) | 0.26 (8.4) | 0.15 (5.8) | | −0.24 (1.7) | −0.004 (0.05) | 0.11 | 0.29 (11.3) | 0.14 (5.5) | | −0.14 (1.0) | −0.03 (17.1) | 0.19 |
| (OC67-2) | 0.26 (8.4) | 0.15 (5.8) | | | −0.009 (2.7) | 0.11 | 0.29 (11.3) | 0.14 (5.4) | | | −0.04 (48.3) | 0.19 |
| (OC67-3) | 0.29 (9.5) | | | | −0.03 (33.4) | 0.08 | 0.33 (13.4) | | | | −0.05 (259.5) | 0.16 |
| **Mature earnings (ln $Y_{73}$)** | | | | | | | | | | | | |
| (Y-1) | 0.017 (2.2) | | 0.026 (4.1) | 0.05 (1.8) | 0.007 (4.0) | 0.03 | 0.048 (6.0) | | 0.038 (3.8) | 0.032 (0.8) | 0.002 (1.1) | 0.09 |
| (Y-2) | 0.019 (7.4) | | 0.025 (3.9) | | 0.0005 (0.7) | 0.03 | 0.048 (6.0) | | 0.038 (3.9) | | −0.002 (4.8) | 0.08 |
| (Y-3) | 0.026 (3.5) | | | 0.05 (1.5) | 0.006 (1.5) | 0.02 | 0.059 (8.3) | | | 0.026 (0.7) | −0.001 (1.6) | 0.07 |
| (Y-4) | 0.003 (3.6) | | | | 0.003 (9.2) | 0.01 | 0.059 (8.2) | | | | −0.0009 (5.2) | 0.07 |

[a] See notes to table 6.1.

brothers, and with and without the difference in occupational status which is suggested by the recursive model presented in Chapter 2 and used in section 6.3 and in Chapter 7.

The marital status variable is of most significance in the earning equations, which is consistent with the results for individuals which are discussed in the previous section.

The inclusion of the relevant recursive occupational status differences increases the $\bar{R}^2$ for both mature occupational status and mature earnings for both monozygotic and dizygotic twins. All of the coefficient estimates are significantly positive at standard levels. These results, therefore, reinforce the conclusion from the equations for individuals that the occupational status measures have significant roles which remain when schooling and many other factors are controlled for.

A comparison of the estimates for the coefficients of the recursive occupational status variables across the regressions for the two types of twins and for individuals gives some insight into the order of magnitude of biases due to failure to control for genetics and various aspects of environment. For mature occupational status there is no substantial bias if the ten background characteristics which are discussed in the previous section are ignored. Controlling for all common environment, however, results in a decline of the estimated direct impact of initial occupational status of over one-quarter, from 0.20 to 0.14. The estimate remains about the same if genetics also are controlled for.

For the determinations of the logarithm of mature earnings, the estimated coefficient of mature occupational status also is not affected substantially by the inclusion of the ten observable background variables.

We now turn to the estimates of the direct impact of the years of schooling. For the difference between twins, as in the equations for individuals, this is apparently the most important single variable (in terms of $\bar{R}^2$) in most of our relations. The role of schooling in the determination of the various indices of socio-economic success, moreover, is of particular interest because of the controversy over the impact of schooling on intra- and intergenerational mobility and equality which is reviewed in section 1.1 above.

Under the assumption of no substantial problems with measurement error, a comparison across the alternative estimates of the coefficients of schooling in the relation for initial occupational status suggests several possible sources of biases.[8] Introducing the ten background variables in the relations for individuals causes a drop of about 14% from 0.42 to 0.37. Controlling for common environment across brothers causes a decline to 0.28, 33% below the original estimate. Also, controlling for genetics lowers the estimate to 0.21, 50% of the original level.

Under the same assumption, the estimate of the direct effect of schooling on mature occupational status drops 25% from 0.35 to 0.26 when initial occupational status is controlled for (independently of whether or not the ten background characteristics are included). Controlling for all common environment and genetics does not cause further significant changes. If we consider the total effects, the coefficient estimate drops a total of 16% from 0.35 to 0.29, with most of the decline occuring when genetics are controlled for.

Such patterns suggest the possible existence of fairly large positive biases in standard estimates of the impact of schooling on early occupational status attainment, but only a modest bias for mature occupational status. The declining bias over the life cycle

---

[8]Bielby, Hauser and Featherman (1976, p. 31) estimate measurement errors for years of schooling and other variables using data from three interviews conducted in a space of six months. They obtain estimates of the ratio of the variance in the measurement error to the total variance of 30, 11, and 4%. The 11% figure is from a personal interview conducted with any adult member of the family. Thus, some of this measurement error reflects inaccurate answers given by spouses. The other two surveys were conducted by mail, in which case presumably the respondent answered, or by telephone directly with the respondent. While the range of 4–30% is very wide, we think that the 30% is an outlier. This estimate differs from those obtained in the other samples by the largest amount. Moreover, the 30% figure is in marked contrast to the measurement errors in parental education which are less than 10% in the same sample. The Bielby et al. study allows for measurement error correlated over time. For other studies with larger samples but with no estimated serial correlation in measurement error, see their bibliography.

is consistent with the results discussed in section 6.3, where the coefficients on most measured background variables are smaller in absolute value for $OC_{67}$ than $OC_i$. Thus, not controlling for these variables would cause a smaller bias in estimates for later in the work career.

For the earnings functions, under the same assumption about measurement error, the original estimate of the schooling coefficient in the relation for individuals is 0.080. The estimated direct effect drops 15% to 0.068 when mature occupational status is added and a total of 24% to 0.059 when both mature occupational status and the set of ten observable background characteristics are included. Controlling for common environment with mature occupational status included leads to an estimate of 0.048, 40% below the original value. Also, controlling for genetics leads to a value of 0.017, only 21% of the original estimate!

If we consider the total effects, the initial coefficient drops from 0.08 to about 0.07 when the ten background variables are included, to about 0.06 when common environment is controlled for, and to 0.026 once genetics also are controlled for. We obtain basically the same value if we limit the sample to pairs with only one years difference in school. This value is only about 30% of the original estimate.

As we noted briefly in Chapter 5, misclassification of MZ and DZ pairs causes us to still have genetic variation for some pairs in the MZ within-pair equation and to eliminate genetic variation in some pairs in the DZ within-pair equation. Assuming a 5% random misclassification, the true coefficient on schooling in the MZ equation would be 0.022 while the corresponding coefficient in the DZ equation would be 0.063. Such adjustments do not greatly alter our previous comments but, if anything, reinforce the statements concerning possible bias in standard estimates of the effects of years of schooling. Under the assumption of no measurement error, the standard procedures may result in very large upward biases indeed of the impact of schooling on the distribution of earnings! The size of the bias on the schooling coefficient depends on the ratio of the variance of measurement error to the variance of the true schooling variable or the noise to signal ratio. As noted in subsection 4.2.1, this ratio differs in the equations based on individuals and on within pair differences because the correlation of true schooling for twins is not zero.

In table 6.3 we present the value of the noise-to-signal ratio that will cause the unbiased estimate of the coefficients on schooling in equations for $OC_i$, $OC_{67}$ and ln $Y_{73}$ to be the same in the equations based on individuals and on within-pair differences. These cal-

Table 6.3
Measurement error that reconciles within, between estimates of education coefficients, assuming no omitted variable bias.

| Coefficient on $S$ in bivariate equations based on | In equation for $OC_i$ | $OC_{67}$ | ln $Y_{73}$ |
|---|---|---|---|
| Individual | 0.42 | 0.35 | 0.080 |
| Within MZ | 0.21 | 0.29 | 0.027 |
| Within DZ | 0.28 | 0.33 | 0.059 |
| $\sigma_w^2/\sigma_s^2$ needed to equate individual and within pair estimates if no omitted variable bias | | | |
| for MZs | 0.15 | 0.05 | 0.20 |
| for DZs | 0.28 | 0.03 | 0.22 |
| *Implied true cross-twin correlation for schooling* | | | |
| MZs | 0.87 | 0.80 | 0.92 |
| DZs | 0.69 | 0.56 | 0.66 |

culations assume that there is no bias arising from the omission of ability or any other variable and that the correlation between measurement error and true schooling is zero. The estimated noise-to-signal ratio is presented for three equations because measurement error would bias the coefficient in the same proportion in all three equations, *ceteris paribus*.

In the equations for ln $Y_{73}$, the noise-to-signal ratio necessary to equalize the coefficients found in the within-pair and individual equations are about 20 and 22% for MZs and DZs, respectively. If measurement error were indeed this large, the unbiased estimate of the effect of schooling would be 0.096 and 0.098 for MZs and DZs, respectively, which are not implausible in and of themselves.

Other considerations, however, suggest that a noise-to-signal ratio of about 0.2 is too large, and that there is a substantial bias from omitted variables. First, if the noise-to-signal ratio is 0.2, as shown in table 6.3, the true correlation in schooling would be estimated as 0.91 which implies that there is virtually no differences in schooling for MZ twins, despite whatever differences occurred in the household and in the military.

Secondly, such a noise-to-signal ratio implies that the average absolute measurement error for each observation is about 1.25 years. This seems large, especially when the average absolute difference in parental education, reported by the twins, is about 0.85 years and the noise-to-signal ratio for parents' education is about 0.92 for father's education and 0.92 and 0.85 for mother's education for MZs and DZs, respectively. It seems likely that the twins know their own education better than their parents' education.

Thirdly, as shown in table 6.3, the noise-to-signal ratio required to equalize the coefficients in the within-pair and individual equations for schooling in the $OC_{67}$ equation is 0.05 or less. Yet these equations use exactly the same schooling series and would be biased by the same proportion if there were no omitted variable bias. To reconcile the results for $OC_{67}$ and $\ln Y_{73}$ and to maintain that there is no omitted variable bias in the $\ln Y_{73}$ equation, it would be necessary that there be a negative bias from omitted variables in the $OC_{67}$ equations. But since $OC_{67}$ can be considered a proxy for or transform of earnings, it would seem that the omitted variable bias would have the same sign as in the $\ln Y_{73}$ equation.

Fourthly, the results in table 6.3 assume that there is no omitted variable bias. The well known result, which is given in Chapter 4, is that an omitted variable will cause a bias if it has a nonzero coefficient in both the true and the auxiliary equation, i.e. in the earnings and in the schooling equations. In this sample we have already shown that a host of family background variables are related to schooling and to earnings even after controlling for schooling. Below we show that a measure of cognitive skills is also related to schooling and to earnings, even after controlling for schooling. Moreover, numerous other studies have shown similar nonzero coefficients for the same and related variables. Thus, it is unreasonable to maintain that the difference between the equations based on individuals and on within-pair data is attributable to measurement error alone.

In table 6.4 we present estimates of the effect of schooling on earnings obtained by adjusting the MZ within-pair estimate by assumed values of the noise-to-signal ratio. As the assumed value

Table 6.4
Estimates of effect of $S$ on ln $Y_{73}$ from MZ within-pair equations, adjusted for noise-to-signal ratio.

| Calculated coefficient | Assumed value of $\sigma_w^2/\sigma_s^2$ | Estimated value of true coefficient |
|---|---|---|
| 0.027 | 0 | 0.027 |
| | 0.05 | 0.034 |
| | 0.10 | 0.044 |
| | 0.125 | 0.051 |
| | 0.150 | 0.060 |
| | 0.175 | 0.073 |
| | 0.20 | 0.092 |

of the noise-to-signal ratio increase, the estimate of the effect of schooling rises at an accelerating rate. If the noise-to-signal ratio is 10 or 12.5%, the estimate of the effect of schooling increases from 0.027 to 0.045 or to 0.052. For these noise-to-signal ratios, adjusted estimates of the effects of schooling from equations based on data for individuals is about 0.09 if there is no omitted variable bias. If the noise-to-signal ratio is 10–12.5%, the bias in the MZ within-pair equations is large but the bias in the individual equations is even bigger, especially when it is recalled that the estimate of 0.08 is also biased downward by measurement error.

We think it unlikely that the noise-to-signal ratio is greater than 10% for several reasons. First, there is solid evidence in this

sample and elsewhere that there is an omitted variable bias in the
equation that relates schooling to earnings. From table 6.3 we
know that the upper limit to the noise-to-signal ratio is 20%, and it
seems unlikely that the true value is more than half way to the
upper limit, especially given the results for $OC_{67}$.

Based on all these considerations we conclude that it is necessary to control for differences in both genetic endowments and in
family environment in studying the effects of schooling on earnings and that not doing so leads to large biases.

## 6.5. Estimates for individuals in subsample for which data on cognitive ability is available

Because of an act of nature (i.e. a fire in the St. Louis military
record repository) we do not have measures of cognitive ability
for most of our sample. In the estimates for the total sample given to
this point in the present chapter and in the next chapter, therefore,
cognitive ability is controlled for when genetic and environmental
factors are controlled for. With this technique it is not possible to
identify the separate contribution of cognitive ability, nor to what
extent its exclusion alone may cause biases in the estimated
parameters of observable variables.

However, for the subset of the sample which entered the Navy
as enlisted men, a measure of verbal cognitive skill, the General
Classification Test (see Chapter 5) generally is available. Let us
denote this measure as $GCT$ or $Y_5$.

The Navy commonly is thought able to be more selective than
the Army. Before turning to regressions which include the $GCT$
variable, therefore, it is useful to inquire whether or not the
structure of the relations appears to be the same for the Navy
sample members as for the whole sample. Table 6.5 has the same
estimated relations as does table 6.1, but it is based on only the
893 individuals in the Navy. A comparison between these two
tables indicates some differences, especially for some of the
estimated coefficients of the background variables. With respect
to the overall implications and the coefficients of the recursive

Table 6.5

Ordinary least squares regression estimates for four indicators of socioeconomic success for 893 individuals in the Navy.[a]

| | $s$ | $OC_i$ | $OC_{67}$ | Age | Raised rural | Cath. | Jew | Born South | No. siblings alive, 1970 | $S_F$ | $S_M$ | $OC_F$ | Constant | $\bar{R}^2$ |
|---|---|---|---|---|---|---|---|---|---|---|---|---|---|---|
| **Years of schooling** | | | | | | | | | | | | | | |
| (S-1) | | | | -0.032 (-0.891) | -0.155 (-0.749) | -0.620 (-2.74) | 1.34 (2.36) | -0.067 (-0.267) | -0.160 (-3.71) | 0.066 (1.93) | 0.119 (3.06) | 0.024 (5.72) | 13.1 (6.99) | 0.145 |
| **Initial occupation** | | | | | | | | | | | | | | |
| ($OC_i$-1) | 0.377 (19.0) | | | | | | | | | | | | -1.03 (-3.85) | 0.287 |
| ($OC_i$-2) | | | | 0.039 (1.50) | 0.095 (0.639) | -0.118 (-0.722) | 0.546 (1.34) | 0.114 (0.633) | -0.137 (-4.41) | 0.030 (1.20) | 0.07 (2.48) | 0.017 (5.40) | 0.954 (0.705) | 0.101 |
| ($OC_i$-3) | 0.343 (16.1) | | | 0.05 (2.19) | 0.149 (1.13) | 0.095 (0.659) | 0.086 (0.24) | 0.136 (0.865) | -0.082 (-2.98) | 0.007 (0.316) | 0.029 (1.16) | 0.008 (2.99) | -3.55 (-2.90) | 0.304 |
| **Mature occupation** | | | | | | | | | | | | | | |
| ($OC_{67}$-1) | 0.364 (18.5) | | | | | | | | | | | | 1.68 (0.628) | 0.276 |
| ($OC_{67}$-2) | 0.298 (12.9) | 0.177 (5.39) | | | | | | | | | | | 3.51 (1.32) | 0.298 |
| ($OC_{67}$-3) | | | | -0.0273 (-1.04) | -0.0421 (-0.280) | -0.305 (-1.85) | 0.128 (3.11) | -0.0645 (-0.357) | -0.0866 (-2.77) | 0.0311 (1.24) | 0.0137 (0.483) | 0.0120 (3.87) | 5.96 (4.36) | 0.061 |
| ($OC_{67}$-4) | 0.288 (12.0) | 0.177 (5.32) | | -0.0250 (-1.10) | -0.0143 (-0.11) | -0.105 (0.737) | 0.800 (2.24) | -0.0655 (-0.419) | -0.0162 (-0.590) | 0.0067 (0.31) | -0.0331 (-1.34) | 0.0020 (0.736) | 2.00 (1.64) | 0.299 |
| **Mature earnings** | | | | | | | | | | | | | | |
| ($\ln Y_{73}$-1) | 0.072 (13.3) | | | | | | | | | | | | 8.71 (118.5) | 0.164 |
| ($\ln Y_{73}$-2) | 0.061 (9.61) | | 0.03 (3.28) | | | | | | | | | | 8.71 (119.1) | 0.173 |
| ($\ln Y_{73}$-3) | | | | -0.001 (-0.119) | -0.056 (-1.48) | 0.032 (0.769) | 0.667 (6.51) | 0.025 (0.550) | -0.028 (-3.59) | 0.007 (1.13) | 0.016 (2.32) | 0.003 (3.31) | 9.47 (2.79) | 0.114 |
| ($\ln Y_{73}$-4) | 0.052 (7.97) | | 0.03 (2.74) | 0.002 (0.255) | -0.046 (-1.32) | 0.071 (1.84) | 0.566 (5.84) | 0.030 (0.705) | -0.018 (-2.37) | 0.003 (0.487) | 0.010 (1.48) | 0.001 (1.34) | 8.64 (26.4) | 0.218 |

[a] See notes to table 6.1.

variables such as schooling and occupational status, however, the two tables seem quite similar. Thus, for our basic purposes the Navy portion of the sample does not seem to be substantially different from the rest of the sample.

However, a comparison of tables 6.1 and 6.5 does not answer the question completely because we do not have the *GCT* data for all of the Navy members of our sample. To add *GCT* to our system we must further restrict our subsample to 609 of the 893 individuals included in table 6.5. Table 6.6 gives the ordinary least squares estimates of the same relations as in table 6.1 and 6.5 but with only the 609 members of the Navy for whom we have the *GCT* data included in the subsample. A comparison between tables 6.1 and 6.5 reveals, once again, some differences in some of the estimated coefficients of the background variables, but the same general overall patterns for these variables. However, the estimates of the coefficients of years of schooling in the initial occupation and the logarithms of mature earnings relations are substantially less in table 6.6 than in table 6.1 or 6.5. Since these coefficients are of primary interest to our study, this discrepancy is bothersome. It implies that the members of the Navy subset for which we have the *GCT* data are not random representatives of our total sample. The apparent explanation is that the *GCT* data are only available for those who entered the Navy as enlisted men. Indeed, if a dummy variable for being an officer is included in eq. (1) in table 6.5, the coefficient on years of schooling drops to 0.062. It seems likely that those with high education who entered as enlisted men had less motivation or drive. Thus, the availability of *GCT* data censors the sample and biases downward the education coefficient. Heckman (1976) has shown that it is possible to obtain unbiased estimates in censored samples by using the inverse of the Mills ratio, which is a transform of the probability of an observation being censored out of the sample. Since this probability is one for an officer, this dummy variable serves an analogous function.

While the estimate of the level of the schooling coefficient in the subsample with *GCT* data is not to be trusted, it is possible that the estimate of the *bias* from omitting *GCT* is appropriate.

Table 6.6

Ordinary least squares regression estimates for four indicators of socioeconomic success for 609 individuals in Navy for whom *GCT* scores exist.[a]

| | $S$ | $OC_i$ | $OC_{67}$ | Age | Raised rural | Cath. | Jew | Born South | No. siblings alive, 1970 | $S_F$ | $S_M$ | $OC_F$ | Constant | $\bar{R}^2$ |
|---|---|---|---|---|---|---|---|---|---|---|---|---|---|---|
| **Years of schooling** | | | | | | | | | | | | | | |
| ($S$-1) | 0.343 (14.5) | | | -0.117 (-2.44) | -0.117 (-0.472) | -0.833 (-3.08) | 1.54 (2.32) | -0.09 (-0.302) | -0.132 (-2.61) | 0.015 (0.356) | 0.129 (2.48) | 00.21 (3.92) | 17.6 (7.02) | 0.131 |
| **Initial occupation** | | | | | | | | | | | | | | |
| ($OC_i$-1) | | | | -0.008 (-0.244) | 0.202 (1.18) | -0.245 (-1.31) | 0.421 (0.918) | 0.202 (0.981) | -0.147 (-4.22) | 0.001 (0.028) | 0.062 (1.73) | 0.016 (4.47) | -0.618 (-1.98) | 0.255 |
| ($OC_i$-2) | | | | | | | | | | | | | 3.58 (2.07) | 0.097 |
| ($OC_i$-3) | 0.311 (12.3) | | | 0.028 (0.953) | 0.238 (1.55) | 0.014 (0.085) | -0.058 (-0.142) | 0.230 (1.25) | -0.106 (-3.39) | -0.004 (-0.148) | 0.022 (0.683) | 0.010 (2.99) | -1.88 (-1.17) | 0.279 |
| **Mature occupation** | | | | | | | | | | | | | | |
| ($OC_{67}$-1) | 0.354 (15.0) | | | | | | | | | | | | 0.339 (1.09) | 0.269 |
| ($OC_{67}$-2) | 0.288 (10.7) | 0.191 (4.82) | | | | | | | | | | | 0.457 (1.49) | 0.295 |
| ($OC_{67}$-3) | | | | -0.0548 (1.63) | 0.0315 (0.181) | -0.463 (-2.44) | 1.39 (3.0) | 0.0743 (0.356) | -0.102 (-2.87) | 0.0448 (1.47) | 0.0258 (0.71) | 0.074 (1.99) | 7.15 (4.08) | 0.077 |
| ($OC_{67}$-4) | 0.269 (9.63) | 0.183 (4.52) | | -0.217 (-0.735) | 0.262 (0.172) | -0.194 (-1.16) | 0.902 (2.21) | 0.0616 (0.338) | -0.391 (-1.25) | 0.0405 (1.53) | -0.0202 (-0.634) | -0.0012 (-0.367) | 1.77 (1.11) | 0.299 |
| **Mature earnings** | | | | | | | | | | | | | | |
| (ln $Y_{73}$-1) | 0.058 (8.99) | | | | | | | | | | | | 8.87 (103.6) | 0.116 |
| (ln $Y_{73}$-2) | 0.041 (5.52) | | 0.005 (4.38) | | | | | | | | | | 8.85 (104.8) | 0.142 |
| (ln $Y_{73}$-3) | | | | -0.021 (-2.60) | -0.037 (-0.875) | -0.012 (-0.262) | 0.650 (5.69) | 0.064 (1.24) | -0.025 (-2.93) | -0.000 (-0.032) | 0.015 (1.67) | 00.02 (2.01) | 10.6 (24.5) | 0.114 |
| (ln $Y_{73}$-4) | 0.032 (4.25) | | 00.04 (3.68) | -0.016 (-1.95) | -0.035 (-0.853) | 0.033 (0.738) | 0.545 (4.95) | 0.064 (1.30) | -0.017 (-2.05) | -0.003 (-0.353) | 0.010 (1.13) | 00.01 (0.980) | 9.70 (22.7) | 0.191 |

[a] See notes to table 6.1.

The necessary conditions are that the effect of *GCT* on earnings (or on any other indicator), which is the slope coefficient on *S* in a *GCT* equation, be the same in the subsample and in the population.

Under the assumption that such conditions prevail, let us examine what happens when we add *GCT* to our recursive model of socioeconomic indicators for the 609 individuals used for table 6.4. Table 6.5 gives the relevant results. In this table *GCT* basically is treated as a prerecursive variable to the four-indicator recursive model discussed above. Therefore, *GCT* is added to each of the relations for our previous four indicators. This treatment may be incorrect since at the time of the administration of the General Classification Test different individuals had different amounts of schooling. If prior schooling affected the test score results, then part of the total effect of schooling is included in the estimated coefficient for *GCT*. Griliches and Mason (1972) solve the same problem by noting that post-test schooling cannot influence the previous *GCT* scores. Let the B and A subscripts indicate before and after the test date. Thus, in an equation such as

$$Y = b(S_A - S_B) + cS_B + dGCT + u$$
$$= B(S_A) + (c - b)S_B + dGCT + u, \qquad (6.1)$$

the coefficient on $(S_A - S_B)$ is an estimate of the total effect of schooling given previously attained levels of cognitive skills. In our data set, education at time of entry into the Navy and education as of 1974 correspond, respectively, to B and A. Therefore, in table 6.7 we include alternative relations with some including years of schooling prior to entry in the Navy. However, the estimated coefficient of this variable is never significantly different from zero.[9]

One question of interest in regard to table 6.7 is to what extent are variations in our background variables consistent with varia-

---

[9]Taubman and Wales (1972) also conclude that in the NBER-TH sample pretest differences in schooling has little affect on the variety of tests given to men in the Air Force in 1943. Griliches and Mason (1972) reach a similar conclusion.

Table 6.7

Ordinary least squares regression estimates for five indicators for 609 individuals in Navy for whom *GCT* scores exist.[a]

| | S | $S_B$ | $OC_i$ | $OC_{67}$ | GCT | Age | Raised rural | Cath. | Jew | Born South | No. siblings alive, 1940 | $S_F$ | $S_M$ | $OC_F$ | Constant | $\bar{R}^2$ |
|---|---|---|---|---|---|---|---|---|---|---|---|---|---|---|---|---|
| **Cognitive ability (*GCT*)** | | | | | | | | | | | | | | | | |
| IQ-1 | | | | | | 0.12 (0.7) | −1.96 (2.3) | −0.76 (0.8) | 7.96 (3.6) | −2.7 (2.7) | −0.45 (2.7) | −0.08 (0.6) | 0.67 (3.9) | 0.47 (2.6) | 41.7 (5.0) | 0.139 |
| IQ-2 | | 3.07 (13.6) | | | | −0.24 (1.7) | −1.6 (2.2) | 0.19 (0.2) | 4.8 (2.4) | −1.8 (2.0) | −0.11 (0.7) | −0.17 (1.3) | .41 (2.7) | 0.27 (1.7) | 27.6 (3.7) | 0.342 |
| **Years of Schooling (*S*)** | | | | | | | | | | | | | | | | |
| S-1 | | | | | 0.162 (15.96) | | | | | | | | | | 4.66 (8.74) | 0.343 |
| S-2 | | | | | 0.147 (13.93) | −0.134 (−3.22) | 0.171 (0.788) | −0.721 (−3.06) | 0.369 (0.632) | 0.307 (1.178) | −0.066 (−1.49) | 0.027 (0.726) | 0.03 (0.64) | 0.14 (2.98) | 11.41 (5.15) | 0.343 |
| **Initial occupation (*$OC_i$*)** | | | | | | | | | | | | | | | | |
| $OC_i$-1 | | | | | 0.073 (9.55) | | | | | | | | | | 0.070 (0.175) | 0.129 |
| $OC_i$-2 | 0.298 (10.62) | | | | 0.025 (2.94) | | | | | | | | | | −1.32 (−3.37) | 0.265 |
| $OC_i$-3 | 0.297 (9.31) | 0.003 (0.043) | | | 0.024 (2.73) | | | | | | | | | | −1.33 (−2.60) | 0.264 |
| $OC_i$-4 | | | | | 0.063 (7.91) | −0.015 (−0.488) | 0.326 (1.98) | −0.196 (−1.10) | −0.082 (−0.187) | 0.372 (1.89) | −0.119 (−3.56) | 0.006 (0.209) | 0.019 (0.558) | 0.013 (3.82) | 0.941 (0.561) | 0.181 |
| $OC_i$-5 | 0.292 (9.44) | | | | 0.023 (2.68) | 0.021 (0.713) | 0.279 (1.82) | 0.00 (0.00) | −0.183 (−0.443) | 0.288 (1.57) | −0.101 (−3.23) | −0.002 (−0.057) | 0.011 (0.351) | 0.010 (2.92) | −2.17 (−1.36) | 0.287 |
| $OC_i$-6 | 0.281 (8.47) | −0.033 (−0.524) | | | 0.024 (2.73) | 0.026 (0.833) | 0.279 (1.82) | −0.002 (−0.012) | −0.173 (−0.42) | 0.283 (1.53) | −0.103 (−3.27) | −0.001 (−0.022) | 0.012 (0.377) | 0.010 (2.92) | −2.22 (−1.38) | 0.286 |

**Mature occupation ($OC_{67}$)**

| | (1) | (2) | (3) | (4) | (5) | (6) | (7) | (8) | (9) | (10) | (11) | (12) | (13) | Constant | $R^2$ |
|---|---|---|---|---|---|---|---|---|---|---|---|---|---|---|---|
| ($OC_{67}$-1) | | | | 0.0732 (9.53) | | | | | | | | | | 1.157 (2.87) | 0.129 |
| ($OC_{67}$-2) | 0.313 (11.18) | | | 0.0225 (2.70) | | | | | | | | | | −0.302 (−0.773) | 0.277 |
| ($OC_{67}$-3) | 0.307 (9.63) | 0.0237 (0.398) | | 0.0214 (2.45) | | | | | | | | | | −0.432 (−0.85) | 0.276 |
| ($OC_{67}$-4) | 0.259 (8.63) | | 0.181 (4.54) | 0.018 (2.18) | | | | | | | | | | −0.0627 (−0.162) | 0.299 |
| ($OC_{67}$-5) | 0.253 (7.55) | 0.0232 (0.397) | 0.181 (4.54) | 0.0170 (1.96) | | | | | | | | | | −0.191 (−0.378) | 0.298 |
| ($OC_{67}$-6) | 0.243 (7.92) | | | 0.0642 (7.91) | −0.0622 (1.94) | 0.157 (0.943) | −0.414 (−2.29) | 0.883 (1.97) | 0.247 (1.24) | −0.0727 (−2.144) | 0.0500 (1.73) | −0.0176 (−0.501) | 0.0043 (1.22) | 4.473 (2.63) | 0.163 |
| ($OC_{67}$-7) | 0.243 (7.92) | | 0.174 (4.28) | 0.0173 (2.02) | −0.0268 (−0.908) | 0.0590 (0.386) | −0.204 (−1.23) | 0.808 (1.97) | 0.108 (0.588) | −0.0361 (−1.15) | 0.0423 (1.60) | −0.280 (−0.876) | −0.0013 (−0.408) | 1.532 (0.963) | 0.302 |
| ($OC_{67}$-8) | 0.238 (6.81) | 0.0211 (0.341) | 0.174 (4.28) | 0.0165 (1.86) | −0.0298 (−0.967) | 0.0590 (0.386) | −0.203 (−1.22) | 0.802 (1.96) | 0.111 (0.606) | −0.0348 (−1.10) | 0.0417 (1.57) | −0.0286 (−0.891) | −0.0013 (−0.405) | 1.567 (0.982) | 0.301 |

**Mature earnings ($\ln Y_{73}$)**

| | (1) | (2) | (3) | (4) | (5) | (6) | (7) | (8) | (9) | (10) | (11) | (12) | (13) | Constant | $R^2$ |
|---|---|---|---|---|---|---|---|---|---|---|---|---|---|---|---|
| ($\ln Y_{73}$-1) | | | | 0.018 (9.49) | | | | | | | | | | 8.68 (85.9) | 0.128 |
| ($\ln Y_{73}$-2) | 0.036 (4.72) | | | 0.013 (5.54) | | | | | | | | | | 8.51 (80.8) | 0.157 |
| ($\ln Y_{73}$-3) | 0.04 (4.65) | −0.017 (−1.06) | | 0.013 (5.60) | | | | | | | | | | 8.61 (62.4) | 0.158 |
| ($\ln Y_{73}$-4) | 0.023 (2.74) | | 0.04 (3.88) | 0.012 (5.15) | | | | | | | | | | 8.52 (81.8) | 0.177 |
| ($\ln Y_{73}$-5) | 0.027 (2.96) | −0.018 (−1.14) | 0.04 (3.90) | 0.012 (5.25) | | | | | | | | | | 8.62 (63.2) | 0.177 |
| ($\ln Y_{73}$-6) | | | | 0.015 (7.44) | −0.023 (−2.93) | −0.008 (−0.199) | −0.001 (−0.018) | 0.531 (4.31) | 0.104 (2.10) | −0.019 (−2.24) | −0.001 (0.135) | 0.005 (0.553) | 0.01 (1.26) | 9.93 (23.6) | 0.188 |
| ($\ln Y_{73}$-7) | 0.017 (2.06) | | 0.04 (3.27) | 0.010 (4.47) | −0.019 (−2.39) | −0.017 (−0.410) | 0.026 (0.585) | 0.494 (4.54) | 0.090 (1.85) | −0.015 (−1.82) | −0.001 (−0.177) | 0.005 (0.577) | 0.01 (0.849) | 9.58 (22.7) | 0.216 |
| ($\ln Y_{73}$-8) | 0.021 (2.23) | −0.015 (−0.891) | 0.04 (3.28) | 0.011 (4.54) | −0.017 (−2.03) | −0.017 (−0.413) | 0.025 (0.565) | 0.498 (4.57) | 0.087 (1.79) | −0.016 (−1.92) | −0.001 (−0.118) | 0.005 (0.622) | 0.01 (0.839) | 9.56 (22.6) | 0.216 |

[a] See notes to table 6.1.

tions in *GCT*. Relations *GCT*-1 and *GCT*-2 provide some insight into this question, although of course they do not allow any decomposition between genetic and environmental sources. The estimates imply that being Jewish results in a higher score of from 4.8 to 8.0 points, which is a considerable contribution since the mean of the *GCT* score is about 50 and the standard deviation is 10. Other significantly positive coefficient estimates are for schooling of the mother (but not of the father) and perhaps the occupational status of the father. These results suggest that family environment is important in determining *GCT* and support Leibowitz's (1974) conjecture about the more important direct role of the mother than of the father in creating that environment. Significantly negative coefficients are for being born in the South, raised rural, and perhaps the number of siblings. Years of schooling prior to entering the Navy is significantly positively associated with performance on the *GCT* test (the sample correlation between the two is 0.55), but the direction of causality is not clear.

Our basic interest in table 6.7, however, is in regard to the impact of adding *GCT* to the relations for the four original indicators. Does it contribute significantly to explaining variance in these indicators? Does its exclusion appear to bias the coefficient estimates of other variables?

The answer to the first question clearly is yes. For the alternatives explored the estimated coefficient of the *GCT* variable is significantly positive. In the mature earnings relation, for example, an increase in *GCT* of 10 points or one standard deviation leads to a 10% increase in estimated earnings. In all cases, therefore, the background variables and recursive system of indicators by themselves are inadequate in representing the cognitive abilities which are captured by this variable.

On the other hand, with the possible exception of the years of schooling relation, the *GCT* variable in itself does not replace the other variables in the system. Many of the background variables and the recursive indicators continue to have significantly non-zero coefficient estimates. Therefore, this measure of cognitive ability does not represent all of the qualities leading to socioeconomic success which are captured by the other variables.

This brings us to the question of the extent to which excluding IQ affects the estimated coefficients of other variables. A comparison of the most inclusive relations in tables 6.6 and 6.7 suggests that there are some substantial effects on the coefficient estimates of a few of the background variables. In the years of schooling equation, for example, being Jewish and the number of siblings seem to represent the same cognitive ability as does *GCT* in that both become insignificant when *GCT* is added. However, most of the coefficients of the background variables are fairly robust to the inclusion of *GCT*.

For most of the recursive indicator variables the estimated bias due to the exclusion of *GCT* also is not very large. The differences in the estimated coefficients of years of schooling in the occupational status relations or of occupational status variables in the mature occupational status and earnings relation is 0.04 or less, generally implying a bias of 10–15% at most.

However, for the years of schooling coefficient in the mature earnings relation, the estimated difference of 0.011–0.022 implies a much larger percentage bias. Under the conditions noted above, this absolute difference also is an estimate of the bias due to the exclusion of *GCT* from the estimates of all Navy responders in table 6.5 or of all of our sample in table 6.1. This reasoning leads to an estimate of bias of about 15–30% in the estimate of the coefficient of the years of schooling in the larger sample if *GCT* is excluded.

Because of the lack of representativeness of the Navy men in our sample for whom we have *GCT* data, in table 6.8 we present one last set of estimates. These are for the earnings relation alone since only in the earnings relation is there evidence of a large bias in the estimated coefficient for schooling if *GCT* is excluded. These regressions are for all Navy pairs where both siblings have positive reported earnings in 1973. The observations used are the pair's average on each variable. The average *GCT* data were derived as follows. In the 224 pairs where each sibling had a *GCT* score, we averaged them. In the 161 pairs where only one brother had a score, it was used as the pair average. In the 16 pairs where

Table 6.8

Ordinary least squares regression estimates for average logarithm of mature earnings for 404 pairs of twins, both in Navy.[a]

| Eq. No. | S | Age | GCT | $S_B$ | Cath. | Jew. | Raised rural | Born South | No. siblings alive, 1940 | $S_F$ | $S_M$ | $OC_F$ | Constant | $\bar{R}^2$ |
|---|---|---|---|---|---|---|---|---|---|---|---|---|---|---|
| Y1 | 0.076 (10.8) | -0.0063 (0.8) | | | | | | | | | | | 9.0 (22.9) | 0.23 |
| Y2 | 0.062 (7.5) | -0.0059 (0.8) | 0.0087 (3.2) | | | | | | | | | | 8.7 (21.8) | 0.25 |
| Y3 | 0.051 (6.0) | -0.00056 (0.08) | 0.0059 (2.2) | | 0.055 (1.2) | 0.516 (4.3) | -0.029 (0.6) | 0.024 (0.5) | -0.024 (2.7) | 0.0010 (0.1) | 0.0048 (0.6) | 0.0019 (1.9) | 8.6 (21.6) | 0.31 |
| Y4 | 0.046 (5.0) | -0.0033 (0.4) | 0.0060 (2.3) | 0.012 (1.4) | 0.054 (1.2) | 0.47 (3.7) | -0.028 (0.6) | 0.028 (0.6) | -0.024 (2.7) | 0.00013 (0.002) | -0.0036 (0.4) | 0.0019 (1.9) | 8.7 (21.6) | 0.32 |

[a]See notes to table 6.1.

neither brother had a *GCT* score, both were assigned 52.5 which is the average for all Navy responders with *GCT* data.[10]

In the first equation the coefficient on schooling is 0.076 which is very similar to that obtained in the whole sample. In eq. (2), when we add the *GCT* measure to eq. (1), the *GCT* variable has a highly significant coefficient of 0.009 and the coefficient on schooling drops to 0.062. When the background variables are added in eq. (3), the education coefficient falls to 0.0509, which is a decrease of 33% from (1). When in eq. (4) we add premilitary education, the coefficient on education as of 1974 is 0.046. When we add an officer dummy to eq. (3) the coefficient on education is 0.048.

What do we conclude from these explorations of the role of *GCT* in regressions for the subset of our sample for which we have data?

First, a measure of cognitive ability has a large, positive and significant estimated coefficient in the equations for all four of our basic socioeconomic indicators. For example, in an earnings equation for white men about age 50, with education and a variety of measures of family background held constant, a one standard deviation increase in *GCT* leads to about a 10% increase in earnings.

Secondly, not controlling for the *GCT* leads to small biases, if any, for most variables in most of our relations. However, it does lead to large differences in the coefficients of several background variables (i.e. being Jewish, number of siblings and possibly father's occupation) in the schooling equation. More important for policy purposes it leads to a bias as large as 30–35% in the schooling coefficient in the earnings equation. The size of this bias

---

[10]This methodology is subject to at least two criticisms. First it must cause random measurement error since the cross-sibling correlation for *GCT* for responders are only 0.76 and 0.46 for MZs and DZs, respectively. Secondly, there may be a systematic measurement error since those who entered as officers were supposed to be above average in intelligence. However, since only about one-half the men with no *GCT* scores left the service as officers and since the average *GCT* of the 161 siblings whose brother did not have a *GCT* score was about 54, some of the systematic error is eliminated.

is in conformity with other studies such as Fägerlind (1975), Olneck (1977) and Taubman and Wales (1974) in which the men in the sample have ten or more years of work experience. It is not in conformity with the multitude of studies in which the men have seven or less years of work experience. While none of the studies that has examined the importance of cognitive abilities on earnings are random samples of the population and while a multitude of different cognitive ability tests have been used, our new findings support the idea that the coefficient on cognitive ability in an earnings equation is near zero only when people have few years of work experience. If so, conclusions on the importance of controlling cognitive ability from samples of young men are inappropriate for later life cycle stages.

Thirdly, the bias as large as 30–35% in the coefficient estimate for the years of schooling in the mature earnings relation is up to roughly half of the bias of 70% in this coefficient estimate indicated by the MZ within-pair estimates of section 6.4. However, as discussed in that section, a plausible degree of measurement error could account for a significant proportion of the remainder of the difference between the individual estimates in table 6.1 and the MZ within-pair estimates in table 6.2. Thus, it appears that ordinary least squares regressions which control for cognitive ability and measured aspects of family background may provide good estimates of the true effects of years of schooling on earnings.

Fourthly, even though our measure of cognitive ability is significant and important in our estimated relations for the four socioeconomic indicators, a comparison of the consistency of these relations and of those discussed in the next chapter with variations in these indicators suggest that we here are not including important factors related to genetics and common environment. There apparently remain quite important unmeasured aspects of ability, motivation, and/or financing capability which are related to the family and which have substantial roles in determining socioeconomic success.

# CHAPTER 7

# ESTIMATES OF THE LATENT VARIABLE MODEL

## 7.1. Introduction

In the previous chapter we presented and discussed ordinary least squares estimates for schooling, $S$, initial occupational status, $OC_i$, mature occupational status, $OC_{67}$, and the logarithm of mature earnings, $\ln Y_{73}$. While the results obtained from treating the twins as individuals are similar to those obtained in other samples, the results obtained from the MZ within-pair equations are startlingly different. The estimates from the MZ within-pair equations, however, may still be biased if the noncommon environment that leads to differences in education (or other right-hand-side variables) also has direct effects on earnings or occupational achievement, or if the right-hand-side variables are subject to measurement error (section 4.2). As was indicated in Chapter 4, we can investigate these problems with a latent variable technique. The latent variable method we use also allows us in certain circumstances to partition the variance of any of our dependent variables into its genetic, common, and noncommon environment components. Unfortunately, the full model we would like to estimate has too many parameters to be identified. Therefore we cannot nest all interesting hypotheses. Thus, in this chapter we examine the basic model given in Chapter 4. In the appendix we present a number of alternatives including one in which we assume that there are no genetic effects.

The findings of the latent variable model analysis include the following. The estimates of the coefficients of the observed variables in the structural equations obtained in all of the alternatives with various restrictions are quite similar to those obtained in the MZ within-pair equations. There is no significant deterioration in the fit of the model when we restrict noncommon environment from being a latent variable. The family effect, the sum of genetic and family environment effects for the four dependent variables, has four distinct components or factors. A model which is restricted to have no genetic elements fits the data less well than our model with genetic effects, although a direct comparison of statistical significance is not available. The sum of genetic and family environment effects accounts for roughly one-half of the variance in earnings and occupation and three-quarters of the variance in schooling. These estimates are the same in all models with various restrictions. The separate contributions of genetic and family environment change as we alter certain assumptions. In the estimates we prefer, genetics account for more than half of the family effects.

We also estimate a model in which we allow for measurement error. If we make the strong assumption that only years of schooling is subject to measurement error, we estimate that such an error accounts for about three-quarters of the variance in the portion of schooling initially attributable to noncommon environment and that the effect of schooling on earnings is substantially greater than in our MZ within-pair and in our latent variable models with no measurement error. We do not, however, place much faith in this result for reasons discussed in subsection 4.3.3. On the other hand, if we assume that the variance of measurement error is proportionately the same for schooling, initial and mature occupational status, the coefficients on education are doubled or tripled. Even these results seem to attribute too much weight to measurement error since they yield estimates of the total effect of education greater than those obtained in section 6.5 when we hold constant *GCT* scores (a measure of cognitive abilities and measured family background).

When we include a measure of cognitive skills in our latent variable model we find that such a measure or its genetic and common environment components have statistically significant and noticeable effects. However, much of the family effect does not flow through cognitive skills. We also find that once genetics and environment are controlled, it is not necessary to control for cognitive skills in measuring the effect of education on earnings.

## 7.2. Our basic latent variable model

As was indicated in Chapter 4, in our basic model we assume that there are four genetic latent variables, but only one environmental latent variable. We justify the inclusion of only one environmental latent variable by the observation that all investments in skills are approximately proportional to family income adjusted for tastes if all prices and interest rates are assumed to be basically constant across and within families. We also assume that all the latent variables are uncorrelated with one another. Another restriction which we impose in our model is that initial occupation has no direct effects on mature earnings, but only an indirect effect that is transmitted through mature occupation. We impose the further restriction that environments are equally correlated across both types of twins, i.e. with $\rho^* = \sigma_{N_1 N_1^*}/\sigma_{N_1}^2$ for MZs and $\rho' = \sigma_{N_1 N_1'}/\sigma_{N_1}^2$ for DZs, we have $\rho^* = \rho'$. We justify this assumption on the grounds that any greater similarity of environments of MZs due to conditioning investments in human capital on G are incorporated in the estimate of genetic effects. With these particular restrictions the model contains 25 unknown parameters.

The maximum likelihood estimate of this model is given in the appendix in table 7A.1. The estimate of $\rho^* = \rho'$ in this model is 0.9 with a standard error of 0.1. This estimated coefficient is not significantly different from 1.0. When $\rho^* = \rho' = 1$, only common environment is latent. Restricting $\rho^* = \rho'$ to be 1, we obtain the maximum likelihood estimates given in table 7.1. We can use the likelihood ratio test to determine if imposing this restriction has significantly worsened the fit of the model. Twice the difference in the logarithm of the value of the likelihood function of the models is 0.5, which with one degree of freedom is far from significant at

## Table 7.1

Basic model with $\rho^* = \rho' = 1.0$, $\lambda \neq 1/2$ (24 parameters).

|  | $G_1$ | $N_1$ | $G_2$ | $G_3$ | $G_4$ | $u_1$ | $u_2$ | $u_3$ | $u_4$ | $S$ | $OC_i$ | $OC_{67}$ |
|---|---|---|---|---|---|---|---|---|---|---|---|---|
| **Reduced form equations** | | | | | | | | | | | | |
| $S$ | 1.85 (15.9) | 1.98 (17.5) | | | | 1 | | | | | | |
| $OC_i$ | 0.68 (5.5) | 1.16 (11.7) | 1.16 (18.5) | | | 0.21 (6.0) | 1 | | | | | |
| $OC_{67}$ | 0.69 (6.3) | 0.78 (8.4) | 0.37 (5.1) | 0.82 (13.8) | | 0.29 (8.9) | 0.14 (5.4) | 1 | | | | |
| $\ln Y_{73}$ | 0.17 (5.9) | 0.19 (7.7) | 0.098 (6.0) | 0.019 (0.8) | 0.31 (26.2) | 0.026 (3.4) | 0.0044 (3.5) | 0.031 (4.7) | 1 | | | |
| **Structural equations** | | | | | | | | | | | | |
| $S$ | 1.85 (15.9) | 1.98 (17.5) | | | | 1 | | | | | | |
| $OC_i$ | 0.30 (1.9) | 0.75 (5.7) | 1.16 (18.5) | | | | 1 | | | 0.21 (6.0) | | |
| $OC_{67}$ | 0.113 (0.1) | 0.090 (1.0) | 0.20 (2.3) | 0.82 (13.8) | | | | 1 | | 0.26 (7.9) | 0.14 (5.4) | |
| $\ln Y_{73}$ | 0.12 (3.3) | 0.13 (5.2) | 0.087 (5.2) | −0.0068 (0.3) | 0.31 (26.2) | | | | 1 | 0.016 (2.3) | | 0.031 (4.7) |

**Other estimates**

$\lambda = 0.34$ (6.1)

$$\sigma_{u_1}^2 = 2.17$$
$$(22.6)$$
$$\sigma_{u_2}^2 = 2.75$$
$$(24.4)$$
$$\sigma_{u_3}^2 = 2.45$$
$$(25.1)$$
$$\sigma_{u_4}^2 = 0.127$$
$$(23.1)$$

---

*Normalizations and restrictions*: A, B, C, D, E, F.
*Functional value*: + 13431.87.

*Restrictions and normalizations*:

A is $\sigma_{G_1}^2 = \sigma_{G_2}^2 = \sigma_{G_3}^2 = \sigma_{G_4}^2 = \sigma_N^2 = 1$.
B is $\sigma_{B_2}^2 = \sigma_{N_3}^2 = \sigma_{N_4}^2 = 0$.
C is $\sigma_{N_1 G_1} = 0$.
D is $\sigma_{N_i G_i} = 0, i = 2, 3, 4.$
E is $\sigma_{N_i N_i} = \sigma_{G_i G_j} = 0, i = 1 \ldots 4, j = 1 \ldots 4.$
F is $\rho' = \rho^* = 1$.
G is $\lambda_i = 1/2, i = 1 \ldots 4.$

The figures in parentheses underneath the point estimates are absolute values of ratios of parameter estimates to estimated asymptotic standard errors.

$S$ is years of schooling.
$OC_i$ is initial full time civilian occupational status, Duncan scale.
$OC_{67}$ is occupational status in 1967, Duncan scale.
$\ln Y_{73}$ is the logarithm of 1973 earnings.

The actual likelihood function values are given by a functional value noted in the table, aside from a constant.

the 5% level. Thus, we cannot reject the hypotheses that non-common environment is not a latent variable. This has two implications. First, in the MZ within-pair equations no bias occurs from not controlling noncommon environment. Secondly, in this special case it is possible to identify some models using twin data that are not identified using siblings, cf. Chamberlain (1977).

For purposes of discussion of coefficients we use table 7.1 in which $\rho^* = \rho' = 1$. Consider first the coefficients of the observed variables for the structural equations. The estimates obtained from the latent variable method are close to those obtained from the MZ within-pair equations estimated by ordinary least squares, which are reproduced in table 7.2. Similarly, once we adjust for

Table 7.2
Coefficients from structural equations based on
MZ within-pair data.

| Dependent variable | $\Delta S$ | $\Delta OC_i$ | $\Delta OC_{67}$ |
|---|---|---|---|
| $\Delta OC_i$ | 0.21 | | |
| $\Delta OC_{67}$ | 0.26 | 0.15 | |
| $\Delta \ln Y_{73}$ | 0.019 | | 0.025 |

*Source*: Chapter 6, table 6.2

the fact that the OLS within-pair regressions yield estimates of twice the noncommon environment variance, the estimates of the residual variances or noncommon environment are nearly identical (table 6.2). These coefficient and variance estimates are very close because they are based on almost the same information and assumptions.

Next let us examine the latent variables. We discuss the relative contribution of genetics and environment later in this chapter. Our estimates indicate that both the first genetic component and the common environment have significant coefficients in all of the structural equations except $OC_{67}$. In other words, these indices have direct effects on earnings and initial occupational achievement over and above any indirect effects that flow through education and occupational achievement in the earnings equations. Also, there is another genetic factor which effects initial occupational achievement and which has direct effects in subsequent achievement and earnings. However, the specific genetic effect that enters the equation for later occupational achievement does not have a significant direct effect on earnings.

We impose a triangular format on our genetic variables. As we indicated in sub-section 2.4.2, in such a format the coefficient on the $i$th genetic indicator is nonzero if the $i$th indicator has a different genetic basis than the previous indicators. The statistical significance of the coefficients of $G_2$–$G_4$ indicates that each of the four dependent variables has a distinct genetic basis.

The overall goodness of fit can be gauged by the likelihood function and the closeness of the estimated covariances to the actual values. These two sets of covariances are displayed in table 7.3. The estimated covariances are close to the actual ones in all instances. There are no obvious differences in fit for individuals or cross siblings or for MZs or DZs.

In our basic model we do not assume random mating nor that our genetic effects are additive, as often are assumed in conventional twins models. Instead we have $\sigma_{G_iG_i'} = \lambda\sigma_{G_i}^2$. The implications of letting $\lambda$ vary from 0.5 is given by comparing the estimates in table 7A.2 in the appendix with those in table 7.1. The former is identical to the latter except that $\lambda$ is restricted to 0.5. The model in table 7A.2 is nested in the one for table 7.1. Twice the difference in the logarithm of the value of the likelihood function of the models is (7.1), which is significant in the chi square test with one degree of freedom at the 1% level. Thus, our basic model fits the data significantly better because of allowing for the possibility of assortative mating and/or nonadditive genetic effects.

There are at least two implications of $\lambda$ less than 0.5. First, a comparison of the results in the two tables suggest that a $\lambda$ restricted to 0.5 tends to increase the role of $G$, and to reduce the role of $N_1$. That is, the oft-used assumption in the more conventional twin model of random mating and nonadditive genetic effects tends to shift weight from the common environment factor

Table 7.3
Actual and estimated covariances for individuals and across siblings in basic model in table 7.1.

| | Individuals | | | | | | | | Cross siblings | | | | | | | |
| | Actual | | | | Estimated | | | | Actual | | | | Estimated | | | |
| | $S$ | $OC_i$ | $OC_{67}$ | $\ln Y_{73}$ | $S$ | $OC_i$ | $OC_{67}$ | $\ln Y_{73}$ | $S$ | $OC_i$ | $OC_{67}$ | $\ln Y_{73}$ | $S$ | $OC_i$ | $OC_{67}$ | $\ln Y_{73}$ |
|---|---|---|---|---|---|---|---|---|---|---|---|---|---|---|---|---|
| **MZs** | | | | | | | | | | | | | | | | |
| $S$ | 9.16 | | | | 9.48 | | | | 7.01 | | | | 7.31 | | | |
| $OC_i$ | 3.92 | 6.02 | | | 3.98 | 5.99 | | | 3.47 | 3.16 | | | 3.54 | 3.15 | | |
| $OC_{67}$ | 3.56 | 2.40 | 4.72 | | 3.46 | 2.32 | 4.59 | | 2.90 | 1.87 | 2.02 | | 2.82 | 1.80 | 1.90 | |
| $\ln Y_{73}$ | 0.71 | 0.45 | 0.40 | 0.28 | 0.75 | 0.47 | 0.41 | 0.30 | 0.65 | 0.42 | 0.31 | 0.15 | 0.69 | 0.45 | 0.32 | 0.17 |
| **DZs** | | | | | | | | | | | | | | | | |
| $S$ | 9.76 | | | | 9.48 | | | | 5.32 | | | | 5.09 | | | |
| $OC_i$ | 4.04 | 5.95 | | | 3.98 | 5.99 | | | 2.79 | 1.98 | | | 2.72 | 1.97 | | |
| $OC_{67}$ | 3.34 | 2.25 | 4.45 | | 3.46 | 2.32 | 4.59 | | 1.94 | 1.13 | 0.91 | | 1.98 | 1.21 | 1.05 | |
| $\ln Y_{73}$ | 0.78 | 0.50 | 0.42 | 0.32 | 0.75 | 0.47 | 0.41 | 0.30 | 0.52 | 0.31 | 0.22 | 0.095 | 0.48 | 0.30 | 0.21 | 0.08 |

to the common genetic factor, as compared with the estimates from our more extended version. The same restriction of $\lambda$ equal to 0.5 tends to reduce the estimates of the role of schooling in the determination of the other three indicators. The other coefficients of both observed and latent variables are not altered significantly.

Secondly, $\lambda$ being less than 0.5 is important for inter-generational mobility which is one of the topics of Chapter 8. In section 3.3 we introduced the concepts of "broad" and "narrow" heritability in the context of discussing the DZ and the parent–child genotypic correlations. For the reader's convenience we reproduce the formulae for these genotypic correlations for DZs in 7.1 and for parent–child in 7.2:

$$c' = 1/2d(1 + bhd^2) + 1/4(1 - d), \qquad (7.1)$$

$$c_{PC} = 1/2d(1 + b), \qquad (7.2)$$

where

$h^2$ = ratio of total genetic variance to total phenotypic variance or broad heritability,

$d$ = ratio of additive genetic variance to total genetic variance,

$b$ = phenotypic correlation of parents, and

$c$ = the genotypic correlation where the subscript indicates the relative involved (PC is parent–child).

Our estimate of the genotypic correlation, $\lambda$, is 0.34. From the model given in table 7.1 we can estimate $h^2 = 0.45$ for ln $Y_{73}$ (see section 7.3 for details).[1] Thus, we have $0.34 = 1/2d(1 + 0.45bd) + 1/4(1 - d)$. Since $-1 \le b \le 1$ and $0 \le d \le 1$, we have enough information to establish feasible ranges for $d$, $b$, and $c_{PC}/2$. Some solutions are given in table 7.4 in which we assume a value of $b$ and solve (7.1) for $d$. We then use the estimated $b$ and $d$ which are feasible to estimate $c_{PC}$ in (7.2).

In this table feasible estimates of the phenotypic correlation for parents (assortive mating) range from 1 to $-\frac{2}{3}$. The available

---

[1] Since $d$ is also bounded between 0 and 1, we can usually eliminate one of the multiple roots.

*Socioeconomic success*

Table 7.4
Converting broad heritability to narrow heritability.

| Phenotypic correlations of parents | Implied ratio of additive to total genotypic variation | Implied parent–child genotypic correlation |
| --- | --- | --- |
| 1.00 | 0.31 | 0.31 |
| 0.50 | 0.33 | 0.25 |
| 0.25 | 0.38 | 0.24 |
| 0.00 | 0.40 | 0.20 |
| −0.25 | 0.44 | 0.16 |
| −0.5 | 0.53 | 0.13 |
| −0.67 | 1.00 | 0.17 |

*Source*: table 7.1 and text.

literature indicates positive assortive mating for traits such as education and IQ and negative assortive mating for personality traits such as extroversion (Vandenberg, 1972). It is not obvious *a priori* what is an appropriate average value for *b*.

If there is no assortive mating, the nonadditive portion of genetic variation does not affect or is not passed on to subsequent generations (compare eqs. (7.1) and (7.2) with *b* equal to zero). In table 7.4 *d* ranges from 0.31 to 1 and increases as the estimate of assortive mating falls. Again it is not obvious to us *a priori* what is an appropriate value of *d*.

The intergenerational genotypic correlation which is given in the last column of this table ranges from 0.17 to 0.31. In a model such as table 7A.2 in the appendix in which there is random mating and only additive genetic effects, the intergenerational genotypic correlation is one-half. Thus, the model estimated in table 7.1 indicates smaller genetic correlations between parent and offspring. However, both models (7.1) and table 7A.1 can be made equally consistent with any parent–child phenotypic correlations for earnings since the latter also incorporates the unobserved parent–child environmental correlation.

Our basic model in table 7.1 restricts $\sigma_{G_iG_i}/\sigma_G^2 = \lambda$ for all *i*. A more general model would have a seperate $\lambda_i$ for each of the genetic indices. In table 7A.3 in the appendix we allow for two

$\lambda$'s. The first applies to $S$, $OC_i$ and $OC_{67}$, while the last applies only to $\ln Y_{73}$. Twice the difference in the logarithm of the likelihood function of this model compared with (7.1) is 0.2. Thus, there is no significant nor noticeable improvement in the fit by allowing for two $\lambda$'s. The estimates of the $\lambda$'s are 0.38 for $\ln Y_{73}$ and 0.29 for the other three variables, with standard errors of 0.08. Thus, the two estimates are not significantly different from each other, nor from the value obtained in table 7.1. The use of 0.38 rather than 0.34 raises the estimate of $d$ and $c_{PC}$ for every value of $b$ in table 7.4.

In Chapter 5 we indicated that the techniques used to classify twins as MZs or DZs are subject to about 5% error. If this classification error were random, the MZ and DZ correlation coefficients would be over and understated by about 0.02, respectively. In table 7A.4 in the appendix we present results for the reduced form equations based on data adjusted on the assumption of such random misclassification. As is indicated in Chapters 4 and 5, compared with the estimates in table 7.1 this adjustment raises the contribution of genetics and lowers the coefficient of the observed variables. The changes, however, are small. Since we cannot be sure that misclassification is random and since the differences between tables 7.1 and 7A.4 are small, we ignore misclassification error from this point on.

Thus far we have imposed the restriction that the genetic endowments and common environment are uncorrelated. Yet there are a variety of circumstances in which we would expect $G$ and $N$ to be correlated. For example, we argued in Chapter 2 that an important element in family environment is family income which affects the levels of nutrition, schooling, and composition of goods and services enjoyed by the children and which can be correlated with parental $G$. Similarly, mothers who are more educated in part because of their genetic endowments also may be more effective producers of skills or values associated with socioeconomic success in their children.

We showed in section 4.3.3 that the model is identified if $\sigma_{G_1 N_1}$ is nonzero. In practice, however, when we allow $\sigma_{G_1 N_1}$ to be non-zero, our estimates have not converged to a stable set of values.

The problem, possibly for the reason given in section 4.3.3, is that the likelihood function is very flat, which can be demonstrated by solving the model for various fixed values of $\sigma_{N_1 G_1}$. Table 7A.5 in the appendix, for example, contains our estimates when $\sigma_{N_1 G_1}$ is restricted to 0.6. Compared to table 7.1 the value of the likelihood function has only changed by 0.3. Twice this difference is not significantly different from that of the model in table 7.1 at the 5% level, using a chi-square test with one degree of freedom. The only significant parameter estimates that change as $\sigma_{N_1 G_1}$ goes from 0 to 0.6 are the coefficients of $N_1$, which decrease. While we cannot distinguish well between models with zero and high $\sigma_{N_1 G_1}$, it is comforting to realize that the entire trade-off is with the coefficient estimates of one variable.

All the latent variable models discussed thus far have four genetic and one environmental variables. However, we noted in Chapters 3 and 4 that it is possible to explain the difference in MZ–DZ cross-sibling correlations on any variable by differences in $\rho^*$ and $\rho'$ for that variable. We can identify a model with four environmental indices in which we have $\rho^* = \sigma_{N_i N_i^*}$ and $\rho' = \sigma_{N_i N_i'}$, $i = 1, \ldots, 4$ provided that we impose some restriction such as $\gamma_5 = 0$.

Estimates for a model with four environmental variables, each with a common $\rho^*$ and $\rho'$, and with $\gamma_5 = 0$ are given in table 7A.6. By construction, this model must have different coefficients on the latent variables than the earlier models with four genetic indices and one environmental index. Thus, a primary question to ask is how do the coefficients on the observed variables in this model compare with the corresponding ones in the mixed genetic-environmental model? The answer is that the coefficients on the observed variables are nearly identical to the coefficients obtained in those versions of the mixed model in which $\rho^* = \rho'$ are not restricted to one (such as in table 7A.1). Thus, it appears that by using latent variable techniques we can obtain approximately the same coefficients on the observed variables whether we think family effects arise because of a combination of genetics and environment or solely because of environment.

The pure environmental model also is like the mixed genetic-environmental models in that four separate factors are needed to span the space covered by the four dependent variables. This pure environmental model differs from the mixed models in that it fits the data less well – the logarithm of the likelihood function differs by fifteen from the best fitting mixed model which uses four more parameters. Unfortunately, since the pure environmental model is not nested in any of the mixed models, we cannot determine if this difference is significant.

To aid in the comparison of the goodness of fit of the two models, we present the estimated covariances from the pure environmental model in table 7A.7. On an absolute basis this model fits the data well. However, compared to the results in table 7.3 the pure environmental model does not fit as well. The major differences are denoted by an "a" or a "b" superscript in table 7A.7. If there is an "a", the pure environmental model fits at least 1% better, while if there is a "b" the mixed model fits at least 1% better. In the panels for individuals, there is a stand-off with improvements in MZs offset by losses for the same elements for DZs. In the cross-sibling portion of the table, there are only two a's but eight b's. The mixed model fits the DZ cross-sibling covariance better.

One final variant of our basic latent variable model which merits mention includes measurement error in our observed variables. In Chapter 4 we noted that measurement error may give rise to substantially greater problems in the within-pair equations and by extension the latent variable models. We also note that it would be possible to allow for measurement error in one observed variable if $\gamma_s = 0$ and if $\rho^* = \rho' = 1$. We have obtained startling results for the coefficient for years of schooling in the earnings equation. This coefficient has been of substantial interest for many years for reasons discussed in Chapter 1. Therefore, we have respecified our model assuming that $T = S + w$, where $w$ is the measurement error uncorrelated with the true variables and across brothers, $S$ is true schooling, and $T$ is observed schooling.

Our results are given in table 7A.8 in the appendix. The parameters of primary interest are the total effects of schooling which are given by the coefficients of $u_1$, and the size of $\sigma_w^2$ and

$\sigma_{u_1}^2$. In table 7A.8 $\sigma_w^2$ is 1.5 while $\sigma_{u_1}^2$ has declined from about 2.2 in the other tables to 0.7. Thus, this model estimates that nearly all of the observed variation in schooling with MZ twin pairs arises because of measurement error. The coefficients on $u_1$ are much bigger than in the MZ within-pair equations, being as large as in the equations for individuals in the case of ln earnings, and even larger than this for mature occupation.

These results are difficult to believe, especially when it is recalled that in section 6.5 we showed that controlling for cognitive ability and measured family background causes a substantial drop in the schooling coefficient in the earnings and occupations equations and that there would be a large reduction even if $\sigma_w^2$ were 1.51.

The problem with these results may be that $\sigma_{\Delta S}^2$ becomes too small once we allow for measurement error. Alternatively, the assumption that only $S$ is measured with error may be causing a problem.

To examine the latter possibility we have reworked the analysis assuming that the schooling, initial and mature occupational status variables all are measured with error. In this run we restrict the noise-to-signal ratio to be the same for $S$, $OC_i$, and $OC_{67}$. The results, which are given in table 7A.9 in the appendix, indicate a reduction in $\sigma_w^2$ to about 1.45 which is about two-thirds of the variance in noncommon environment. The estimates for the effects of education also are reduced, but are still greater than those obtained when controlling for cognitive skills and measured aspects of family background and greater than those in table 6.1 for $OC_i$ and $OC_{67}$. Therefore, we reject the estimates in tables 7A.8 and 7A.9.

## 7.3. Relative importance of genetics and environment

In table 7.5, which is derived from table 7.1, genetics accounts for about 30% of the variance in schooling and occupational status and 45% of the variance in the logarithm of 1973 earnings. Common environment, $N$, accounts for 42% of the variance in

Table 7.5
Sources of variances of schooling, initial and later occupational status, and earnings; basic model.

| Percent of total arising from | $S$ | $OC_i$ | $OC_{67}$ | $\ln Y_{73}$ |
|---|---|---|---|---|
| $\sigma^2_{G_1}$ | 36% | 08% | 11% | 10% |
| $\sigma^2_{G_2}$ | | 23 | 03 | 03 |
| $\sigma^2_{G_3}$ | | | 15 | * |
| $\sigma^2_{G_4}$ | | | | 32 |
| $\Sigma\,\sigma^2_{G_i}$ | 36 | 31 | 29 | 45 |
| $\sigma^2_{N_1}$ | 41 | 22 | 13 | 12 |
| $\sigma^2_{u_1}$ | 23 | 02 | 04 | 01 |
| $\sigma^2_{u_2}$ | | 46 | 01 | * |
| $\sigma^2_{u_3}$ | | | 53 | 01 |
| $\sigma^2_{u_4}$ | | | | 42 |

*Source*: table 7.1.
 *implies less than 0.5%.
 Totals may not add to 100% because of rounding.

schooling, 22% in initial occupation, and 10% of 1967 occupation and the logarithm of 1973 earnings. The remainders, which are attributable to specific environment, are 25–55% of the total.

Of the genetic effects, most of the total impact is attributable to the index introduced in an equation for a particular indicator, e.g. $G_3$ for $OC_{67}$. However, the first genetic index has noticeable effects on all four indicators while the second accounts for 3% of the variance in $OC_{67}$ and $\ln Y_{73}$.

The variance decomposition can be sensitive to the restrictions imposed on the estimates. When $\sigma_{G_1N_1}$ is not restricted to zero, the coefficients on $N_1$ vary greatly, but others are unchanged. An example is given in appendix table 7A.5.

The estimates of the genetic contribution are affected by our assumptions about assortive mating and dominance. As can be inferred from table 7A.2, estimates of the effects of the $G_1$ index are about 25% greater than in table 7.5.

In table 6.1 we presented some equations which include a number of commonly available proxies for $G$ and $N$. The $\bar{R}^2$ in the reduced form equations, which indicate the proportion of the variance of the dependent variable attributable to these background variables, are far smaller – generally one-quarter or less – than the contribution of the family effects obtained from the latent variable model. Thus, the measured variables are incomplete proxies in controlling for family effects and poor proxies for judging the importance of the family.

Perhaps the best way to summarize this section is to say that all of our various models (except the pure environmental one) suggest that genetic endowment, common environment, and specific environment all contribute to schooling and labor market success. Common environment appears more important for schooling and early occupation, while genetics are more important for earnings and mature occupation. If these results can be taken as even approximately correct, they imply that even extreme policies to ensure equality of opportunity by eliminating *all* differences between families in common environment (including those due to the family income) would not eliminate much of the family contribution to the welfare of offspring. Of course, since we do not know what exactly is meant by common environment, it is difficult to eliminate all differences.

These results, of course, are obtained from a particular sample of white male veterans born between 1917 and 1927. This sample has a different mean and variance in earnings and education than either the population as a whole or the white men of the same age group. This noncomparability may mean that our results, especially those for the partition of the variance, do not apply to the cohort or for the population as a whole. Moreover, even if they do apply to the current population, there is no reason to consider any of these effects fixed for reasons explained in more detail in section 3.5.

## 7.4. The effects of cognitive skills

Thus far in this chapter we have controlled for unobserved genetic and environmental variables by statistical techniques. But, as indicated in Chapters 5 and 6, for those in the Navy we have available data on the *GCT*, which is a measure of cognitive skills. In section 6.5 it is shown that the *GCT* and the available measures of family background together provide adequate controls for the omitted ability variables when estimating the effect of schooling on earnings. In this section we first examine the extent to which the estimate of the education coefficient of the coefficients on the unobserved and observed variables. At this point we consider the relative contributions of the various unobserved variables to the variances of the four dependent variables. While the previous tables contain the total effects (in the reduced forms) and the direct effects (in the structural equations), we only summarize and discuss the total effects here.

Until now we have examined our results primarily in terms of if the stability in the earnings equation is affected by holding *GCT*, genetics, and common environment constant. Secondly, we estimate the extent to which the *G* and *N* effects in the previous sections of this chapter are attributable to cognitive skills. Thirdly, we estimate if the underlying genetic and environmental bases of the *GCT* test are the same or different from those that underlie the four previous indicators. Finally, we provide an estimate, which can be compared with others in the literature, of the contributions of genetics and common environment to the *GCT* variable.

We remind the reader that the *GCT* test is only available for those who entered the Navy as enlisted men. It was shown in section 6.5 that fairly similar results are obtained using the Navy subsample as in our full sample. But we obtain substantially different parameter estimates for education when only those Navy people with *GCT* data are used. However, we also find both that the coefficients of *GCT* and that the changes in the other coefficients when holding *GCT* constant are the same whether the people with the *GCT* data or the full Navy sample (with, when necessary, estimated *GCT* data) are used. Given the above findings, we decided to integrate the *GCT* data into the analysis as follows. We augment the covariances calculated from the full sample for the previous four indicators as given, for example, in table 7.3, by various covariances involving *GCT* calculated from the 146 MZ and 78 DZ pairs for which both siblings have *GCT* data. In our estimation of standard errors we do not allow for the fact that there are substantially fewer observations for the *GCT* data; hence, we have overstated the $t$ statistics on all parameters relating to this variable.

We incorporate the *GCT* data into our analysis by converting our model into one of five indicators where *GCT* enters the four other structural equations and where the fifth equation is

$$GCT = H_1G_1 + H_2G_2 + H_3G_3 + H_4G_4 + H_5G_5 + H_6N_1 + u_5, \qquad (7.3)$$

where $H_j$, $j = 1, \ldots, 6$, are parameters to be estimated.

The results are given in table 7.6. The estimates of coefficients are very similar to corresponding ones in table 7.1 in which *GCT* is not included. Thus, once $G$ and $N$ are controlled, there is no additional benefit from controlling *GCT*.

In table 7.7 we present the partition of the variances of the five indicators based on table 7.6. For *GCT* we calculate that genetics, common environment, and noncommon environment account for 35, 37, and 26%, respectively. The available estimates in the literature generally estimate genetics to be a larger proportion than this. There are several possible reasons for our lower estimate. First, the *GCT* test was given at time of induction into the Navy while most other studies are based on tests given earlier in life. Variations in teenage and early adult environment may contribute to vocabulary, the major element in the *GCT*. Secondly, other studies use different measures of cognitive skills which may be more highly related to genetic endowments. Scarr and Weinberg (1977) present some evidence that vocabulary development is more highly correlated with family environment than mathematical skills or abstract reasoning. Thirdly, the other studies use different techniques than we do. Fourthly, the results in this section have been based on those pairs for whom *GCT* scores are available and who answered our survey. The cross-twin correlation for all the pairs with *GCT* data is the same for MZ pairs, but lower by about 0.1 for DZ pairs. Thus, in the full sample genetics would account for more of the variance in *GCT* than in the subsample used.

The partition of the variance of the *GCT* variable indicates that

## Table 7.6
### Latent variable estimates of basic model, five indicators (35 parameters).

| | $G_1$ | $N_1$ | $G_2$ | $G_3$ | $G_4$ | $G_5$ | $u_1$ | $u_2$ | $u_3$ | $u_4$ | $u_5$ | $S$ | $OC_i$ | $OC_{67}$ | $GCT$ |
|---|---|---|---|---|---|---|---|---|---|---|---|---|---|---|---|
| *Reduced form equations* | | | | | | | | | | | | | | | |
| S | 1.75 (19.3) | 2.06 (24.0) | 0.00094 | 0.000041 | 0.00116 | 0.00412 | 1 | | | | 0.008 | | | | |
| $OC_i$ | 0.78 (7.05) | 1.06 (12.3) | 1.20 (22.9) | -0.00021 | -0.006 | 0.021 | 0.20 (6.02) | 1 | | | 0.041 (0.39) | | | | |
| $OC_{67}$ | 0.72 (7.48) | 0.75 (9.93) | 0.36 (5.60) | 0.81 (13.0) | -0.044 | 0.16 | 0.29 (9.07) | 0.14 (5.29) | 1 | | 0.30 (2.98) | | | | |
| $\ln Y_{73}$ | 0.14 (6.07) | 0.22 (12.0) | 0.094 (6.67) | 0.030 (1.31) | 0.30 (2.48) | 0.056 | 0.027 (3.63) | 0.004 | 0.028 (4.23) | 1 | 0.11 (4.57) | | | | |
| GCT | 0.12 (2.65) | 0.57 (20.9) | 0.12 (-2.17) | -0.005 (-0.07) | -0.145 (-3.13) | 0.51 (18.2) | | | | | 1 | | | | |
| *Structural equations* | | | | | | | | | | | | | | | |
| S | 1.74 | 2.05 | | | | 0.51 | 1 | | | | | 0.20 | | | 0.008 |
| $OC_i$ | 0.42 | 0.62 | 1.2 | | | | | 1 | | | | 0.26 | 0.14 | | 0.04 |
| $OC_{67}$ | 0.12 | -0.11 | 0.23 | 0.81 | | | | | 1 | | | 0.019 | | 0.028 | 0.30 |
| $\ln Y_{73}$ | 0.076 | 0.099 | 0.096 | 0.008 | 0.32 | | | | | 1 | | | | | 0.10 |
| GCT | 0.12 | 0.56 | -0.12 | -0.005 | -0.145 | 0.51 | | | | | 1 | | | | |

*Other estimates:*

$\sigma^2_{u_1} = 2.20$ (22.5)  $\sigma^2_{u_2} = 2.72$ (24.6)

$\sigma^2_{u_3} = 2.42$ (25.0)  $\sigma^2_{u_4} = 0.124$ (23.1)

$\sigma^2_{u_5} = 0.227$ (23.1)  $\lambda = 0.322$ (8.25)

*Normalizations and restrictions:* A, B, C, D, E, F and $G_5$ uncorrelated with $N_1$, $G_j$, $u_j$, $j = 1,\ldots,4$, $i = 1,\ldots,5$.

*Functional value:* = +14135.8.

*Notes:* see table 7.1.

Table 7.7
Sources of variances of schooling, initial and later occupational status, earnings, and *GCT*.

|  | Schooling (%) | Initial occupation (%) | 1967 occupation (%) | 1973 earnings (%) | GCT score (%) |
|---|---|---|---|---|---|
| $\sigma^2_{G1}$ | 32 | 10 | 11 | 6 | 2 |
| $\sigma^2_{G2}$ | 0 | 24 | 3 | 3 | 2 |
| $\sigma^2_{G3}$ | 0 | 0 | 14 | 0 | 0 |
| $\sigma^2_{G4}$ | 0 | 0 | 0 | 30 | 2 |
| $\sigma^2_{G5}$ | 0 | 0 | 1 | 1 | 30 |
| $\Sigma\,\sigma^2_G$ | 32 | 34 | 29 | 40 | 36 |
| $\sigma^2_{N1}$ | 45 | 19 | 12 | 16 | 37 |
| $\sigma^2_{u1}$ | 23 | 1.5 | 4 | 0 |  |
| $\sigma^2_{u2}$ |  | 45 | 1 | 0 |  |
| $\sigma^2_{u3}$ |  |  | 53 | 1 |  |
| $\sigma^2_{u4}$ |  |  |  | 41 |  |
| $\sigma^2_{u5}$ | 0 | 0 | 1 | 1 | 26 |

*Source*: table 7.6. $\lambda = 0.322$, $\rho^* = \rho' = 1$.

roughly one-third is attributable to specific environment and another one-third to a genetic index, $G_5$, specific to the *GCT* variable. This $G_5$ index has only modest effects in the reduced forms of the other four indicators.

Let us assume that the *GCT* is a good measure of cognitive skills. Thus, it seems that parents affect their child's cognitive skill development differently from other skills and that much of the effect of parents on their offspring's earnings does not flow through cognitive skills. On the other hand, results in this chapter and in section 6.5 indicate that controlling for *GCT* and observable family background is adequate when estimating the effects of education on earnings.

## Appendix

Estimates for variants for basic latent variable model which are mentioned in the text. Because of computational costs, standard errors were not calculated for some parameters in some runs.

Basic four-indicator model with $\rho^* = \rho' \neq 1$ (25 parameters).

| | $G_1$ | $N_1$ | $G_2$ | $G_3$ | $G_4$ | $u_1$ | $u_2$ | $u_3$ | $u_4$ | $S$ | $OC_i$ | $OC_{67}$ |
|---|---|---|---|---|---|---|---|---|---|---|---|---|
| **Reduced form equations** | | | | | | | | | | | | |
| S | 1.85 (15.9) | 2.07 (13.2) | | | | 1 | | | | | | |
| $OC_i$ | 0.67 (5.5) | 1.22 (10.3) | 1.16 (18.3) | | | 0.12 (0.9) | 1 | | | | | |
| $OC_{67}$ | 0.70 (6.3) | 0.82 (7.8) | 0.37 (5.1) | 0.82 (13.9) | | 0.27 (5.2) | 0.14 (5.3) | 1 | | | | |
| $\ln Y_{73}$ | 0.17 (5.9) | 0.20 (7.3) | 0.09 (4.6) | 0.022 (0.9) | 0.31 (26.3) | 0.0096 (0.4) | 0.0042 (3.2) | 0.030 (4.3) | 1 | | | |
| **Structural-equations** | | | | | | | | | | | | |
| S | 1.85 (15.8) | 2.07 (13.2) | | | | 1 | | | | | | |
| $OC_i$ | 0.45 (1.7) | 0.97 (3.0) | 1.16 (18.3) | | | | 1 | | | 0.12 (0.9) | | |
| $OC_{67}$ | 0.1348 (0.9) | 0.119 (0.9) | 0.204 (2.1) | 0.820 (13.8) | | | | 1 | | 0.28 (6.1) | 0.14 (5.0) | |
| $\ln Y_{73}$ | 0.15 (2.8) | 0.17 (2.8) | 0.079 (4.1) | -0.002 (-0.095) | 0.31 (26.3) | | | | 1 | 0.00165 (0.07) | | 0.030 (4.3) |

**Other estimates**

$\lambda = 0.34$ (6.1)  $\rho^* = \rho' = 0.90$ (10.3)

$\sigma^2_{u_1} = 1.76$ (3.8)  $\sigma^2_{u_2} = 2.67$ (18.3)

$\sigma^2_{u_3} = 2.45$ (25.0)  $\sigma^2_{u_4} = 0.12$ (20.0)

*Normalizations and restrictions*: A, B, C, D, E.
*Functional value*: = +13431.61.
*Notes*: see tables 7.1 and 7.2.

## Table 7A.2
### Basic model except random matching and only additive genetic effects ($\lambda = 1/2$).

| | $G_1$ | $N_1$ | $G_2$ | $G_3$ | $G_4$ | $u_1$ | $u_2$ | $u_3$ | $u_4$ | $S$ | $OC_i$ | $OC_{67}$ |
|---|---|---|---|---|---|---|---|---|---|---|---|---|
| *Reduced form equations* | | | | | | | | | | | | |
| S | 2.090 | 1.710 | | | | | | | | | | |
| | (20.5) | (13.7) | | | | | | | | | | |
| $OC_i$ | 0.847 | 1.043 | 1.143 | | | 1 | | | | | | |
| | (7.0) | (8.2) | (17.1) | | | | | | | | | |
| $OC_{67}$ | 0.814 | 0.658 | 0.361 | 0.794 | | 0.290 | 0.149 | 1 | | | | |
| | (7.3) | (5.4) | (4.8) | (13.0) | | (5.7) | (8.8) | | | | | |
| $\ln Y_{73}$ | 0.210 | 0.150 | 0.102 | 0.016 | 0.300 | 0.024 | 0.0045 | 0.030 | 1 | | | |
| | (7.8) | (5.1) | (5.6) | (0.6) | (23.1) | (3.1) | (3.6) | (3.2) | | | | |
| | | | | | | | | | | | | |
| *Structural equations* | | | | | | | | | | | | |
| S | 2.090 | 1.710 | | | | | | | | | | |
| | (20.5) | (13.7) | | | | | | | | | | |
| $OC_i$ | 0.436 | 0.706 | 1.143 | | | 1 | | | | 0.197 | | |
| | (2.7) | (5.7) | (17.1) | | | | | | | (5.7) | | |
| $OC_{67}$ | 0.144 | 0.058 | 0.192 | 0.794 | | | 1 | | | 0.261 | 0.149 | |
| | (0.9) | (0.5) | (2.0) | (13.0) | | | | | | (5.7) | (8.8) | |
| $\ln Y_{73}$ | 0.155 | 0.105 | 0.091 | −0.0078 | 0.300 | | | | 1 | 0.015 | | 0.030 |
| | (4.2) | (3.8) | (5.0) | (0.3) | (23.1) | | | | | (1.9) | | (3.2) |

*Other parameter estimates*

$\sigma^2_{u1} = 2.18$    $\sigma^2_{u3} = 2.49$
   (22.6)       (26.2)

$\sigma^2_{u2} = 2.80$    $\sigma^2_{u4} = 0.13$
   (25.2)       (24.0)

*Normalizations and restrictions*: A, B, C, D, E, F, G.
*Functional value*: = +13435.44.

## Table 7A.3

Basic four-indicator model with two DZ genotypic correlations and $\rho^* = \rho' = 1$ (25 parameters).

| | $G_1$ | $N_1$ | $G_2$ | $G_3$ | $G_4$ | $u_1$ | $u_2$ | $u_3$ | $u_4$ | $S$ | $OC_i$ | $OC_{67}$ |
|---|---|---|---|---|---|---|---|---|---|---|---|---|
| *Reduced form equations:* | | | | | | | | | | | | |
| $S$ | 1.81 (13.2) | 2.011 (15.9) | | | | 1 | | | | | | |
| $OC_i$ | 0.650 (4.9) | 1.17 (11.9) | 1.165 (18.6) | | | 0.207 (6.0) | 1 | | | | | |
| $OC_{67}$ | 0.679 (5.9) | 0.792 (8.5) | 0.368 (5.1) | 0.824 (13.8) | | 0.294 (9.0) | 0.143 (5.3) | 1 | | | | |
| $\ln Y_{73}$ | 0.169 (5.9) | 0.192 (8.1) | 0.098 (6.1) | 0.018 (0.79) | 0.308 (25.7) | 0.026 (3.3) | 0.0044 (3.5) | 0.031 (4.7) | 1 | | | |
| *Structural equations* | | | | | | | | | | | | |
| $S$ | 1.81 | 2.01 | | | | 1 | | | | | | |
| $OC_i$ | | 0.757 | 1.165 | | | | 1 | | | 0.207 | | |
| $OC_{67}$ | | 0.093 | 0.20 | 0.824 | 0.308 | | | 1 | | 0.264 | 0.143 | |
| $\ln Y_{73}$ | | 0.135 | 0.087 | −0.0074 | 0.308 | | | | 1 | 0.016 | 0.143 | 0.031 |

*Other estimates:*

$\lambda = 0.32 \quad \lambda_1 = 0.37$
$(3.9) \quad\quad (4.8)$

$\sigma^2_{u_1} = 2.16 \quad \sigma^2_{u_2} = 2.74$
$(22.6) \quad\quad (24.2)$

$\sigma^2_{u_3} = 2.44 \quad \sigma^2_{u_4} = 0.127$
$(24.8) \quad\quad (22.7)$

*Normalizations and restrictions:* A, B, C, D, E, F.
*Functional value* = 13431.76.
*Notes:* see tables 7.1 and 7.2.

Table 7A.4

Basic model with data adjusted for random misclassification (24 parameters).

| | $G_1$ | $N_1$ | $G_2$ | $G_3$ | $G_4$ | $u_1$ | $u_2$ | $u_3$ | $u_4$ | $S$ | $OC_i$ | $OC_{67}$ |
|---|---|---|---|---|---|---|---|---|---|---|---|---|
| *Reduced form equations* | | | | | | | | | | | | |
| S | 1.90 | 1.98 | | | | 1 | | | | | | |
| $OC_i$ | 0.71 | 1.15 | 1.20 | | | 0.19 | 1 | | | | | |
| $OC_{67}$ | 0.71 | 0.78 | 0.37 | 0.86 | | 0.29 | 0.14 | 1 | | | | |
| ln $Y_{73}$ | 0.17 | 0.19 | 0.094 | 0.021 | 0.32 | 0.021 | 0.0043 | 0.034 | 1 | | | |

*Other estimates*

$\sigma^2_{u_1} = 1.98$    $\sigma^2_{u_2} = 2.65$
$\sigma^2_{u_3} = 2.39$    $\sigma^2_{u_4} = 0.121$
$\lambda = 0.28$

*Normalizations and restrictions:* A, B, C, D, E, F.
*Functional value:* = 13383.77.
*Notes:* see table 7.1.

## Table 7A.5
### Basic model with $\sigma_{N_iG_i} = \sigma_{N_iG_i} = 0.6$ (24 parameters).

| | $G_1$ | $N_1$ | $G_2$ | $G_3$ | $G_4$ | $u_1$ | $u_2$ | $u_3$ | $u_4$ | $S$ | $OC_i$ | $OC_{67}$ |
|---|---|---|---|---|---|---|---|---|---|---|---|---|
| *Reduced form equations* | | | | | | | | | | | | |
| $S$ | 1.853 | 1.148 | | | | 1 | | | | | | |
| | (15.6) | (8.6) | | | | | | | | | | |
| $OC_i$ | | 0.799 | 1.184 | | | 0.205 | 1 | | | | | |
| | | (6.4) | (21.7) | | | (5.99) | | | | | | |
| $OC_{67}$ | | 0.466 | 0.362 | 0.822 | | 0.294 | 0.144 | 1 | | | | |
| | | (4.0) | (5.5) | (14.2) | | (5.94) | (8.9) | | | | | |
| $\ln Y_{73}$ | | 0.113 | 0.097 | 0.020 | 0.309 | 0.026 | 0.0045 | 0.0308 | 1 | | | |
| | | (3.8) | (6.6) | (0.89) | (26.9) | (3.4) | (3.5) | | | | | |
| *Structural-equations* | | | | | | | | | | | | |
| $S$ | 1.85 | 1.15 | 1.184 | | | 1 | | | | 0.205 | | |
| $OC_i$ | 0.3009 | 0.5631 | 0.1909 | 0.822 | | | 1 | | | 0.264 | 0.144 | |
| $OC_{67}$ | 0.597 | 0.0471 | 0.0856 | 0.071 | | | | 1 | | 0.0198 | | 0.0308 |
| $\ln Y_{73}$ | 0.1498 | 0.079 | | | 0.309 | | | | 1 | | | |

*Other estimates*

$\lambda = 0.34$
$\quad(6.2)$

$\sigma^2_{u_1} = 2.17 \quad \sigma^2_{u_2} = 2.74$
$\qquad\quad(24.6) \qquad\qquad(24.5)$

$\sigma^2_{u_3} = 1.24 \quad \sigma^2_{u_4} = 0.127$
$\qquad\quad(25.1) \qquad\qquad(23.0)$

*Normalizations and restrictions*: A, B, D, E, F; $\sigma_{G_iN_i} = 0.6$.
*Functional value*: $= +13431.93$.
*Notes*: see table 7.1.

Table 7A.6
A pure environmental variable model (21 parameters).

| | $N_1$ | $N_2$ | $N_3$ | $N_4$ | $u_1$ | $u_2$ | $u_3$ | $u_4$ | $S$ | $OC_i$ | $OC_{67}$ |
|---|---|---|---|---|---|---|---|---|---|---|---|
| *Reduced form equations* | | | | | | | | | | | |
| $S$ | 2.76 (31.5) | | | | 1 | | | | | | |
| $OC_i$ | 1.36 (23.2) | 1.17 (18.8) | | | 0.095 (0.9) | 1 | | | | | |
| $OC_{67}$ | 1.07 (20.8) | 0.34 (5.2) | 0.79 (12.3) | | 0.26 (5.4) | 0.15 (5.3) | 1 | | | | |
| $\ln Y_{73}$ | 0.26 (20.1) | 0.09 (5.0) | 0.026 (11.2) | 0.30 (19.3) | 0.0053 (0.2) | 0.0042 (3.1) | 0.029 | 1 | | | |
| *Structural-equations* | | | | | | | | | | | |
| $S$ | 2.76 | | | | 1 | | | | | | |
| $OC_i$ | | 1.17 | | | | 1 | | | 0.095 | | |
| $OC_{67}$ | | | 0.79 | | | | 1 | | 0.25 | 0.15 | |
| $\ln Y_{73}$ | | | 0.003 | 0.30 | | | | 1 | -0.0021 | | 0.029 |

*Other estimates*

$\sigma_{u_1}^2 = 1.75$　$\sigma_{u_2}^2 = 2.73$
　(4.2)　　　(16.11)
$\sigma_{u_3}^2 = 2.51$　$\sigma_{u_4}^2 = 0.129$
　(24.3)　　(13.5)
$\rho^* = 0.94$　$\rho' = 0.61$
　(14.9)　　(18.84)

*Normalizations and restrictions*: C, D, E, and $\sigma_{N_1}^2 = \sigma_{N_2}^2 = \sigma_{N_3}^2 = \sigma_{N_4}^2 = 1$.
*Functional value*: = +13447.27.
*Notes*: see table 7.1.

Table 7A.7

Estimated covariances for individuals and across siblings in pure environmental model in table 7A.6.

| | | Individuals | | | | Cross siblings | | | |
|---|---|---|---|---|---|---|---|---|---|
| | | $S$ | $OC_i$ | $OC_{67}$ | $\ln Y_{73}$ | $S$ | $OC_i$ | $OC_{67}$ | $\ln Y_{73}$ |
| MZs | $S$ | 9.37[a] | | | | 7.22[a] | | | |
| | $OC_i$ | 3.92[a] | 5.96 | | | 3.56 | 3.05[b] | | |
| | $OC_{67}$ | 3.42[b] | 2.30[b] | 4.57 | | 2.80 | 1.76[b] | 1.79[b] | |
| | $\ln Y_{73}$ | 0.74 | 0.47 | 0.41 | 0.30 | 0.69 | 0.43 | 0.31 | 0.16 |
| DZs | $S$ | 9.37[b] | | | | 4.65[b] | | | |
| | $OC_i$ | 3.92[b] | 5.96 | | | 2.29[b] | 1.96 | | |
| | $OC_{67}$ | 3.42[a] | 2.30[a] | 4.57 | | 1.80[b] | 1.13[a] | 1.15[b] | |
| | $\ln Y_{73}$ | 0.74 | 0.47 | 0.41 | 0.30 | 0.44[b] | 0.28[b] | 0.20[b] | 0.10 |

[a] $\dfrac{|u^*| - |u'|}{\text{actual}} \geq 0.01$.

[b] $\dfrac{|u'| - |u^*|}{\text{actual}} \geq 0.01$, where $|u'|$ is the absolute value of actual minus estimated in table 7.1, and $|u^*|$ is the absolute value of actual minus estimated in table 7A.6.

## Table 7A.8
### Basic model with measurement error in schooling (25 parameters).

| | $G_1$ | $N_1$ | $G_2$ | $G_3$ | $G_4$ | $u_1$ | $u_2$ | $u_3$ | $u_4$ | $S$ | $OC_i$ | $OC_{67}$ |
|---|---|---|---|---|---|---|---|---|---|---|---|---|
| *Reduced form equations* | | | | | | | | | | | | |
| $S$ | 2.09 | 1.71 | | | | 1 | | | | | | |
| | (20.50) | (13.70) | | | | | | | | | | |
| $OC_i$ | 0.84 | 1.05 | 1.14 | | | 0.64 | 1 | | | | | |
| | (6.998) | (8.24) | (16.86) | | | (1.24) | | | | | | |
| $OC_{67}$ | 0.81 | 0.66 | 0.36 | 0.79 | | 0.94 | 0.051 | 1 | | | | |
| | (7.26) | (5.42) | (4.78) | (12.98) | | (1.22) | (0.41) | | | | | |
| $\ln Y_{73}$ | 0.21 | 0.15 | 0.093 | 0.020 | 0.030 | 0.078 | 0.0010 | 0.021 | 1 | | | |
| | (7.71) | (5.18) | (4.42) | (0.80) | (23.66) | (1.29) | (0.46) | (1.22) | | | | |

*Other estimates*

$\sigma^2_{u_1} = 0.67 \quad \sigma^2_{u_2} = 2.61$
$\sigma^2_{u_3} = 2.13 \quad \sigma^2_{u_4} = 0.129$
$\sigma^2_w = 1.51$

*Normalizations and restrictions*: A, B, C, D, E, F, G.
*Functional value*: = 13435.14.
*Notes*: see table 7.1.

Table 7A.9

Basic model with proportional measurement error ($\sigma_w^2/\sigma_{Y_j}^2$ is same for first three indicators) (25 parameters).

| | $G_1$ | $N_1$ | $G_2$ | $G_3$ | $G_4$ | $u_1$ | $u_2$ | $u_3$ | $u_4$ | $S$ | $OC_i$ | $OC_{67}$ |
|---|---|---|---|---|---|---|---|---|---|---|---|---|
| *Reduced form equations* | | | | | | | | | | | | |
| $S$ | 2.09 | 1.71 | | | | 1 | | | | | | |
| | (20.51) | (13.71) | | | | | | | | | | |
| $OC_i$ | 0.84 | | 1.14 | | | 0.59 | 1 | | | | | |
| | (7.0) | | (18.50) | | | (0.96) | | | | | | |
| $OC_{67}$ | 0.81 | | 0.36 | 0.79 | | 0.87 | 0.09 | 1 | | | | |
| | (7.26) | | (4.78) | (12.98) | | (0.95) | (0.48) | | | | | |
| $\ln Y_{73}$ | 0.21 | 0.15 | 0.093 | 0.02 | 0.30 | 0.072 | 0.0029 | 0.032 | 1 | | | |
| | (7.71) | (5.19) | (4.44) | (0.80) | (23.66) | (0.10) | (0.42) | | | | | |

*Other estimates*

$\sigma_{u1}^2 = 0.72$  $\sigma_{u2}^2 = 1.78$
$\sigma_{u3}^2 = 1.46$  $\sigma_{u4}^2 = 0.129$
$\sigma_w^2 = 1.45$  $\sigma_s^2/\sigma_{Y_i}^2$  $Y_i = S, OC_i, OC_{67}$

*Normalizations and restrictions*: A, B, C, D, E, F, G.
*Functional value*: = 13435.14.
*Notes*: see table 7.1.

# CHAPTER 8

# SOME MAJOR IMPLICATIONS OF THE LATENT VARIABLE ESTIMATES: INTERGENERATIONAL SOCIAL MOBILITY AND EQUALITY OF OPPORTUNITY VERSUS EQUALITY OF OUTCOME

## 8.1. Introduction

We now use the results of Chapter 7 to examine two important issues which have had little or no prior empirical investigation.

In section 8.2 we consider the implications of our estimates for intergenerational social mobility. Our estimates indicate that there is considerable intergenerational mobility even though family effects are quite important for the intragenerational distribution of socioeconomic success.

In section 8.3 we focus on the question of the contribution of equality of opportunity to the equality of outcome. We first discuss alternative definitions of equality of opportunity and indicate why we favor one which does not incorporate inequalities of genotype. Given this definition, our estimates imply that inequality of opportunity accounts for less than 20% of the variance in outcomes. Thus, equalizing opportunities in this sense would to a limited degree equalize outcomes without necessarily requiring any inefficient disincentives. However, total family effects, including genetics, account for about 60% of the variance of outcomes. Therefore to obtain the goal of those who wish to reduce the degree of inequality beyond that included in our preferred definition, the trade-off between efficiency and equity inherent in transfer and compensatory programs has to be faced.

## 8.2. Social mobility

In previous chapters we investigated the effects of various measured and unmeasured variables on *intra*generational inequality in schooling, occupational status, and earnings. But in our survey in Chapter 1 we indicated that people judge the fairness of a society, in part, by its degree of *inter*generational social mobility or immobility.

There are a variety of reasons, detailed below, why information on intragenerational inequality does not indicate the sources of, or the effects of various policies on, intergenerational inequality or social mobility. In this section we examine a number of issues connected with social mobility.

### 8.2.1. Social mobility and immobility

Social mobility is defined by the extent of agreement between the income (or some other indicator) of a child and his or her parents. There are a number of ways of portraying or measuring this sameness. For example, in subsection 8.2.4 we present a table which contains the probability of the offspring being in the same tenth of the earnings distribution as were his or her parents. A useful summary measure of this table or of social mobility in general is the intergenerational correlation coefficient, $c_{PC}$, introduced in Chapter 3. As in section 3.3, assume a model for the present discounted value of lifetime earnings in which

$$Y_P = G_P + N_P, \tag{8.1}$$

$$Y_C = G_C + N_C, \tag{8.2}$$

where

$G$    is an overall genetic index,

$N$  is an overall environmental index which includes family and individual specific environment,

$P$  is for parent, and

$C$  is for child.

Then in equilibrium, in which the prices and the variance of $G$ and $N$ remain constant from one generation to the next, the phenotypic correlation of parent and child is

$$c_{PC} = \frac{\sigma_{G_C G_P}}{\sigma_G^2} h^2 + \frac{\sigma_{N_P N_C}}{\sigma_N^2} e^2 + \frac{\sigma_{G_P N_C} + \sigma_{G_C N_P}}{\sigma_G \sigma_N} he, \qquad (8.3)$$

where

$h^2$ = broad heritability = $\sigma_G^2/\sigma_Y^2$, and

$e^2$ = environmentability = $\sigma_N^2/\sigma_Y^2$.

We also showed in section 3.3 that when assortive mating on phenotypes occurs, in equilibrium

$$c_{PC}^g = \frac{\sigma_{G_C G_P}}{\sigma_G^2} = \tfrac{1}{2} d(1 + b), \qquad (8.4)$$

where

$b$ = the phenotypic correlation of parents or assortive mating, and

$d$ = the ratio of additive to total genotypic variance.

Suppose for simplicity that $\sigma_{G_P N_C} = \sigma_{G_C N_P} = 0$. Then since $e^2 + h^2 = 1$, social mobility or $c_{PC}$ is a weighted average of the intergenerational genotypic and environmental correlations.

In eq. (8.3) $c_{PC}$ can range from $+1$ to $-1$. If $c_{PC}$ equals 1, a child's income can be predicted exactly from his or her parents' and there is complete immobility or no social mobility. If $c_{PC}$ equals 0, there is no (linear) relationship between child's and parents' income and complete social mobility. If $c_{PC} = -1$, a child's income can be predicted exactly from his or her parents'. A parent with the highest income has a child with the lowest and a grandchild with the highest income. Thus, there is complete cyclical immobility. The further $c_{PC}$ is from 0, the smaller is social mobility.

Increases in $\sigma_{G_P G_C}/\sigma_G^2$ or $\sigma_{N_P N_C}/\sigma_N^2$ raise $c_{PC}$. The parent–child genetic correlation need not be fixed. For example, changes in marriage or in fertility patterns, both of which may be influenced by social policies, can alter this correlation. Even if this correlation is fixed, $c_{PC}$ can be altered by changing $h^2$, $e^2$, or the parent–child environmental correlation which can be influenced by a variety of factors. For example, the child-rearing practices experienced by a person while a child can influence the choice of such practices when he or she becomes a parent. Such practices may be a function of variables like after-tax family income which can be altered by public policy.

The effects of these intergenerational genetic and environmental correlations are related to, but are not the same as, the previous estimates of the effects of genetics and environment on the intragenerational variance in earnings and other variables.

Part of this difference occurs because of differences in the formula for intra- and intergenerational correlations. For example, the DZ genetic correlation given in section 3.3 is

$$\sigma_{GG'}/\sigma_G^2 = c_{DZ}^g = \tfrac{1}{2} d(1 + bdh^2) + \tfrac{1}{4}(1 - d). \tag{8.5}$$

Generally (8.5) differs from and in this sample is an upper bound to (8.4). Also, we expect $\sigma_{N_P N_C}$ to differ from and be less than $\sigma_{NN'}$, because the twins share the same womb, usually are brought up together, and are reared in the same social milieu.

While we expect $\sigma_{N_P N_C}$ to be smaller than $\sigma_{NN'}$, we still expect $\sigma_{N_P N_C}$ to be positive because the parents' environment in (8.1) incorporates their own childhood experiences which may effect their tastes and preferences for types of child rearing. Moreover, *per capita* family income provided by parents while a person is being raised may effect his or her subsequent preferences for number of children and expenditures per child. (For models of this type see Easterlin, 1975, or Cavalli-Sforza and Feldman, 1973).

Thus, on both environmental and genetic grounds, we expect $c_{PC}$ to be no greater than the corresponding cross-sibling phenotypic correlation. Since we are assuming that $\sigma_Y^2$, $\sigma_G^2$ and $\sigma_N^2$ are constant from one generation to another, the argument above suggests that $\sigma_{Y_P Y_C} \leq \sigma_{YY}$.

The intergenerational correlations also differ from an analysis of he intragenerational contributions of genetics, family, and other environments for two additional reasons. Within a generation we know that $h^2 + e^2 = 1$ if $\sigma_{NG} = 0$. In the intergenerational correlation formula in (8.3), only part of $h^2$ and of $e^2$ enter into $c_{PC}$.

Finally intergenerational correlations depend on the ratio of the covariance of $Y_P Y_C$ to the variance of $Y$. It is certainly possible or the necessarily positive variance of $Y$ to be accompanied by a covariance which can be positive, negative, or zero. Moreover, Conlisk (1974), in a model examined in more detail below, has shown that some policies could increase the covariance but decrease the variance. Such policies reduce intragenerational inequality but increase social immobility.

## 3.2.2. *Estimating $c_{PC}$ using DZ twins*

In principle it is possible to estimate social mobility for any variable of interest. The major limitation in making such estimates is the lack of appropriate data. Of course many samples have information on parents' and offspring's completed years of schooling and parents' occupational status and offspring's current occupational status. A few samples such as that used by Sewell and Hauser (1975) have parents' and children's current earnings. But no sample has data on parents' and children's present discounted value of lifetime earnings or even earnings at the same age for the two generations.

Consider the relationship of $c_{PC}$ and the cross-sibling correlation for DZ pairs, $c'$. As was shown in section 3.3, the formula for $c' = c^g_{PC}$ is

$$c' = \frac{\sigma_{GG'}}{\sigma_G^2} h^2 + \frac{\sigma_{NN'}}{\sigma_N^2} e^2 + 2 \frac{\sigma_{NG'}}{\sigma_N \sigma_G} he. \tag{8.6}$$

Again for simplicity assume all genotypic, environmental correlations are zero. Thus, both $c_{PC}$ and $c'$ are weighted averages with weights of $h^2$ and $e^2$.

We maintain that $\sigma_{NN'} \geq \sigma_{N_P N_C}$. We now demonstrate that in nearly all cases $\sigma_{GG'}/\sigma_G^2 \geq \sigma_{G_PG_C}/\sigma_G^2$. Subtracting (8.4) from (8.5, yields

$$c_{DZ}^g - c_{PC}^g = \frac{\sigma_{GG'}}{\sigma_G^2} - \frac{\sigma_{G_CG_P}}{\sigma_G^2} = w = \tfrac{1}{4}(1-d) - \tfrac{1}{2}db\,(1-dh^2). \quad (8.7)$$

We know that $0 \leq d \leq 1$, $h^2 \leq 1$, and $-1 \leq b \leq 1$. If $b \leq 0$, it is clear that $w \geq 0$. If $b > 0$, $w \geq 0$ if

$$\tfrac{1}{2} \geq \frac{db\,(1-dh^2)}{1-d}. \qquad (8.7a)$$

The inequality in (8.7a) need not hold. There are combinations of $b$, $d$, and $h^2$, such as $b$ and $d$ high and $h^2$ low, for which (8.7a) and $w$ are negative. We have an estimate of $h^2$ and estimates of $d$ conditional on $b$. Thus, we can estimate whether $w$ is positive. Our estimates suggest that a positive value of $w$ is not likely.

It is possible to adjust $c'$ to obtain a better estimate of $c_{PC}$. In table 7.4 we used the theoretical formula for $c_{DZ}^g$ along with estimates of both this correlation coefficient and $h^2$ to estimate values for pairs of $b$ and $d$ using (8.5). Using (8.7) and estimates of $h^2$, $d$, and $b$, we can adjust the $c'$ in (8.6) by replacing $c_{DZ}^g$ with $c_{PC}^g$.

Of course earnings and other variables vary over the life cycle.[1] Suppose current income $Y_t$ is expressed as

$$Y_t = \hat{Y} + v_t, \qquad (8.8)$$

where

$\hat{Y}$   is the permanent or lifetime variable, and
$v_t$   is transitory income (including life cycle variations) which is uncorrelated with $\hat{Y}$.

Then with $\hat{Y}$ and $v_t$ uncorrelated

$$\sigma_{Y_tY_t} = \sigma_{\hat{Y}\hat{Y}'} + \sigma_{v_tv_t}, \qquad (8.9)$$

---

[1]Lillard and Willis (1976) estimate $\sigma_{\hat{Y}\hat{Y}}/\sigma_Y^2$ to be about 0.75 for earnings for all males continuously reporting earnings for seven years in the Michigan Income Dynamic Sample. For whites around age 50 we suspect that the permanent figure is higher.

$$c'_t = \frac{\sigma_{Y_t Y'_t}}{\sigma^2_{Y_t}} = \frac{\sigma_{\hat{Y}\hat{Y}'}}{\sigma^2_{\hat{Y}}} \frac{\sigma^2_{\hat{Y}}}{\sigma^2_{Y_t}} + \frac{\sigma_{v_t v'_t}}{\sigma^2_{v_t}} \frac{\sigma^2_{v_t}}{\sigma^2_{Y_t}}. \qquad (8.10)$$

Since $\sigma^2_{\hat{Y}} + \sigma^2_{v_t} = \sigma^2_{Y_t}$, in (8.10) $c'_t$ is a weighed average of the cross-twin correlation in $\hat{Y}$ and $v_t$. If $v_t v'_t$ were zero, $c'_t$ would be a downward biased estimate of the cross-sibling correlation in lifetime earnings because $\sigma^2_{\hat{Y}}/\sigma^2_{Y_t} < 1$ owing to the existence of transitory income. The greater is the relative importance of transitory income $(\sigma^2_{v_t}/\sigma^2_Y)$, the greater is this bias. But $v$ includes life cycle variations in annual earnings. It seems likely that siblings' investments in on-the-job training are correlated, so $\sigma^2_{v_t v'_t} > 0$. The closer is $\sigma_{v_t v'_t}/\sigma^2_{v_t}$ to $\sigma_{\hat{Y}\hat{Y}'}/\sigma^2_{\hat{Y}}$ the smaller is the bias. We suspect that the bias from using $Y_t$ rather than $\hat{Y}$ is not large. Therefore, we generally continue to treat $c'$ as an upper bound estimate for the $c_{PC}$ based on the present discounted value of lifetime earnings, etc.

## 8.2.3. Estimates of social mobility

In this subsection we present and discuss our estimates of the intergenerational correlation for several variables. For both education and occupational status we have data on the twins' parents as supplied by the twins. For these variables and for earnings we also can use the estimate suggested in subsection 8.2.2.

In table 8.1 the direct estimate of the intergenerational correlation is 0.3 for education and 0.2 for occupational status.[2] The DZ cross-twin estimates for these two variables are 0.55 (0.52) and 0.21 (0.18), respectively, with the numbers in parentheses including the correlation for misclassification error given in section 5.6. The DZ estimate for occupational status is about equal to the direct intergenerational estimate. Possible explanations for this include that there is greater measurement error in the status

[2]This estimate is in line with others from the same cohort. See Taubman and Wales (1974).

Table 8.1
Intergenerational correlation coefficients.

|                                              | $c_{PC}$ | $c'$        | Adjusted $c'^a$ |
|----------------------------------------------|----------|-------------|-----------------|
| Years of education (father, child)           | 0.30     | 0.55(0.52)  | 0.49            |
| Years of education (mother, child)           | 0.30     | 0.55(0.52)  | 0.49            |
| Years of education (mid parent, child)       | 0.30     | 0.55(0.52)  | 0.49            |
| Occupational status[b] (father, child)       | 0.21     | 0.21(0.18)  | 0.18            |
| In earnings (mid parent, child)              | n.a.     | 0.30(0.38)  | 0.25            |

[a]Calculated as $c' + (c_{PC}^g - c_{DZ}^g) h^2$ for an assumed assortive mating of 0.50, which is approximately at the observed value of 0.55 for education of parents.
[b]Duncan scale.
n.a. = not available.

measures for brothers than for fathers,[3] the annual versus lifetime problem discussed above, sampling fluctuations, and/or that $c_{DZ}^g$ is less than $c_{PC}^g$.

Table 8.2 presents estimates for the ratio of the additive to total genetic variance, $d$, the parental phenotypic correlation or assortive mating coefficient, $b$, and the parent–child genotypic correlation. (See section 7.2 for details.) For the most part the estimates of $d$ are 0.5 or lower, while the parent–child genotypic correlations are 0.31 or lower. The value of the DZ genotypic correlation used in these calculations is 0.34 ($\lambda$ in table 7.1). Without additional information, it is not possible to choose among the various estimates in table 8.2. The DZ cross-sibling correlation is a weighted average of the cross-sibling genetic and environmental correlations. Hence, if we replace the DZ genetic correlation with the parent–child genetic correlation, we obtain a

[3]Father's occupational status is constructed as the average of the two brothers' answers (after conversion to the Duncan scale). Averaging should reduce measurement error.

Table 8.2
Estimated range of $c_{PC}^g$, for education, occupational status, and ln earnings.

| Assumed values for $b$ | Estimated values | | | | | |
|---|---|---|---|---|---|---|
| | Education | | Occupational status[a] | | ln earnings | |
| | $d$ | $c_{PC}^g$ | $d$ | $c_{PC}^g$ | $d$ | $c_{PC}^g$ |
| 1.00 | 0.10 | 0.1 | 0.30 | 0.30 | 0.31 | 0.31 |
| 0.50 | 0.20 | 0.15 | 0.33 | 0.25 | 0.33 | 0.25 |
| 0.25 | 0.30 | 0.18 | 0.33 | 0.21 | 0.38 | 0.24 |
| 0.00 | 0.40 | 0.20 | 0.40 | 0.20 | 0.40 | 0.20 |
| −0.25 | 0.40 | 0.15 | 0.45 | 0.17 | 0.44 | 0.16 |
| −0.50 | 0.50 | 0.12 | 0.50 | 0.12 | 0.53 | 0.13 |
| −0.73 | 0.50 | 0.08 | 0.50 | 0.08 | 1.00 | 0.17 |

[a] $h^2 = 0.31$ and 0.29 for mature and initial occupations. This column is calculated for $h^2 = 0.30$.
Note when there are two values of $d$, the one in the unit interval is shown.
*Source*: Table 7.4 and text in section 7.2.

better estimate of the parent–child phenotypic correlation. For education, we have a direct estimate of $b$ of 0.55. In our model there are four latent genetic variables and these variables need not have the same assortive mating coefficients, especially if people choose mates on both earnings and nonearnings grounds. Suppose, however, that we use an estimate of $b$ of 0.5 for education, earnings, and occupation. Then we can replace $c_{DZ}^g$ with $c_{PC}^g$ in (8.6) to obtain an estimate of $c_{PC}$. The results are given in the last column of table 8.1. The estimate for education is somewhat closer to the direct estimate of 0.3, while the estimate for occupation is a bit below the direct estimate, perhaps for the reasons given above.

We can push the analysis one step further. Given our estimates of $c_{PC}$, $h^2$, and $c_{PC}^g$, we can solve for the parent–child environmental correlation in (8.3). This is given by 0.38 and 0.15 for education and occupation, respectively. From table 7.5 we can calculate the proportion of total environmental variance that is common to the twins as $\sigma_N^2/(\sigma_N^2 + \Sigma\sigma_{u_i}^2)$. For education and occupation this is 64 and 30%, respectively (with the latter averaged over initial and 1967 occupations). Thus, parent–child environmental correlations are large relative to the corresponding genotypic correlations, but roughly one-half the size of environmental correlations of twins.

We cannot be as specific for earnings. But assuming that the covariance between $G$ and $N$ terms is zero, we can use (8.3), our estimate of $h^2$, and the estimates of $\sigma_{G_C G_P}/\sigma_G^2$ in table 8.2 conditional on various values of $b$. For all the values of $b$, we calculate that genetics contribute about 0.06 to 0.13 to the $c_{PC}$ estimate of 0.25. Of course, the remaining part of the estimated $c_{PC}$ comes from $\sigma_{NN'}$ rather than $\sigma_{N_C N_P}$. But all in all our estimates suggest that genetics do not play a large role in intergenerational links even if they do play an important role in intragenerational differences.

The above calculations, of course, are based on a number of assumptions which include that society is in a steady state equilibrium. Since, for example, the distribution of education was different for the twins than for their parents, the results should be treated as at best rough orders of magnitude.

### 8.2.4. Intergenerational handicaps and advantages

The previous subsection showed that there is a positive correlation between the parents' and their child's education, occupational status, and earnings. Thus, children who come from below average families are more likely to remain below average, etc. It is not obvious, however, how much of an advantage or handicap is conveyed by an intergenerational correlation of, say, 0.3.

As an aid in judging the implications of such a correlation, let us examine table 8.3 which indicates the probability of a child falling into the same tenth of the distribution as does his or her parents.[4] If the parent–child correlation, $r$, is zero, the prob-

---

[4] The calculations assume parent and child distributions are bivariate normally distributed with the mean 0 and variance 1 for both generations. The calculations assume that the parent is at the point of the particular tenth which divides its area in half. There are only trivial differences which result if the parent is placed at the midpoint of the interval or at either end.

Table 8.3
Probability of a child being in the same tenth of the income distribution as his or her parents.

| Parents' income tenth | If parent–child correlation, $r$, is: | | | | | |
|---|---|---|---|---|---|---|
| | 0 | 0.1 | 0.3 | 0.5 | 0.7 | 0.9 |
| Bottom | 0.1 | 0.131 | 0.204 | 0.298 | 0.428 | 0.676 |
| 2nd | 0.1 | 0.111 | 0.135 | 0.165 | 0.217 | 0.371 |
| 3rd | 0.1 | 0.105 | 0.116 | 0.134 | 0.168 | 0.280 |
| 4th | 0.1 | 0.102 | 0.108 | 0.121 | 0.148 | 0.243 |
| 5th | 0.1 | 0.101 | 0.105 | 0.116 | 0.141 | 0.229 |
| 6th | 0.1 | 0.101 | 0.105 | 0.116 | 0.141 | 0.229 |
| 7th | 0.1 | 0.102 | 0.108 | 0.121 | 0.148 | 0.243 |
| 8th | 0.1 | 0.105 | 0.116 | 0.134 | 0.168 | 0.280 |
| 9th | 0.1 | 0.111 | 0.135 | 0.165 | 0.217 | 0.371 |
| Top | 0.1 | 0.131 | 0.204 | 0.298 | 0.428 | 0.676 |

*Note*: parent and child are assumed to have a bivariate normal distribution with mean 0, variance 1, and $r$ is as specified. The calculations assume that the parents' earnings are at the point of the particular tenth which divides its area in half, i.e. at the twentieth-tile.

ability of the child being in the same tenth as his or her parents is 10% at all income levels. When $r = 0.3$, the probability of the child being in the same decile as his or her parents is always greater than 10% and the differential is greater the further we move from the median. For example, 20% of those offspring whose parents are in the top decile are themselves in the top tenth. As $r$ increases, the probability of the child being in the same tenth as are his or her parents also increases.

Table 8.4 gives the probability of a child's position in the income distribution being greater than or equal to his or her parents' position. When $r = 0.3$, 85% of the children whose parents are in the second tenth have incomes which place them in the second tenth or higher while the remaining 15% are in the lowest decile. Again, when $r = 0.3$, 59% of those whose parents are in the middle fifth have earnings that place them that high in the distribution.

To summarize the results in table 8.4, it is useful to consider parents below the average and those in the fifth to top tenth. For

Table 8.4
Probability of a child having the same or higher income as
his or her parents.

| Parents' income tenth | If parent–child correlation, $r$, is: | | | | |
|---|---|---|---|---|---|
| | 0.1 | 0.3 | 0.5 | 0.7 | 0.9 |
| Bottom | 1.00 | 1.00 | 1.00 | 1.00 | 1.00 |
| 2nd | 0.88 | 0.85 | 0.81 | 0.78 | 0.79 |
| 3rd | 0.78 | 0.75 | 0.72 | 0.70 | 0.70 |
| 4th | 0.69 | 0.67 | 0.65 | 0.64 | 0.66 |
| 5th | 0.60 | 0.59 | 0.59 | 0.59 | 0.63 |
| 6th | 0.50 | 0.52 | 0.53 | 0.55 | 0.60 |
| 7th | 0.41 | 0.44 | 0.47 | 0.51 | 0.58 |
| 8th | 0.32 | 0.37 | 0.42 | 0.47 | 0.57 |
| 9th | 0.23 | 0.29 | 0.35 | 0.43 | 0.58 |
| 10th | 0.13 | 0.20 | 0.30 | 0.43 | 0.68 |

*Note*: see table 8.3 for notes.

low-income parents, the probability that their offspring have income greater than their own decreases as $r$ increases till $r = 0.7$ and then rises slightly. For the wealthier parents, the probability of their offspring having higher incomes increases as $r$ increases. When $r$ is small parents have little association with their children's outcome and the numbers in table 8.4 for $r = 0.1$ are like those that would be obtained from a univariate normal table. As $r$ increases a child is more likely to be where his or her parents are, which explains the difference in results for those above and below the middle tenth. The results for $r = 0.9$ for low-income parents occur because the children are so like their parents.

In tables 8.3 and 8.4 the calculations assume that the parents are at the point in a tenth that divides its area in half, i.e. the twentieth-tile. Alternative calculations which assume either that the parents are at the bottom, the top, or the numerical midpoint of the decile yield nearly identical results.

### 8.2.5. *Altering social mobility and intragenerational inequality*

In this subsection we examine various policies that can be used to alter both social mobility and intragenerational inequality. A useful framework within which to explore these issues is provided by a model presented in Conlisk (1974).[5] In our notation his model can be expressed as

$$Y_C = A_C + \alpha Y_P + u_c, \tag{8.11}$$

$$A_C = G_C + \beta Y_P + v_C, \tag{8.12}$$

$$G_C = \gamma G_P + w_C, \tag{8.13}$$

where

$A$    is "ability" scaled to have a unit coefficient,
$G$    is a genetic index scaled to have a unit coefficient,
$Y$    is income,
$u$    is a random variable,
$v$    is a random variable,
$w$    is a random variable,
$P$    is parent, and
$C$    is child.

In a steady state the same equations hold for each generation.

We can solve this differential equation model for $\sigma_Y^2$, $\sigma_{Y_P Y_C}$, and $c_{PC}$, where the last term is defined as $\sigma_{Y_P Y_C}/\sigma_Y^2$. Assuming that $u$ and $w$ and $v$ and $w$ are uncorrelated with each other within a generation, that none of the random variables are correlated across generations, and imposing the normalization that $\sigma_G^2 = 1$, Conlisk shows that the steady solution of this model is:[6]

$$\sigma_Y^2 = [\sigma^2 + (2\mu - 1)]/[1 - (\alpha + \beta)^2], \tag{8.14}$$

$$c_{PC} = \alpha + \beta + \lambda \mu \gamma / \sigma_Y^2, \tag{8.15}$$

where

$\sigma^2 = \sigma_u^2 + \sigma_v^2 + 2\sigma_{uv}$,
$\lambda \; = (1 - \gamma)^2$,
$\mu \; = [1 - \lambda (\alpha + \beta)]^{-1}$.

[5]Recently biologists have also begun to examine models in which there is inheritance of the phenotype through family environment as well as inheritance of genes of DNA. See Cavalli-Sforza and Feldman (1973).
[6]Stability requires $\alpha + \beta < 1$, $\gamma < 1$. See Conlisk (1974).

Conlisk also shows that

$$\frac{\partial c_{PC}}{\partial (\alpha + \beta)} = \frac{\sigma^2 [\sigma^2 + 2\lambda\mu + \mu^2 (\lambda - 1)[1 - (\alpha + \beta)^2]] + \lambda\mu^2}{[\sigma^2 + \lambda (2\mu - 1)]^2},$$

(8.16)

$$\frac{\partial c_{PC}}{\partial \sigma^2} = \frac{-\lambda\mu\gamma}{[1 - (\alpha + \beta)^2][\sigma_u^2]^2} < 0,$$

(8.17)

$$\frac{\partial \sigma_Y^2}{\partial (\alpha + \beta)} = \frac{2 [\lambda\gamma\mu^2 + (\alpha + \beta) \sigma_Y^2]}{1 - (\alpha + \beta)^2} > 0,$$

(8.18)

$$\frac{\partial \sigma_Y^2}{\partial \sigma^2} = \frac{1}{1 - (\alpha + \beta)^2} > 0.$$

(8.19)

In this model $\alpha$ and $\beta$ indicate the effects of the systematic part of family environment, which here is assumed to be family income, on ability and income. Policies of equalization of opportunity can reduce $\alpha$ or $\beta$. From (8.16) we see that a reduction in these parameters reduces the parent–child correlation. But from (8.18) such a reduction lessens $\sigma_Y^2$ or intragenerational inequality. Other parts of the environment are included in the random terms, $u$, $v$, and $w$. From (8.17) and (8.19) we observe that a decrease in $\sigma^2$ will increase $c_{PC}$ but reduce $\sigma_Y^2$. The different effects of $\sigma^2$ and $\alpha + \beta$ on $c_{PC}$ occur because environments correlated over generations add to parent–child phenotypic correlations, while nonsystematic environmental variation reduce parent–child correlations. However, both types of environment add to the variance in $Y$.

Unfortunately, our model does not generate exactly the parameters needed in Conlisk's model since we calculate the total family effect and not just that dependent on $Y_P$. Put another way, we have calculated that for years of schooling $\sigma_{N_P N_C}/\sigma_N^2$ is 0.38 but $\sigma_{NN'}/\sigma_N^2$ is 0.64; thus, parent–child environmental correlations differ from the total family environmental correlations.

On the other hand if equality of opportunity means a zero environmental correlation over generations, then from (8.3) $c_{PC} = c_{PC}^g h^2$. We know that for earnings $h^2 = 0.45$, and that $c_{PC}^g$ in table 8.2 ranges from 0.13 to 0.31. Thus, such an equality of opportunity policy would yield a $c_{PC}$ ranging from 0.06 to 0.14, which estimates are close to complete social mobility. If this equality of opportunity program also set the effect of family environment on $\sigma_Y^2$ to zero, then $\sigma_Y^2$ would be reduced by 12% and $\sigma_G^2$ as a ratio of the new $\sigma_Y^2$ would be about 50%. In other words, there still would be substantial variation within a generation attributable to one's parents even if there were small intergenerational links.

### 8.3. Equality of opportunity and equality of outcome

Several reasons for wishing to distinguish equality of outcome and equality of opportunity are intimately bound up with the issues of equality and efficiency. On the one hand some people argue that the fairness or humaneness of a society should be judged in terms of how unequal is the distribution of income or, more broadly, economic welfare. Others argue that fairness should be examined not in terms of outcome, but in terms of whether each individual has the same chances in a race.[7] In this view it is not fair to deny a person the chance to develop his or her skills and capabilities just because his or her parents *cannot* or *will not* invest in their offspring's human capital.

Many people are concerned about inequality in income distribution because of the low standard of living with its debilitating effects for those in the left-hand tail of the distribution and because of the conspicuous consumption and power of those in the right-hand tail of the distribution. Yet even individuals who acknowledge the legitimacy of either of these concerns criticize some income distribution schemes on the grounds that their financing and eligibility rules create so much economic inefficiency that society is better off tolerating the inequality of outcomes. But if the source of the unequal outcomes is inequality of opportunity, it is often possible to increase efficiency while reducing inequality. For example, government loan guarantees may eliminate those

---

[7]See Brittain (1977, ch. 1). There is some question as to the appropriateness of allowing innate or genetic abilities to influence the winning of the race.

capital market imperfections that inhibit socially profitable investments in human capital. Indeed, precisely on these grounds Okun (1975) voices the hope that much of inequality is due to lack of opportunity.[8] However, if inequality of opportunity is not a major component of inequality in outcomes, hard choices on the "big trade-off" between equality and efficiency have to be made.

## The concept of equality of opportunity

Equality of outcome is defined as everyone having the same income or, more broadly, economic welfare.[9] This definition seems to be universally accepted. Equality of opportunity, however, is often defined differently by various writers. Klappholz (1972) provides a summary of some of these views. A major issue, on which there is ongoing debate, is the treatment of advantages and disadvantages conferred by genetic endowments. Several writers, who are in favor of more income redistribution or related policies, include differences in ability arising from genetic endowments in their definition of inequality of opportunity and in their argument of the need for more governmental action. Examples include Brittain (1977) and Sewell (1971).

Others, whose philosphical and political views span a wide spectrum, have argued that genetic differences are not part of inequality of opportunity. Examples include Becker (1975), Bowen (1977), Okun (1975), and Tawney (1961). Okun, for example, says on p. 76, "Differences in natural abilities are generally accepted as relevant characteristics that are being tested in the race rather than as unfair headstarts and handicaps. The inheritance of natural abilities is on one side of the line of unequal opportunity, and the advantages of family position clearly on the other". Okun on the same page also asks, "Does the unequal

[8]See Okun (1975, p.83)

[9]Sometimes it is defined in terms of income equalling needs for each person. Needs can be defined in terms of utility or economic welfare. See Klappholz (1972) or Sen (1973).

opportunity line begin at difference in prenatal influences? Or at the benefits of better childhood health care, achievement-oriented training, educational attainment, family assistance in job placement, inheritance of physical property?" Our answer to this question, which is only partially dictated by the available data, is that inequality of opportunity begins in the womb, with prenatal conditions which are subject to policy influences.

There obviously is not unanimity as to the definition of equality of opportunity. We think, however, the distinction made by Becker, Bowen, Tawney, and Okun in which genetic endowments are not part of inequality of opportunity is the more meaningful one. It is more meaningful partly because it corresponds to common usage, as when programs such as Head Start are advocated, and because it generates a greater social consensus in defining equity. Moreover, and perhaps more importantly, elimination of handicaps arising from family environment need not involve efficiency costs, whereas offsetting poor genes does. Of course the Brittain and Sewell value judgement that substantial inequality of outcomes based on whom one's parents are is grounds for redistribution need not be incorrect, but this is simply a different issue from how important is inequality of opportunity given our preferred definitions.

Becker presents a model which was discussed in Chapter 2. In his model the optimal investment in human capital depends on prices, interest rates, family income, tastes, and genetic endowments. As was shown in Chapter 2, Becker models inequality of opportunity as arising because of imperfect capital markets which alter the shape and position of the marginal supply of funds curve.

We argued in Chapters 2 and 4 that the across-family variation in common environment estimates the contribution of differences in family income to investment in human capital. In this chapter we treat this estimate as indicating the extent of inequality of opportunity. We also try to refine the estimate for factors not discussed previously.

Table 7.5 presented the total (the sum of direct and indirect) contributions of the various $G$, $N$, and $u$ variables to each of the four dependent variables in our model. As shown in the table, common environment accounts for 12 and 41% of the variance of the ln of 1973 earnings and of schooling, respectively. The relative size of these two percentages is not surprising. Presumably parents have much greater impact over schooling decisions of their offspring than over many postschooling decisions. Moreover, the variance in schooling makes only a small contribution to the variance of earnings.

These results suggest that inequality of opportunity has a substantial impact on the variance of schooling, one type of investment in human capital, but only a very modest impact on the variance in ln earnings. The number taken at face value would indicate that even if it had been possible to eliminate all the variance in family environment when this cohort was being reared, the inequality in the ln earnings outcome would not have been reduced greatly. This conclusion and its generalization to the population are, however, subject to certain qualifications. We begin with some that are relevant to the cohort studied and then consider the difficulties in generalizing to other cohorts.

The combined effect of genetics and common environment for any variable is given by the cross-twin correlation $c^*$, for MZ twins. The genetic component is given by multiplying the difference between the MZ and DZ cross-twin correlation, $c^* - c'$, by an (estimated) constant $k$ which exceeds 1. The common environment estimate is then given by

$$\frac{1}{k}\left[c' - \left(1 - \frac{1}{k}\right)c^*\right].$$

If our estimates of $c^*$ and/or $c'$ are biased, then our estimates of genetic and/or common environment may be biased. Unfortunately our estimates of $c^*$ and $c'$ may be affected by response bias. For example, both brothers may be more likely to answer our survey only if neither is an exceptionally low-wage earner. We would expect that such response bias would raise both $c^*$ and $c'$, since one success/one failure combinations may be under-represented. The genetic effect may be under- or overestimated since it depends on the size of the response bias for both

$c^*$ and $c'$, but it seems likely that we overestimate common environment since $(1 - 1/k)$ is less than 1.

Another possible difficulty with our results arises from measurement error. Assuming that such measurement error is uncorrelated for twins, both $c^*$ and $c'$ are understated – presumably by the same percentage amount. In this instance both genetic and common environmental effects are underestimated.

Measurement error usually refers to wrong numbers being written down. Transitory income refers to correct numbers for annual earnings being recorded, but annual earnings deviating from the proper concept of normal, permanent, or (the present discounted value of) lifetime earnings. Thus, transitory income can be thought of as another type of measurement error.

Using the Michigan Panel of Income Dynamics, which is a nationwide random sample, Lillard and Willis (1978) estimate that for white males permanent income constitutes about 80% of the variance in annual earnings. The remainder includes both transitory effects and measurement error. Their 80% figure should be a lower bound for our sample for two reasons. First, their sample includes young people whose earnings grow most rapidly and irregularly while our sample includes only men about age 50. The rapid growth of the young counts as transitory income in their methodology. Secondly, we expect that transitory income of brothers is correlated because of choices of similar occupations, on-the-job training, etc. These considerations suggest that the permanent component of the variation in income may be about 90% of the total. Adjusting for measurement error and transitory income, common environment accounts for about 15% instead of 12% of the variance in earnings. (If the permanent component is 80% the estimate for common environment rises to 17%.)

Our estimates are based on men aged 50. It is possible that common environment is more important earlier in the life cycle. However, long-term longitudinal samples suggest otherwise. For example, Taubman (1975) reports that in the NBER-TH sample the total $R^2$ in an equation with many variables is greater when the men in that sample were about 47 years old than when they were about 33 years old. Moreover, Fägerlind (1975) in his Malmo

sample shows simple and total correlations increasing continuously with age as the men in his sample (for whom data has been
gathered every five years) aged from about 20 to about 50 years
old.

There are several reasons to question whether our results
generalize to other groups. First, the sample design requires
everyone who was sent a questionnaire to have been in the
military, to be alive in 1974, and not to have been uncoopertive in
previous studies. Exclusion of people who did not meet these
requirements may mean that $c^*$ and $c'$ are not appropriate for the
population as a whole. It is not obvious, however, whether this
biases our estimate of the common environment upwards or
downwards.

Another difficulty in generalizing from our results is that the
distribution of genetics and environment may not be the same in
our cohort as in others. The genetic distribution may differ
because of changes in migration patterns and because not enough
time has passed since recent waves of migrations for genetic
distributions to be in equilibrium. What we suspect to be more
important is that the distribution of family environment may have
changed. For example, the distribution of income, parental
education, and number of siblings, which presumably are important elements in family environment, probably are different in
younger cohorts. But we also suspect that for more recent cohorts
these environmental variables are distributed more equally.[10]
Clearly it would be nice to have other samples which could help
resolve and replicate these findings. But even given the above
qualifications, it appears that variation in common environment
across families only accounts for a very modest proportion of the
variation in earnings.

In this section we provide an estimate of the contribution of
inequality of opportunity, defined as the ratio of the variance in
common environment to the variance in earnings. We estimate
inequality of opportunity to account for less than 20% of the

---

[10]However, Jencks and Brown (1977) reports MZ and DZ cross-twin correlations
for a recent cohort that are similar to ours.

variance in outcomes, but that who one's parents are accounts for about 60% of the variance in outcomes. To attain the goal of those who wish to reduce the remaining degree of inequality beyond that due to common environment, compensatory and transfer programs have to be used. The trade-off between efficiency and equality has to be faced.

# CHAPTER 9

# CONCLUSIONS

The question of what determines intragenerational socioeconomic inequalities and intergenerational socioeconomic mobility is indeed an important one. Better understanding the nature of these determinants provides a firmer basis for evaluating the fairness and openess of society, judging the effectiveness and efficiency of policies, exploring to what extent the liberal creed of equality of opportunity leads to equality of outcomes, and investigating to what degree there is upward mobility and rewards for merit, with probable attendant positive effects on political stability and on the quality of leadership.

In the past decade there has been an explosion of effort to explore these determinants. As the review in section 1.2 indicates, however, these studies generally have been flawed by a number of problems. (1) Many possibly important variables, such as a whole range of family effects and noncognitive (and often cognitive) abilities and motivations, have been excluded. (2) Estimated coefficients of included variables, such as schooling, probably have been biased due to correlations with significant excluded variables. (3) Cross-section data has been used to investigate time series phenomena without evidence that the necessary conditions exist to justify such an interpretation. (4) The results which have been obtained relate only to marginal changes, not large ones. (5) The underlying structural supply and demand relations are not identified.

In this book we believe that we have made a major step

forward in estimating the determinants of intragenerational socioeconomic inequalities and intergenerational socioeconomic mobilities. Although we continue to have the last two problems mentioned above, we have developed a data set and methodologies which permit a substantial advancement in lessening the first three problems and, to a much lesser extent, the fourth. The results which we obtain are sometimes quite different from those presented by others, with far-reaching implications for understanding society and for planning policy.

The data set which we use is a major longitudinal source never before examined by social scientists: the NAS–NRC twin sample, which includes 2478 pairs of white twin brothers who were born in 1917–27, served in the military, and answered the most recent in a series of questionnaires in 1974. In Chapters 3 and 5 we reviewed the available evidence concerning twins in general and this set of twins in particular. Our qualified conclusions are as follows. (1) The distributions of characteristics of our DZ twins, for whom the twinning rate generally is dependent upon such factors as mother's age and socioeconomic background, are significantly different from those for our MZ twins, for whom the twinning rate is random, only for number of siblings and mother's education. (2) Any special treatment of twins and special interactions between twins probably are relatively unimportant for our purposes in comparison to the overall quality and quantity of material well-being, emotional support, and other aspects of family and childhood environment. (3) The distributions of background characteristics of the twins in our sample do not appear to be substantially different than those for all white male veterans of the same age cohort, although they do differ from nonveterans. Therefore, we somewhat cautiously conclude that the results of this study are applicable to the much bigger population of white male veterans of approximately the same age.

To analyze these data we posit a model which determines four major socioeconomic indicators over the life cycle: schooling, initial occupational status, mature occupational status, and the logarithm of mature earnings. This model is recursive in structure, with genetic and environmental indices entering into each relationship. For a subset of the sample we have data which permits the incorporation of a measure of cognitive ability as an additional prerecursive observable variable. In Chapter 2 we discussed this model structure in detail, with particular emphasis on the relation to the standard human capital approach and the strengths and weaknesses of that approach. In Chapter 3 we discussed the implications of the special genetic relations between twins for our work, and what one legitimately can and cannot conclude from decomposition of the variance of a characteristic into genetic and environmental components (and a covariance between them). We emphasize that the emotionalism surrounding the genetics–environment or nature–nurture controversy has caused overly strong claims to be made by both sides, thus obscuring the limits to what legitimately can be deduced.

We believe that exploring the determination of our four basic socioeconomic indicators gives considerable insights into life cycle socioeconomic developments and into the questions which we pose about intragenerational socioeconomic equality and intergenerational socioeconomic mobility. We can easily think of additional life cycle socioeconomic indicators that might be of about equal importance (e.g. health, marital status, peace of mind, quantity and quality of children). We do not attempt to include them in our model, however, because of lack of data and the additional complexities which expansion of the model would entail for our latent variable, variance components extended twins model.

We first estimate some of the parameters of our model using ordinary least squares techniques. Estimates based on treating the members of the sample as individuals (i.e. with no utilization of the information concerning twin brothers) are similar in most respects to those of previous studies reviewed in section 1.2. If years of schooling and occupational status are not included among the right-hand side variables, many of the standard socioeconomic background variables have significant coefficient estimates with the *a priori* expected sign: positive effects for Jewish religion and parental education and occupational status; negative effects for the number of siblings, Catholic religion, and rural background. However, the Leibowitz (1974) conjecture that the coefficient on the mother's education is larger than that on the father's since most investment in parental time spent with the children is by the mothers, is not supported by our estimates. In several equations age has a negative coefficient which may reflect any or all of the following: the secular trend in years of schooling, the greater disruptions suffered by older men in the Great Depression and the Second World War, and the well-documented peaking of most earnings in the mid and late forties age bracket. The effects of most background variables also tend to decline, if anything, over the life cycle (i.e. be greater for years of schooling and initial occupational status than for mature occupational status and earnings), which seems *a priori* plausible. Perhaps the most surprising result among the background variables occurs in the occupational status equations and is the estimated positive effect of having been born in the South, which may reflect racial discrimination since a number of characteristics associated with the South are being controlled for. Married persons, finally, tend to have higher earnings, but not different occupational status. This result may reflect the need to support multiperson households in an age cohort in which wives often were not employed.

When education and/or occupational status are included as right-hand side recursive variables, their coefficients generally are significant and of the *a priori* expected sign, thus providing support for the recursive structure posited in our analysis. The estimated coefficients of the background variables generally decline in absolute value and sometimes become insignificant. For the subsample for which we have data on cognitive ability, comparing the estimates obtained with and without this variable included, suggests that some biases are introduced if cognitive ability is omitted. For example, the implied bias in the coefficient of years of schooling in the logarithm of earnings relation is 35%. This is a relatively large estimate in comparison to those reported by Griliches and Mason (1972) and in the Welch (1975) survey, although Taubman and Wales (1974, 1975) and Olneck (1977) present estimates about as large. Moreover, Hauser and Daymont (1976) indicate that the bias increases with work experience, which is consistent with our relatively large estimate since we have mature men with much more work experience in our sample than is the case in many other studies.

In broad terms, then, our ordinary least squares estimates for individuals are consistent with the finding of others, with the differences being more in interesting details (such as the size of the bias due to the exclusion of cognitive ability or the effect of having been born in the South) than in basic relations. Such general consistency with other studies is important since it strengthens the interpretation that the results which we obtain from alternative modes of analysis are not an artifact of peculiarities in our sample, but reflect basic underlying problems due to excluded variables which probably are prevalent (but not commonly examined) in most other studies. Like other studies, our ordinary least squares estimates for individuals leave considerable proportions of the variances in the socioeconomic indicators of interest unexplained. This suggests the possibility of the existence of important unobserved variables, the exclusion of which may cause considerable biases in the estimated coefficients of the observed variables.

We next present ordinary least squares estimates between twin brothers. For the DZ within-pair estimates we are holding constant environment which is common to the brothers. For the MZ within-pair estimates we also are holding constant genetics. Analysis of covariance rejects the null hypothesis that the DZ and MZ relations are the same, at least for earnings, suggesting that genetics are important. For both types of twins the within-brother estimates again are consistent with the posited recursive structure in schooling and in occupational status.

Under certain conditions, detailed in section 4.2 and partially tested in Chapter 7, we can use the within-twins regressions in comparison with the individual regressions to estimate the biases which arise if genetics and common environment are not controlled for. For the determination of mature occupational status such a comparison suggest a bias of over one-quarter in the coefficient estimate of initial occupational status if all common environment is not controlled for, and the ten common observable background variable do *not* by themselves provide adequate control for this environment. The failure to control for genetics does not seem to cause a bias in this coefficient. For the coefficient estimate of mature occupational status in the determination of the logarithm of mature earnings, the pattern is basically the same.

Of even greater interest, of course, are the implications of such comparisons for the coefficient estimates of schooling. For the determination of initial occupational status, such comparisons suggest a bias of about 14% for not controlling for the ten observable background variables, of about 33% for not controlling for all of common environment, and of about 50% for not controlling for common environment and genetics. For the determination of mature occupation similar comparisons suggest a smaller total bias of about 12%, mostly occurring if genetics are not controlled for. For the earnings function, finally, the total effect of schooling falls from 0.08 to 0.07 when the ten observed background variables are controlled for, to about 0.06 when all of common environment is controlled for, and to only 0.025 if genetics also are controlled for. This last value is only about 30% of the estimate obtained for individuals in the standard way!

Part of the differences in coefficient estimates in the various ordinary least squares estimates which we present may originate in misclassification of twins or in other measurement errors. Calculations which we presented in Chapter 6, however, suggest that it is unlikely that such sources of error account for differences of the order of magnitude which we obtain. As also is indicated in Chapter 6, part of the differences probably are due to the failure to control for cognitive ability in our estimates based on the total sample. Once again, however, this factor combined with the ten background measures does not account for most of the differences between point estimates, although much of the difference vanishes when the noise-to-signal ratio is 10%.

Therefore, we are led to several major conclusions. Standard methods of estimating the effects of schooling on major socioeconomic indicators probably lead to estimates with substantial upward biases. Controlling for commonly available background variables and measures of cognitive ability reduces such biases, but may leave substantial biases due to the failure to control for other important family effects (whether genetic or environmental in origin) which may alter socioeconomic success through affecting characteristics like noncognitive abilities and motivation. Our current knowledge of such family effects is quite limited, although some initial work in this area has been undertaken by social scientists such as Leibowitz (1974) and Lindert (1976). In any case most past estimates of the impact of schooling on occupational status and on earnings probably have been substantially too high. Given the probable actual estimates, changes such as improvements in capital markets are unlikely to have much impact on the distribution of socioeconomic success. The returns to education in terms of these socioeconomic indicators (independent of other nonpecuniary returns) has been overstated. When it is also considered that the amount of schooling which an individual receives reflects in considerable part family background, the still widespread (although hardly unquestioned) faith in the success of schooling in lessening inequalities and increasing mobility seems dubious indeed. If more equality of outcomes as measured by the distribution of the occupational status and earnings measures is desired by society (as is the case in our own personal value judgements), different means – possibly including direct transfers – need to be utilized to pursue such goals.

These are strong results. To further explore whether or not they are justified and to shed further light on the nature of the role of genetic and environmental family effects, in Chapter 4 we developed new methodology in the form of a latent variable, variance components, extended twin model. If we allow for the inclusion of as many genetic and environmental indices as we have socioeconomic indicators in our recursive model, the system is underidentified. Moreover, as was explored in section 4.3, the identification question is more complicated than simply counting the degrees of freedom, since some of the parameters in the model can be estimated only in particular sub-blocks of the variance–covariance matrix. We therefore define a basic model in which we assume that all structural disturbances are uncorrelated with all other variables (except the dependent variable in the structural relation for which each appears), that there are four genetic and one environmental indices, that all of these indices are orthogonal to each other, that there is assortive mating and/or nonadditive genetic effects, and that the part of environment which directly affects more than one socioeconomic indicator is identically correlated across brothers for both types of twins.

In Chapter 7 we presented nonlinear maximum likelihood estimates of this basic model and of a number of variations of it. These variations suggest that (a) there is a significant improvement in the fit if assortive mating and/or nonadditive genetic effects are allowed; (b) that the part of environment which directly affects more than one socioeconomic indicator is perfectly correlated across brothers (which strengthens the interpretation of the within-twin-pair regression results); (c) that if nonzero covariances are allowed between genetic and environmental indices the primary change is a reduced relative estimated contribution of environment (although we have difficulty in locating the maximum of the likelihood function if a nonzero covariance is allowed); and (d) that a mixed environmental–genetics model probably is preferable to either a pure genetics or a pure environmental model. The point estimates of the observable variables are robust and are about the same as the ordinary least squares estimates for MZ twins. Therefore, the strong conclusions made above about the extent of and implications of biases in the coefficient estimates for schooling and other variables due to the failure to control for family effects are reinforced.

The estimates of the parameters of the model, including the relative variances of the unobserved variables, under somewhat more controversial assumptions also permit the decomposition of the variance in the socioeconomic indicators into genetic and environmental components. The sum of genetics and family environment accounts for about one-half of the variance in earnings and occupational status and three-quarters of the variance in schooling, independent of which of the alternatives discussed in Chapter 7 is used. Such estimates reinforce the emphasis made above on the great importance of total family effects in determining socioeconomic inequality for the relevant population, given the environment which they have experienced. The significance of such family effects permitted substantial intragenerational socio-economic inequality despite some policies, such as extensive schooling, which many people hoped would offset significantly different family backgrounds.

The estimated division of the total family effects into genetic and environmental components depends upon which estimates are used. In the estimates which we prefer on other grounds, genetics accounts for more than half of the total family effects.

The assumptions upon which these estimates are based allow us to quantify the contribution of inequality of opportunity – defined as the effects of differences in family income – to inequality of outcomes. We estimate that no more than 20% of the variance in earnings in this sample of white males is due to inequality of opportunity. Elimination of inequality of opportunity does not involve losses in economic efficiency. But elimination of most of inequality of outcome involves a trade-off with efficiency.

These estimates also permit exploration of intergenerational socioeconomic mobility. As Conlisk (1974) emphasizes, policies or other events which reduce intragenerational inequalities need not necessarily increase intergenerational mobility. In Chapter 8 we discussed this issue and how we can obtain at least orders of magnitude for estimates for intergenerational mobility from the estimates of our extended twin models by the latent variable, variance components, maximum likelihood technique. If equality of opportunity is defined to be a zero environmental correlation across generations (an extreme which is unlikely to be obtained in the near future in the society of the United States), our estimates imply that the introduction of complete equality of opportunity would result in very low intergenerational correlations (e.g. 0.06–0.14 for earnings). They still imply, nevertheless, that genetics account for about half of the intragenerational variance in earnings, with the implications discussed above.

Let us reiterate that our variance decomposition estimates apply for a particular population which experienced and inter-acted with a particular environment. As discussed in Chapter 3, a different environment could have caused a much different decomposition between genetics and environment. Furthermore, the decomposition of the variance does not tell what determines the level of the various socioeconomic indicators. Nevertheless we think that such estimates aid in understanding the determinates of intragenerational inequality and intergenerational mobility for the population which currently has major control over the destiny of our society. As such they provide important supplements to our other significant contributions noted above to the understanding of how our socioeconomic system and important policies relating to schooling have functioned in determining intra- and intergenerational socioeconomic inequalities in the United States in the twentieth century.

# APPENDIX: QUESTIONNAIRES

NAS-NRC-FUA  NATIONAL ACADEMY OF SCIENCES
R-19-8      NATIONAL RESEARCH COUNCIL
MAY 1965    DIVISION OF MEDICAL SCIENCES
            FOLLOW-UP AGENCY

## HEALTH QUESTIONNAIRE

1. Do you have a twin brother?
   ☐ Yes, Living  ☐ Yes, Not Living  ☐ No.
   (If you checked *No* stop here and return form.)

2. What branch of service were you in?
   ☐ Army  ☐ Navy  ☐ Air Force  ☐ Marine Corps  ☐ Coast Guard
   Year entered service _____

3. Service serial number _____

4. Date of birth _____
                (Month)         (Day)        (Year)

5. As children, were you and your twin "as alike as two peas in a pod" ☐ *or* of
   only ordinary family resemblance ☐?

6. In childhood, did your parents, brothers and sisters, or teachers have trouble in
   telling you apart?  ☐ Yes  ☐ No.

7. List any illness, impairment, disability, hospitalization, and operation you have
   had *since separation from military service*, stating the year when it first
   occurred, and giving the name and address of the hospital where you were
   treated.

8. If this was not sent to your permanent address, please give your correct
   address:
   Number and Street _____
   City, zone no., State _____

9. Please give your twin's current address:
   Full name _____
   Street Address _____
   City and State _____

NAS-NRC-MFUA
Form R19-20
January 1974

## Questionnaire for the Twins Study of Education and Earnings

Your participation in this survey is entirely voluntary and you may refuse to answer any question to which you object. Your answers will not be used for other than statistical purposes and the information you provide will not be published in such a way as to identify you personally.

Please indicate by your signature that you have read the above statement.

Signature: _____

1. Are you:

| Single, | Married, | Remarried, | Separated, | Divorced, | Widowed, | Other? |
|---|---|---|---|---|---|---|
| □ | □ | □ | □ | □ | □ | □ |
| 1 | 2 | 3 | 4 | 5 | 6 | 7 |

(7)

2. Year of marriage _____ (8-9)

3. Current age of wife _____ (10-11)

4. For each living child, please indicate sex (M/F) and age starting with the eldest:

| Sex | Age | Sex | Age | Sex | Age | Sex | Age | Sex | Age | Sex | Age | Sex | Age |
|---|---|---|---|---|---|---|---|---|---|---|---|---|---|
| □ | □ | □ | □ | □ | □ | □ | □ | □ | □ | □ | □ | □ | □ |
| (12) | (13-14) | (15) | (16-17) | (18) | (19-20) | (21) | (22-23) | (24) | (25-26) | | | | |
| □ | □ | | | | | | | | | | | | |

(3:7-21)

5. Besides your twin, how many brothers and sisters were alive in 1940? _____ (27)

How many were older than you? _____ (28)

6. In what religion were you and your wife raised:

| | Catholic | Protestant | Jewish | None | Other |
|---|---|---|---|---|---|
| (29) You | ☐ | ☐ | ☐ | ☐ | ☐ |
| (30) Your wife | ☐ | ☐ | ☐ | ☐ | ☐ |
| | 1 | 2 | 3 | 4 | 5 |

7. How many times a month on average do you and your wife attend religious services:

(31) You ———— (32) Your wife ————

8. What is the highest grade of schooling finished by: (Bachelor's Degree is 16, Ph.D. is 19)

You ———— Your father ———— Your mother ———— Your oldest son ————
(33–34) (35–36) (37–38) (39–40)

Your oldest daughter ———— Your wife ———— Her father ———— Her mother ————
(41–42) (43–44) (45–46) (47)

9. Please indicate the type of elementary and high school you and your family attended. If more than one type applies, check each.

| | Elementary School | | | | High School | | |
|---|---|---|---|---|---|---|---|
| | Public | Parochial | Private | | Public | Parochial | Private |
| (49) You | ☐ | ☐ | ☐ | (50) | ☐ | ☐ | ☐ |
| (51) Your wife | ☐ | ☐ | ☐ | (52) | ☐ | ☐ | ☐ |
| (53) Oldest son | ☐ | ☐ | ☐ | (54) | ☐ | ☐ | ☐ |
| (55) Oldest daughter | ☐ | ☐ | ☐ | (56) | ☐ | ☐ | ☐ |
| | 1 | 2 | 3 | | 1 | 2 | 3 |

10. Have you received formal vocational training such as bookkeeping or electrical?

No    Yes          If yes, type_____

(57)  ☐    ☐
      1    2        Number of weeks _____ (58–59)

11. If you and/or your oldest son attended college, please fill in the following. If attended more than one, list the last one.

|  | Name | Last year attended | Highest Degree |
|---|---|---|---|
| Your last undergraduate school | _____ | _____ (60–61) | _____ (62) |
| Your last graduate school | _____ | _____ (63–64) | _____ (65) |
| Your oldest son's last undergraduate school | _____ | _____ (66–67) | _____ (68) |

12. Please describe the precise nature of *first full time* civilian occupation (either before or after service) such as salesman in bakery or welder in shipyard:

(69) You _____

(70) Your eldest child _____

(71) Please describe your father-in-law's normal occupation:

13. If working, are you and your wife employed by:

|  | Private Company | Government | Self-Employed in Own Business | Private Non-Profit Institution |
|---|---|---|---|---|
| (72) You | ☐ | ☐ | ☐ | ☐ |
| (73) Your wife | ☐ 1 | ☐ 2 | ☐ 3 | ☐ 4 |

14. During most of last week, were you:

(74) Working ☐ 1    Not working (but with a job) ☐ 2    Unemployed, looking for work ☐ 3

Unemployed, not looking for work ☐ 4    Retired ☐ 5    Unable to work ☐ 6

15. How many hours did you work last week? _____ (75–76)

How many hours do you normally work a week? _____ (77–78)

☐ 1 (80)

16. How much do you and your wife usually earn before deductions? Please *indicate amount* and then *check pay period* that applies to this amount:

|          |    | per |      | Hour | Week | Month | Year | Other (specify) |
|----------|----|-----|------|------|------|-------|------|-----------------|
| You      | $  | _____ (7–11) | | ☐ | ☐ | ☐ | ☐ | _____ |
|          |    |     |      | 1    | 2    | 3     | 4    |                 |
| Your wife | $ | _____ (13–17) | | ☐ | ☐ | ☐ | ☐ | _____ |
|          |    |     |      |      |      |       |      |                 |

17. During 1973:
    How much did you earn? $ _____ (19–20)

    How much did your wife earn? $ _____ (21–22)

    How much was your family income from all sources? $ _____ (23–24)

18. How do you feel about the job you now have:

    (25) Like it very much ☐ 1        Like it fairly well ☐ 2

    Dislike it very much ☐ 3          Dislike it somewhat ☐ 4

19. If you thought the chances of financial success were about equal would you:

    (26) Prefer to be self-employed ☐ 1    Prefer to be salaried ☐ 2    Indifferent ☐ 3

20. Please check the amount of time your *wife* normally worked during each of the following periods:

|  | Full time | Part time | Intermittently | Did not work |
|---|---|---|---|---|
| (27) Before 1942 | ☐ | ☐ | ☐ | ☐ |
| (28) 1942–1945 | ☐ | ☐ | ☐ | ☐ |
| (29) 1946–1950 | ☐ | ☐ | ☐ | ☐ |
| (30) 1951–1955 | ☐ | ☐ | ☐ | ☐ |
| (31) 1956–1960 | ☐ | ☐ | ☐ | ☐ |
| (32) 1961–1972 | ☐ | ☐ | ☐ | ☐ |
|  | 1 | 2 | 3 | 4 |

21. As best as you can remember, what factors influenced your decision to enter the occupational field you are in at the present time. Check *yes* or *no* to each. (33–40)

|  | Yes 1 | No 2 |
|---|---|---|
| A. Type of school training | ☐ | ☐ |
| B. Type of military training | ☐ | ☐ |
| C. Personal or political contacts | ☐ | ☐ |
| D. Pay offered including fringes | ☐ | ☐ |
| E. Prospects of eventual financial success | ☐ | ☐ |
| F. Chance for interesting work | ☐ | ☐ |
| G. Chance for independent work | ☐ | ☐ |
| H. Person-to-person contact | ☐ | ☐ |

(41–48)

|  | Yes 1 | No 2 |
|---|---|---|
| I. Chance to help others | ☐ | ☐ |
| J. Represented a challenge | ☐ | ☐ |
| K. Job security | ☐ | ☐ |
| L. Provided much free time | ☐ | ☐ |
| M. Liked that kind of work | ☐ | ☐ |
| N. Family business | ☐ | ☐ |
| O. Status | ☐ | ☐ |
| P. No other option | ☐ | ☐ |

Which three of A through P were most important? _____ , _____ , _____

(49)      (50)      (51)

22. Do you have an annual medical check-up?

(52)   No ☐ 1     Yes, by family ☐ 2     Yes, at government, union ☐ 3
               physician           or company clinic

23. If above is yes, when did you begin this practice?

(53)   As a child ☐ 1     After 1945 ☐ 2     Year began _____ (54–55)

24. If *your* medical check-up is with *your* private physician, is the doctor's bill covered by health insurance?

(56)   No ☐ 1     Yes, fully paid by insurance ☐ 2     Yes, partially paid ☐ 3

25. If above is yes, when did this coverage begin?   Year _____ (57–58)

26. Do your wife and children also have at least annual medical check-ups?

(59)   Wife     Yes ☐     No ☐

(60)   Children     Yes ☐ 1     No ☐ 2

27. Social Security Number:

Yours _____ (61–69)         Your wife's _____ (70–78)

☐ 2 (80)

NAS-NRC MFUA
R19-41 FORM 1
DECEMBER 1975

GENETIC COMPONENTS IN ECONOMIC AND SOCIAL
CHARACTERISTICS
SELECTED SERVICE DATA—NAVY TWINS

R-19 STUDY NO. ☐ ☐ ☐
1-6

DOCUMENTS FOUND IN FILE:     1—Yes     2—No

NAVPERS 609 or
Other Enl. Qual. ☐
7

NAVPERS 24/
DSS 221 Enl. ☐
8

NAVPERS 601
Service Rec. ☐
9

NAVPERS 553
Separation ☐
10

EDUCATION (Years)     99 NS ☐ ☐     11-12

STATE OF RESIDENCE AT EAD     99 NS ☐ ☐     13-14

FAMILY BACKGROUND: 1—Yes     2—No     9—NS

Living?
Father ☐ 15
Mother ☐ 16

Parents?
Divorced ☐ 17
Sep. ☐ 18

Has a-
Step-father ☐ 19
Step-mother ☐ 20

RELIGION
1 Protestant
2 Catholic
3 Jewish
4 Other/None  9 NS
☐ 21

QUALIFICATION TESTS:   ∅ GCT, No tag digit; 1 GCT-1; 2 GCT-2; 3 GCT-3; 4 AFQT; 5 AQT;
6 GCT, Not consistent with date of record or asterisk use (give details)

| Test | Score | Yr. | Mo. | Test | Score | Yr. | Mo. | Test | Score | Yr. | Mo. |
|---|---|---|---|---|---|---|---|---|---|---|---|
| ☐ | ☐ | ☐ | ☐ | ☐ | ☐ | ☐ | ☐ | ☐ | ☐ | ☐ | ☐ |
| 22 | 23-25 | 26-27 | 28-29 | 30 | 31-33 | 34-35 | 36-37 | 38 | 39-41 | 42-43 | 44-45 |

APTITUDE TESTS

| Yr. | Mo. | ARI | MAT | CLER | RADIO | MK MECH | MK ELEC |
|-----|-----|-----|-----|------|-------|---------|---------|
| ☐ | ☐ | ☐ | ☐ | ☐ | ☐ | ☐ | ☐ |
| 46-47 | 48-49 | 50-52 | 53-55 | 56-58 | 59-61 | 62-64 | 65-67 |

Code *and* write in if available

| QUALIFICATIONS CLASS | 1ST RECOMMENDATION | 2ND RECOMMENDATION | CARD 1 |
|---|---|---|---|
| ☐ | ☐ | ☐ | ☐ 1 |
| 68 | 69-70 | 71-72 | 80 |

CARD 2

FIRST FULL-TIME CIVILIAN OCCUPATION

TITLE _____  BUSINESS/EMPLOYER _____

    (if code not shown)      DUTIES _____

| DOT Code | YRS. | Code |
|---|---|---|
| ☐☐☐☐☐☐☐☐☐ | ☐ | 9 ≥ 9 |
| 7-15 | 16 | & NS |

| PROFICIENCY SCORE (omit decimal) | CLASS C SCHOOLS 1 Yes   2 No |
|---|---|
| ☐☐ | ☐ |
| 29-30 | 31 |

RATING AND PAY GRADE

☐☐☐☐☐☐☐☐☐☐☐

17-28

## CLASS A AND CLASS B SCHOOLS

### 1ST
| School | Cl | Year |
|--------|-----|------|
| 32–33 | 34 | 35–36 |

### 2ND
| School | Cl | Year |
|--------|-----|------|
| 37–38 | 39 | 40–41 |

### 3RD
| School | Cl | Year |
|--------|-----|------|
| 42–43 | 44 | 45–46 |

### 4TH
| School | Cl | Year |
|--------|-----|------|
| 47–48 | 49 | 50–51 |

## MORE THAN FOUR CLASS A OR B SCHOOLS

1—Yes  2—No

52

## AWARDS AND DECORATIONS

0 None
1 Medal of Honor, Navy Cross, Distinguished Service
2 Silver Star
3 Legion of Merit
4 Distinguished Flying Cross
5 Navy/Marine Corps Medal
6 Bronze Star Medal
7 Air Medal
8 Pers. Commend. Ribbon/Letter
9 Purple Heart Medal
G Good Conduct Medal
U Unit Commendation

53

## JOB PREFERENCE

DOT CODE

54–62

# REFERENCES

Administrator of Veterans Affairs (1969) *Annual Report to Congress, 1968,* U.S. Government Printing Office, Washington, D.C.

Allen, G. and J. Schachter (1970) "Do Conception Delays Explain Some Changes in Twinning Rates?", *Acta. Genet. Med., Gemelloe,* 19, January–April, 30–34.

Allen, Martin, G., et al. (1972) "Schizophrenia in Veteran Twins: A Diagnostic Review", *American Journal of Psychiatry,* 128, no. 8, February, 939–945.

Anastasi, A. (1958) *Differential Psychology,* New York: MacMillan.

Becker, Gary (1958) *The Economics of Discrimination,* Chicago: University of Chicago Press.

Becker, Gary (1964) *Human Capital: A Theoretical and Empirical Analysis with Special Reference to Education,* New York: NBER.

Becker, Gary (1967) "Human Capital and the Personal Distribution of Income", Woytinski Lecture no. 1, Ann Arbor: University of Michigan.

Becker, Gary (1975) *Human Capital,* NBER.

Becker, G. and N. Tomes (1976) "Child Endowments and the Quantity and Quality of Children", *Journal of Political Economy,* 84, August, 5143–5162.

Beebe, G.W. and A.H. Simon (1969) "Ascertainment of Mortality in the U.S. Veteran Population", *American Journal of Epidemiology,* 89, 636–643.

Bendix, R. and S.M. Lypsett, eds. (1966) *Class, Status and Power: Social Stratification in Comparative Perspective,* 2nd edn., Macmillan and Company.

Ben-Porath, Y. (1967) "The Production of Human Capital and the Life Cycle of Earnings", *Journal of Political Economy,* 75, August, 352–365.

Berg, I. (1971) *Education and Jobs: The Great Train Robbery,* Boston: Beacon Hill Press.

Behrman, Jere and Paul Taubman (1975a) "Earnings, Schooling, and Ability: A Multiple Indicator Model Using Twins", University of Pennsylvania, unpublished.

Behrman, Jere and Paul Taubman (1975b) "Nature and Nurture in the Determination of Earnings and Occupational Status", University of Pennsylvania, unpublished.

Behrman, Jere and Paul Taubman (1976) "Intergenerational Transmission of Income and Wealth", *American Economic Review,* 66, no. 2, May, 436–440.

Behrman, Jere, Paul Taubman and Terence J. Wales (1977) "Controlling for and Measuring the Effects of Genetics and Family Environment in Equations for Schooling and Labor Market Success", in: Paul Taubman, ed., *Kinometrics: The Determinants of Socioeconomic Success Within and Between Families,* Amsterdam: North-Holland.

Bielby, W., R. Hauser and D. Featherman (1976) "Response Errors of Nonblack Males in Models of the Stratification Process", Madison: University of Wisconsin, Center for Demography and Ecology Working Paper #76-4.

Blau, P. and O. Duncan (1967) *The American Occupational Structure*, New York: John Wiley and Sons, Inc.

Blaug, Mark, (1976), "Human Capital Theory: A Slightly Jaundiced Survey," *Journal of Economic Literature*, XIV, September, 827–855.

Bloom, B. (1964) *Stability and Change in Human Characteristics*, New York: John Wiley and Sons, Inc.

Blum, Z. (1972) "White and Black Careers During the First Decade of Labor Force Experience Part II: Income Differences", *Social Science Research*, 1, September, 271–292.

Bock, R. and S. Vandenberg (1967) "Components of Heritable Variation in Mental Test Scores", Report no. 22 from the Louisville Twin Study.

Bowen, H. (1977) *Investment in Learning*, San Francisco.

Bowles, S. and H. Gintis (1973) "I.Q. in the U.S. Class Structure", *Social Policy*, January/February, 65–96.

Bowles, Samuel, and Valerie Nelson, (1974), "The Inheritance of I.Q. and the Intergenerational Reproduction of Economic Inequality", *Review of Economics and Statistics*, LVI, 39–51.

British Medical Research Council's Committee on the Aetiology of Chronic Bronchitis (1960) "Standardized Questionnaire on Respiratory Symptoms, College of General Practitioners", *British Medical Journal*, 2, 1665.

Brittain, J. (1977) *The Inheritance of Economic Status*, Brookings Institute.

Bulcock, J., I. Fägerlind and I. Emanuelsson (1974) Education and the Socio-economic Career: U.S.-Swedish Comparisons, Report No. 6, Institute for the Study of International Problems in Education, University of Stockholm.

Burt, C. and M. Howard, (1957), "Heredity and Intelligence: A Reply to Criticisms", *British Journal of Statistical Psychology*, 10, 33–63.

Cavalli-Sforza, L. and W. Bodmer (1971) *The Genetics of Human Populations*, W.H. Freeman and Company.

Cavalli-Sforza, L. and M. Feldman (1973) "Cultural versus Biological Inheritance: Phenotypic Transmission from Parents to Children", *American Journal of Human Genetics*, 25, no. 6, November, 618–637.

Cederloff, R., L. Friberg and Z. Hrubec (1969) "Cardiovascular and Respiratory Symptoms in Relation to Tobacco Smoking: A Study on American Twins, *Arch. Environmental Health*, 18, 934–940.

Cederloff, R., L. Friberg, E. Jonsson and L. Kaij (1961) "Studies on Similarity Diagnosis in Twins with the Aid of Mailed Questionnaires", *Acta Genetics*, 11, 338–362.

Chamberlain, G. (1974) "Education, Income and Ability Revisited", Harvard Institute of Economic Research Discussion Paper no. 302; forthcoming in *Journal of Econometrics*.

Chamberlain, G. (1976) "Unobservables in Earnings Functions: Applications in the Malmo Data", Harvard University, unpublished.

Chamberlain, G. (1977a) "An Instrumental Variable Interpretation of Identification in Variance Components and MIMIC Models", in: Paul Taubman, ed., *Kinometrics: The Determinants of Socioeconomic Success Within and Between Families*, Amsterdam: North-Holland.

Chamberlain, G. (1977b) "Are Brothers as Good as Twins?", in: Paul Taubman, ed., *Kinometrics: The Determinants of Socioeconomic Success Within and Between Families*, Amsterdam: North-Holland.

Chamberlain, G. and Z. Griliches (1975) "Unobservables with a Variance Components Structure: Ability, Schooling, and the Economic Success of Brothers", *International Economic Review*, 16, no. 2, 442–449.

Chamberlain, G. and Z. Griliches (1976) "More on Brothers", Harvard Institute of Economic Research Discussion Paper no. 469.

Coleman, J.S. (1973) "Effects of School on Learning: The IEA Findings", Paper presented at the IEQ-Harvard Conference on Educational Achievement, November.

Coleman, J.S., et al. (1966) *Equality of Educational Opportunity*, Washington, D.C.: U.S. Department of Health, Education and Welfare, Office of Education. 1966.

Conlisk, John (1971) "A Bit of Evidence on the Income–Education–Ability Interrelation", *Journal of Human Resources*, 6, no. 3, 358–362.

Conlisk, John (1974) "Can Equilization of Opportunity Reduce Social Mobility?", *American Economic Review*, March.

de Wolff, P. and A.R.D. Van Slijpe (1973) "The Relations Between Income, Intelligence, Education and Social Background", *European Economic Review*, 4, 235–264.

Duncan, O. (1961) "A Socio-economic Index for all Occupations", in: Albert J. Reiss, ed., *Occupations and Social Status*, New York: Free Press.

Duncan, O. (1968) "Ability and Achievement", *Eugenics Quarterly*, 15, March, 1–11.

Duncan, O., D. Featherman and B. Duncan (1972) *Socioeconomic Background and Achievement*, New York: Seminar Press.

Easterlin, R. (1975) "The Economics and Sociology of Fertility: A Synthesis", in: Charles Tilly, ed., *Historical Studies of Changing Fertility*, Princeton: Princeton University Press.

Eaves, L. (1975) "Testing Models for Variance in Intelligence", *Heredity*, 34.

Enders, T. and C. Stern (1948) "The Frequencies of Twins, Relative to age of Mothers, in American Populations", *Genetics*, 33, May, 263–272.

Eriksson, A.W. and J. Fellman (1967) "Twinning in Relation to Marital Status of Mother", *Acta Genetics*, 17, 385–398.

Eriksson, I. (1970) *Alder och Inkomst*, Stockholm: Allmanna Forlaget.

Erikson, R. (1971) *Upprax for-Hallanden och social rorlightet*, Stockholm: Allmanna Forlaget.

Fägerlind, I. (1975) *Formal Education and Adult Earnings*, Stockholm: Almqvist and Wiksell International.

Fardoust, S. (1978) "Risk-Taking Behavior, Socioeconomic Background, and Distribution of Income: A Theoretical and Empirical Analysis", Ph.D. Dissertation, University of Pennsylvania.

Featherman, D. (1971a) "A Research Note. A Social Structural Model for the Socio-economic Career", *American Journal of Sociology*, 77, September, 923–304.

Featherman, D. (1971b) "The Socioeconomic Achievement of White-Religo-Ethnic Subgroups: Social and Psychological Explanations", *American Sociological Review*, 36, April, 207–222.

Feldman, M. and R. Lewontin (1975) "The Heritability Hang-Up", *Science*, December.

Fisher, F.M. (1966) *The Identification Problem in Econometrics*, New York: McGraw-Hill.

Fisher, R.A. (1918) "The Correlation Between Relatives and the Supposition of Mendelian Inheritance", *Trans. Royal Society*, Edinburgh, 42, 321–341.

Freeman, R. and M. Gordon, eds. (1974) *The Changing Labor Market for Minorities in Higher Education and the Labor Market*, New York: McGraw-Hill.

Gittlesohn, A.M. and S. Milham, (1965) "Observations on Twinning in New York State", *British Journal of Preventive and Social Medicine*, 19, 8–17.

Goldberger, A. (1972) "Maximum-Likelihood Estimation of Regressions Containing Unobservable Independent Variables", *International Economic Review*, 13, 1–15.

Goldberger, A. (1973) "Structural Equation Models: An Overview", in: A. Goldberger and O. Duncan, eds., *Structural Equation Models in the Social Sciences*, New York: Seminar Press.

Goldberger, A. (1975) "Statistical Inference in the Great IQ Debate", Madison: University of Wisconsin, Institute for Research on Poverty.

Goldberger, A. (1976a) "Mysteries of the Meritocracy", in: M.J. Block and G. Dworkin eds., *The IQ Controversy: Critical Readings*, New York: Pantheon.

Goldberger, A. (1976b) "Jensen on Burks", *Educational Psychologist*, 12, no. 1.

Goldberger, A. (1977) "Twin Methods, a Skeptical View," in: P. Taubman, ed., *Kinometrics: Determinants of Socioeconomic Success Within and Between Families*, Amsterdam: North-Holland.

Goldberger, A. and R.C. Lewontin (1976) "Jensen's Twin Fantasy", and other unpublished notes. 1976.

Gordon, R. (1977) "Effects of Father's Occupation and Education on Offspring's IQ Score for Whites of Non-Farm Background", Princeton: Princeton University, mimeo.

Griliches, Z. (1978) "A Partial Survey of Sibling Models", Harvard University, mimeo.

Griliches, Z. and W.M.M. Mason (1972) "Education, Income, and Ability", *Journal of Political Economy*, 80, part II, May/June, S75–S103.

Grossman, M. (1975) "The Correlation Between Health and Schooling", in: N. Terleckyj, ed., *Household Production and Consumption*, New York: NBER.

Gustavsson, S. (1974) "Utbildningens effeckt pa lonen", unpublished manuscript, Stockholm: Institute for Industrial Research.

Halsey, L. (1961) in: A.H. Halsey, ed., *Ability and Educational Opportunity*, Paris: O.E.C.D.

Hauser, R.M. (1970) "Disaggregating a Social Psychological Model of Educational Attainment", *Social Science Review*, 60, June, 409–419.

Hauser, R.M. (1973) "Inequality on Occupational Status and Income", Working Paper no. 73-13, Madison: Center for Demography and Econology, University of Wisconsin.

Hauser, R.M. (1977) unpublished tabulations, personal communication.

Hauser, R. and David L. Featherman (1976) "Equality of Schooling: Trends and Prospects", *Sociology of Education*, 49, no. 2, 99–120.

Hauser, R. and T. Daymont (1977) "Schooling, Ability, and Earnings: Cross

Sectional Findings 8 to 14 years after High School Graduation", *Sociology of Education*, 50, no. 3.

Hauser, R.M., W.H. Sewell and K.G. Lutterman (1973) "Socioeconomic Background and the Earnings of High School Graduates", Working Paper no. 73-22, Madison: Center for Demography and Econology, University of Wisconsin.

Heckman, James (1976) "The Common Structure of Statistical Models of Truncation, Sample Selection, and Limited Dependent Variables and a Sample Estimator for Such Models", *The Annals of Social and Economic Measurement*, 5, 475–492.

Hendricks, H. (1966) "Twinning in Relation to Birth Weight, Mortality, and Congenital Anomolies", *Obstetrics and Gynecology*, 27, January, 47–53.

Herrnstein, R. (1971) "I.Q.", *Atlantic*, 228, September, 43–64.

Hill, C.R. and F.P. Stafford (1977) "Family Background and Lifetime Earnings", in: F. Juster, ed., *The Distribution of Economic Well-Being*, NBER.

Hodge, R.W., P.M. Siegel and P.H. Rossi (1964) "Occupational Prestige in the United States 1925–1963", *American Journal of Sociology*, 70, 286–302.

Hodge, R.W., D.J. Treiman and P.H. Rossi (1966) "A Comparative Study of Occupational Prestige", in: R. Bendix and S.M. Lipset, eds., *Class, Status, and Power*, rev. edn., New York: Free Press.

Hrubec, Z., and Neel, J.V. (1978) "The National Academy of Sciences – National Research Council Twin Registry: Ten Years of Operation" in: W.E. Nance, ed., *Twin Research: Proceedings of the Second International Congress on Twin Studies*, Aug. 29–Sept. 1, 1977, Washington, D.C., Part B. Biology and Epidemiology, Progress in Clinical and Biological Research Volume 24B, New York: Alan R. Liss, Inc., pp. 153–172.

Hrubec, Z., R. Cederlof and L. Friberg (1973) "Respiratory Symptoms in Twins: Effects of Residencs – Associated Air Pollution, Tobacco, and Alcohol Use, and Other Factors", *Arch. Environmental Health*, 27, September, 189–195.

Hrubec, Z., R. Cederlof and L. Friberg (1976) "Background of Angina Pectoris: Social and Environmental Factors in Relation to Smoking", *American Journal of Epidemiology*, 103, January, 16–29.

Hunt, J. McV. (1961) *Intelligence and Experience*, New York: Ronald Press.

Húsen, J. (1959) *Psychological Twin Research*, 1: *A Methodological Study*, Stockholm: Almqvist and Wiksell.

Husen, T. (1950) *Testresultatens prognosvarde*, Stockholm: Almqvist and Wiksell.

Husen, T. *Talent, Equality and Meritocracy, Availability and Utilization of Talent*, The Hague: Martinus Nijhoff.

Husen, T. *Social Influences on Educational Attainments*, Paris: OECD.

Ishikawa, T. (1975) "Family Structures and Family Values in the Theory of Income Distribution", *Journal of Political Economy*, 83, no. 5, October, 987–1008.

Jablon, S. et al. (1967) "The NAS–NRC Twin Panel: Methods of Construction of the Panel, Zygosity Diagnosis, and the Proposed Use", *American Journal of Human Genetics*, 19, 133–161.

Jencks, C. and M. Brown (1977) "Genes and Social Stratification: A Methodological Exploration with Illustrative Data", in: P. Taubman, ed., *Kinometrics: The Determinants of Economic Success Within and Between Families*, Amsterdam: North-Holland.

Jencks, C., et al. (1972) *Inequality, A Reassessment of the Effect of Family and Schooling in America*, New York: Basic Books.
Jensen, A. (1967) "Estimation of the Limits of Heritability of Traits by Comparison of Monozygotic and Dizygotic Twins", *Proceedings of the National Academy of Sciences*, 58, 149.
Jensen, A. (1969) "How Much Can We Boost IQ and Scholastic Achievement?", *Harvard Educational Review*, 39, no. 1, Winter, 1–123.
Jensen, A. (1972) *Genetics and Education*, London: Methuen.
Jensen, A. (1974) "Kinship Correlations Reported by Sir Cyril Burt", *Behavior Genetics*, 4, 1–28.
Jensen, A. (1975) "The Meaning of Heritability in the Behavioral Sciences", *Educational Psychologist*, 11, 171–183.
Jinks, J.L. and L.O. Eaves, (1974), "I.Q. and Inequality", *Nature*, 248, March, 287–289.
Jinks, J.L. and D.W. Fulker (1970) "Comparison of the Biometrical, Genetical, Mava, and Classical Approaches to the Analysis of Human Behavior", *Psychological Bulletin*, 73, no. 5, May, 311–349.
Johansson, L. (1971) *Utbildning: Empirisk del.*, Stockholm: Allmanna Forlaget.
Jöreskog, K. and A.S. Goldberger (1975) "Estimation of a Model with Multiple-Indicators and Multiple Causes of a Single Latent Variable", *Journal of the American Statistical Association*, 708, no. 351, 631–639.
Kadane, J., T.W. McGuire, P.R. Sanday and R. Staelin (1976) "Model of Environmental Effects on the Development of IQ,: *Journal of Educational Statistics*, 1.
Kamin, L.J. (1974) *The Science and Politics of IQ*, Potomic, Maryland: John Wiley and Sons.
Kelley, J. (1973) "Causal Chain Models for the Socioeconomic Career", *American Sociological Review*, 38, August, 481–493.
Klappholz, K. (1972) "Equality of Opportunity, Fairness and Efficiency", in: M. Peston and B. Correy, eds., *Essays in Honour of Lord Robbins*, International Arts and Sciences Press, London: Weidenfeld & Nicholson.
Klevmarken, A. (1972) *Statistical Methods for the Analysis of Earnings Data*, Stockholm: Almqvist and Wiksell.
Klevmarken, A., et al. (1974) *Industritjanstemannens lonestruktur, En studie av loneprofiler for tjansteman med hogre utbildning*, Stockholm: Almqvist and Wiksell.
Koch, H. (1966) *Twins and Twin Relations*, Chicago University Press.
Layzer, David (1974) "Heritability Analysis of IQ Scores: Science or Numerology", *Science*, 183, 1259–1266.
Leibowitz, A. (1974) "Home Investment in Children", *Journal of Political Economy*, 82, no. 2, March/April, S111–S131.
Lewontin, R.C. (1970) "Race and Intelligence", *Bulletin of the Atomic Scientist*, 26, March, 2–8.
Light and Smith (1969) "Social Allocation Models of Intelligence. A Methodological Inquiry", *Harvard Educational Review*, 39, August, 484–510.
Lillard, L. and R. Willis (1978) "Dynamic Aspects of Earnings Mobility", *Econometrica*, September.
Lindert, P. (1976) "Sibling Position and Achievement", University of Wisconsin, mimeo.

Loehhlin, John, Gardner Lindzey and J.N. Spuhler (1975) *Race Differences in Intelligence*, San Francisco: W.H. Freeman & Co.

Majoribanks, K.M. (1970) "Ethnic and Environmental Influences on Levels and Profiles of Mental Abilities", unpublished Ph.D. dissertation, University of Toronto, Canada.

Meade, J. (1973) "The Inheritance of Inequality: Some Biological, Demographic, Social and Economic Factors", *Proceedings of the British Academy*, 59, 1–29.

Mincer, J.B. (1957) *Intelligence in the United States*, New York.

Mincer, J.B. (1958) "Investment in Human Capital and Personal Income Distribution", *Journal of Political Economy*, August.

Mincer, J.B. (1960) "Labor Supply, Family Income, and Consumption", *American Economic Review*, May.

Mincer, J.B. (1962a) "Labor Force Participation of Married Women", *Aspects of Labor Economics*, New York: NBER.

Mincer, J.B. (1962b) "On the Job Training; Costs, Returns, and Some Implications", *Journal of Political Economy*, Supplement, October.

Mincer, J.B. (1969) "Schooling, Age, and Earnings", *Human Capital and Personal Income Distribution*, NBER.

Mincer, J.B. (1970) "The Distribution of Labor Incomes: A Survey with Special Reference to the Human Capital Approach", *Journal of Economic Literature*, 8, March, 1–26.

Mincer, J.B. (1974) *Schooling, Experience, and Earnings*, New York: NBER.

Mittler, P. (1971) *The Study of Twins*, Harmondworth, Middlesex: Penguin Books.

Morgenstern, R. (1973) "Direct and Indirect Effects on Earnings of Schooling and Socio-Economic Background", *Review of Economics and Statistics*, 50, no. 2, May, 225–233.

Mosychuk, H. (1969) "Differential Home Environments and Mental Ability Patterns", unpublished Ph.D. dissertation, University of Alberta, Canada.

Mueser, Peter (1979) "The Effects of Noncognitive Traits", in: Christopher Jencks, et al., *Who Gets Ahead? The Determinants of Economic Success in America*, New York: Basic Books, 122–158 (ch. 5).

Myers, G.C. and A.M. Pitts (1977) "Alternative Projections of the U.S. Male Veteran Population 1970–2000", Working paper from Center for Demographic Studies, Duke University, July, 1976, for report by National Research Council: Health Care for American Veterans, National Academy of Sciences, Washington, D.C.

Nance, W.E. (1976) "Note on the Analysis of Twin Data" (Letter to the Editor), *American Journal of Human Genetics*, 28, 297–299.

Nichols, R.C. and W.C. Bilbro, Jr. (1966) "The Diagnosis of Twin Zygosity", *Acta Genetics*, 16, 265–275.

Olneck, M. (1976a) "The Effects of Education on Occupational Status and Earnings", Institute for Research on Poverty, Discussion Paper no. 358-76, University of Wisconsin, Madison.

Olneck, M. (1976b) "The Determinants of Educational Attainment and Adult Status Among Brothers: The Kalamazoo Study", Ph.D. Thesis, Harvard Graduate School of Education.

Olneck, M. (1977) "On the Use of Sibling Data to Estimate the Effects of Family Background, Cognitive Skills, and Schooling: Results from the Kalamazoo

Brothers Study", in: P. Taubman, ed., *Kinometrics: Determinants of Socio-economic Success Within and Between Families*, Amsterdam: North-Holland.

Okun, A. (1975) *Equality and Efficiency: The Big Tradeoff*, Washington.

Peller, S. (1944) "Studies of Mortality Since the Rennisance, Twins and Single-tons", *Bulletin of the History of Medicine*, 16, 362–381.

Pitts, A.M., R.M. Hillson, G.C. Myers and E.P. Stallard (1977) "Socioeconomic Trends and the Health of the U.S., Male Veteran Population: Past, Present, and Future", Working Paper from Center for Demographic Studies, Duke University, June, 1976, for report by National Research Council: Health Care for American Veterans, National Academy of Sciences, Washington, D.C.

Plowden, A. (1969) *Children and Their Primary Schools*, A Report of the Central Advisory Council for Education (England) II: Research and Surveys, London: Her Majesty's Stationery Office.

Pollin, W., M.G. Allen, A. Hoffer, J.R. Stabenau and Z. Hrubec (1969) "Psychopathology in 15,909 Pairs of Veteran Twins: Evidence for a Genetic Factor in the Pathogensis of Schizophrenia and Its Relative Absence in Psychoneurosis", *American Journal of Psychiatry*, 126, November, 592–610.

Price, B. (1950) "Primary Biases in Twin Studies", *American Journal of Human Genetics*, 2, December, 293–352.

Rainwater, L. (1974) "A Model of Household Heads' Income; 1967–1971", The Joint Center for Urban Studies of MIT and Harvard, mimeo.

Reiss, A.J., Jr., et al. (1961) *Occupations and Social Status*, New York: Free Press of Glencoe.

Robinson, P.M. (1974) "Identification, Estimation, and Large Sample Theory for Regressions Containing Unobservable Variables", *International Economic Review*, 15, no. 3.

Rosen, S. (1976) "A Theory of Life Earnings", *Journal of Political Economy*, August, supplement.

Ross, Stephen, Paul Taubman and Michael Wachter (1977) "Learning by Observing and the Distribution of Wages", University of Pennsylvania, mimeo.

Samuleson, Paul (1964) *Principles of Economics*, McGraw-Hill.

Scarr-Salapetek, S. (1975) "Twin Method: Defense of a Critical Assumption", University of Minnesota, mimeo. 1975.

Scarr, Sandra and Richard Weinberg (1977) *The influence of "Family Background" on Intellectual Attainment: The Unique Contribution of Adoptive Studies to Estimating Environmental Effects*, University of Minnesota.

Schultz, T.W. (1961a) "Investment in Human Capital", *American Economic Review*, 51, no. 1, March, 1–17.

Schultz, T.W. (1961b) "Education and Economic Growth", in: N.B. Henry, ed., *Social Forces Influencing American Education*, Chicago: Chicago University Press.

Seltzer, C.C. and S. Jablon (1977) "Army Rank and Subsequent Mortality by Cause: 23 Year Follow-up", *American Journal of Epidemiology*, 105, June, 559–566.

Sen, A. (1973) *On Economic Inequality*, Oxford: Clarendon Press.

Sewell, W. (1971) "Inequality of Opportunity for Higher Education", *American Sociological Review*, 36, October.

Sewell, W.H. and R.M. Hauser (1972) "Causes and Consequences of Higher Education: Models of the Status Attainment Process", *American Journal of Agricultural Economics*, 54, December, 851–861.

Sewell, W. and R. Hauser (1975) *Education, Occupation and Earnings: Achievement in the Early Career*, New York: Academic Press.

Smith, James and F. Welch (1975) *Black-White Male Earnings and Employment, 1960–1970*, Santa Monica: Rand Corporation Report, R-1666-DOL.

Spaeth, J.L. (1974) "Characteristics of the Work Setting and the Job as Determinants of Income", unpublished manuscript, University of Illinois, Survey Research Laboratory.

Stahl, I. (1973) "Arbetsmarknadsintradetsinformations-problematik", in: *Utvärdering av en högskolereform, in UKA-knoferens i juni 1973*, Rapport nr 2 i UKA"s rapportserie om högre utbildning och forskning, Stockholm: Svenska Utbildningsförlaget Liber.

Stuit, D., ed. (1947) *Personnel Research and Test Development in the Bureau of Naval Personnel*, Princeton University Press, Princeton, N.J.

Summers, A. and B.L. Wolfe (1974) "Equality of Educational Opportunity Quantified: A Production Function Approach", Prepared for Presentation at the Econometric Society Winter Meeting, 27–30 December.

Taubman, Paul (1975) *Sources of Inequality of Earnings*, Amsterdam: North-Holland.

Taubman, Paul (1976) "The Determinants of Earnings; Genetics, Family, and Other Environments", *American Economic Review*, 66, no. 5, December.

Taubman, Paul and Terence J. Wales (1974) *Higher Education: An Investment and a Screening Device*, New York.

Taubman, Paul and Terence J. Wales (1976) "The Path to Labor Market Success: The Role of Unobserved Genetic and Environmental Variables", University of Pennsylvania, mimeo.

Taubman, Paul, Jere R. Behrman and Terence J. Wales (1978) "The Roles of Genetics and Environment in the Distribution of Earnings", in: Z. Griliches et al., eds., *Income Distribution and Economic Inequality*, New York: John Wiley.

Tawney, R. (1961) *Equality*, New York.

Thurow, L. and R.E.B. Lucas (1972) *The American Distribution of Income: A Structural Problem*, Joint Economic Committee, Washington, D.C.

Tinbergen, J. (1956) *Economic Policy: Principles and Design*, 1st edn., Amsterdam: North-Holland.

Tinbergen, J. (1975) *Income Distribution Analysis and Policies*, Amsterdam: North-Holland.

U.S. Department of Commerce, Bureau of the Census (1963) "Methodology and Scores of Socioeconomic Status", Working Paper no. 15, Washington, D.C.

U.S. Department of Health, Education, and Welfare (1950–75) *Vital Statistics of the United States*, Volumes for 1950–1975, U.S. Government Printing Office, Washington, D.C.

U.S. Department of the Navy, Personal communication.

Vandenberg, S. (1968) "The Nature and Nurture of Intelligence", in: D. Glass, ed., *Genetics*, Russell Sage Foundation.

Vandenberg, S. (1972) "Assortive Mating or Who Marries Whom?", *Behavior Genetics*, 2, no. 2-3, 126–157.

Weiss, Y. (1972) "The Risk Element in Occupational and Educational Choices", *Journal of Political Economy*, November/December.

Welch, F. (1975) "Human Capital Theory: Education, Discrimination and Life Cycles", *Papers and Proceedings of American Economic Association*, 65, May, 63–73.

Wilder, C.S. (1973) "Prevalence of Selected Chronic Respiratory Conditions, United States, 1970", *Vital and Health Statistics*, Series 10, no. 84, Department of Health, Education. and Welfare Publication no. (HRA) 74-1511, September.

Williams, T. (1973) "Cultural Deprivation and Intelligence: Extensions of the Basic Model", unpublished Ph.D. dissertation University of Toronto, Canada.

Williams, T. (1974) "Cultural Deprivation and Intelligence", Paper read to Annual Meeting of the American Educational Research Association, New Orleans.

Wolf, R.M. (1964) "The Identification and Measurement of Environmental Process Variables Related to Intelligence", unpublished Ph.D. dissertation, University of Chicago.

Zellner, A. (1970) "Estimation of A Regression Relationship Containing Unobservables", *International Economic Review*, 11, October, 441–454.